The Soci
Rights

The Sociology of Human Rights

An Introduction

MARK FREZZO

polity

First published in 2015 by Polity Press

Polity Press
65 Bridge Street
Cambridge CB2 1UR, UK

Polity Press
350 Main Street
Malden, MA 02148, USA

ISBN-13: 978-0-7456-6010-3
ISBN-13: 978-0-7456-6011-0(pb)

A catalogue record for this book is available from the British Library.

Library of Congress Cataloging-in-Publication Data

Frezzo, Mark.
  The sociology of human rights : an introduction / Mark Frezzo.
     pages cm.
  Includes bibliographical references.
  ISBN 978-0-7456-6010-3 (hardcover) -- ISBN 978-0-7456-6011-0 (papercover) 1. Human rights--Social aspects. 2. Social rights. I. Title.
  JC571.F693 2014
  323--dc23

                        2014016881

Typeset in 11 on 13 pt Scala by
Servis Filmsetting Ltd, Stockport, Cheshire

The publisher has used its best endeavours to ensure that the URLs for external websites referred to in this book are correct and active at the time of going to press. However, the publisher has no responsibility for the websites and can make no guarantee that a site will remain live or that the content is or will remain appropriate.

Every effort has been made to trace all copyright holders, but if any have been inadvertently overlooked the publisher will be pleased to include any necessary credits in any subsequent reprint or edition.

For further information on Polity, visit our website: politybooks.com

Contents

Background to the Book   viii

Introduction: Thinking Sociologically about Human Rights   1
  Fundamental Questions   4
  An Invitation to Human Rights   6
  A Dilemma in Human Rights   7
  The Human Rights Community   8
  The Human Rights Canon   11
  Human Rights, Social Policy, and Law   15
  Special Features of the Book   18

Chapter 1: Defining the Sociology of Human Rights   22
  The Sociological Perspective   23
  What Are Human Rights?   26
  Negative Rights/Civil and Political Rights   27
  Positive Rights/Economic and Social Rights   30
  Cultural and Environmental Rights   32
  Rights Bundling   34
  What is the Sociology of Human Rights?   35
  Sociological Angles on Human Rights   37
  Major Concepts in the Sociology of Human Rights   41
  Science, Values, and Rights Bundles   43
  Globalization and Culture   46
  Summary   49

Chapter 2: Classifying Human Rights   51
  Why Do We Need to Rethink the Categories of Human
    Rights?   53
  Sociological Perspectives   55
  Lumping and Splitting in the Domain of Human Rights   57

Two Ways of Classifying Human Rights   60
Social Movements, Policy, and Law   64
The Circulation of Human Rights   68
Summary   71

Chapter 3: Civil and Political Rights   74
Preliminary Questions about Civil and Political Rights   74
The Legacy of the Enlightenment and the Three-Generations
    Schema   78
Decolonization and Human Rights   81
The Bedrock of the Human Rights Canon?   83
The Role of the UN   85
Where Do Civil and Political Rights Fit?   87
Summary   90

Chapter 4: Economic and Social Rights   93
Economy and Society   94
Preliminary Questions about Economic and Social Rights   97
Liberty, Equality, and the Legacy of the Enlightenment   99
Human Rights and the Political Chessboard   100
The Two Covenants   102
The Relational Character of Human Rights   103
Economic and Social Rights in the US Context   106
Summary   109

**Chapter 5: Rights to Culture, the Environment, and
    Sustainable Development**   111
Solidarity or the Ties that Bind   111
Situating Collective Rights   113
Culture, Environment, and Development   114
The Specificity of Third-Generation Rights   115
Versions of Sustainable Development   117
Origins of Third-Generation Rights   120
Further Questions about Collective Rights   124
Summary   126

Chapter 6: Rights Bundles   128
Oxfam International, Amnesty International, and Rights
    Bundling   128
Alternative Development   130
Angles on Human Rights   132

Historical Origins of Rights Bundling   133
Why Do We Need Rights Bundles?   136
Poverty as a Human Rights Puzzle   140
Formulating Rights Bundles   141
Subsidiarity   142
Three Rights Bundles   143
Summary   146

Conclusion: An Agenda for the Sociology of Human Rights   150
Human Rights, Peace, and Development   151
Social Science and Human Values   152
Rethinking Development   154
Global Governance   155
Rights Conditions, Rights Claims, and Rights Effects   156
A Research Agenda   156
Final Thoughts   163

Suggestions for Further Reading   164
Internet Resources for Consultation   166
Terminology   169
References   176
Index   183

Background to the Book

It makes sense to begin with a reflection on the uses of this book. The fundamental purpose of this book is to furnish readers with the tools to think systematically about human rights in the age of globalization. Far from being a mere academic concern, the question of human rights harbors profound implications not only for interstate relations and state policy, but also for daily life. Needless to say, it is difficult, if not impossible, to imagine studying human rights in abstraction from real-world concerns. After all, how we *think about* human rights has a significant bearing on how we interpret the global, national, and local news that comes to us through the Internet, television, radio, newspapers and magazines, and word of mouth. Furthermore, how we interpret the news has a profound influence on how we act in the world. More precisely, our understanding of human rights has a great effect on our capacity to feel empathy for human beings experiencing interstate war, civil strife, forced migration, human trafficking, violent crime, extreme poverty, religious persecution, cultural exclusion, environmental destruction, and other social problems. The capacity for empathy provides an important basis for human rights – not least because the concept of human rights presupposes an appeal to a *shared* human experience.

Notwithstanding the oft-repeated argument that the wealth of bad news from conflict zones across the world has created pervasive "compassion fatigue" among the populations of the Global North, this book operates from the assumption that the problem is not numbness or a deficit of genuine concern, but rather difficulty in recognizing the connection between human rights "over here" and human rights "over there." As scholarship has demonstrated, globalization can be seen as a process of economic, political, social, and cultural integration that produces increasingly intense connections among the world's peoples. Though aware of these connections – as manifested, for example, in consumption patterns in the Global North, the emergence and growth of the European Union as a transnational "super-state," cultural conflicts within and among nation-states, and the spread of environmental degradation – many of the inhabitants of the Global North are unaware of the actual *human rights* issues that are at stake. However, an encouraging sign can be found in the growing concern in the Global North about a range of issues: minerals and diamonds from conflict areas; the proliferation of armaments and the conscription of children as soldiers in fractured societies; human trafficking and sexual servitude; natural disasters in poor regions; sweatshops in low-wage zones; the plight of immigrants toiling for miserable wages as maids, nannies, farm workers, meatpackers, restaurant workers, and construction workers in wealthy regions; the homogenization of culture and the "stripmallization" of the landscape; and the environmental impacts of mass consumption.

To take an example that links a few of the aforementioned problems, increased consumption in the Global North exerts a decisive influence on labor and environmental conditions in the Global South, with its high concentration of factories, natural-resource extraction areas, and dumping sites for waste from the production and consumption processes (McMichael 2012). More conspicuously, there is mounting evidence in environmental science suggesting that rising sea levels and changing weather patterns, which are associated with the global climate change that is the result of more than 200 years of continuous industrialization to meet increasing consumer demand, have disproportionate effects on the Global South. Even such natural disasters as earthquakes, tsunamis, hurricanes, floods, and mudslides have exaggerated effects on the weaker infrastructures of the Global South. Flaws in the built environment – manifested in potholed roads, broken bridges, erratic power grids, inadequate water systems, insufficient hospitals, limited public transit systems, and spotty communication networks – reflect centuries of inequality among nation-states (from colonialism to the current debt regime). These examples demonstrate the profound connection between human rights "here" in the Global North and "there" in the Global South. It follows that we must devote serious attention not only to the consequences (both deliberate and unintended) of human rights remedies in the Global South, but also to the significant "backflow" of human rights knowledge from poorer, weaker, under-represented nation-states and societies to the luckier parts of the world. This is not only a normative claim; it is also a *social scientific obligation*.

Such issues force us to think more deeply not only about how we are connected to nation-states, societies, peoples, communities, and ecosystems across the planet, but also about what kind of world we wish to inhabit – an issue that has become paramount in the globalization era. While it would be naïve and counter-productive to imagine that we can recreate the world *de novo* according to a blueprint devised by any combination of academics, policymakers, officials of the United Nations (UN), non-governmental organization (NGO) staff, and activists, it would be equally problematic to summarily discount the importance of positive thinking – or what athletes and artistic performers call "creative visualization" – in improving the world. But positive thinking must be grounded in existing idea-systems, institutions, and practices. Accordingly, this book encourages readers not only to imagine a better world in the abstract, but also, and more importantly, to sketch the practical steps to improving existing idea-systems, policy frameworks, institutions, and organizations, whether through engaging in spirited debate with academics and policymakers, pushing for state-level legislation to provide personal protections and social entitlements to citizens, moving to reform the UN system, or proposing to create new global governance organizations (Wilkinson 2005).

Rethinking the Human Rights Canon

This book takes as its point of departure an acknowledgement of the pressing need to rethink, re-apply, and reform the existing human rights canon. This canon consists of a set of treaties, declarations, and pronouncements, and indeed an idea-system built, whether implicitly or explicitly, on the practice of placing human rights into categories: first-generation civil and political rights; second-generation economic and social rights; and third-generation cultural and environmental rights. Notwithstanding the enduring profundity of its central documents (including the celebrated Universal Declaration of Human Rights), the human rights canon has manifested considerable strain under the pressures of globalization, whether economic, political, social, cultural, or environmental. To the end of mitigating the pressure on the canonical texts to meet the demands of contemporary problems, academics and other members of the human rights community have begun to emphasize the overlap among the three categories of rights. This is partly attributable to greater cross-pollination among nation-states, peoples, and cultures on the nature, scope, and applicability of human rights in the era of globalization. In effect, globalization, characterized by its capacity to sweep away old orders and establish new ones, has served to create the conditions not only for new grievances and *rights claims* advanced by social movement organizations (SMOs) and their NGO allies, but also for new *rights effects* manifested in the enactment of policy at the state level. In sum, as political sociologists intervening in the field of human rights might caution us: while globalization may have established new conditions both for the conduct of SMOs and for the proposal of new rights, it still falls to sovereign nation-states either to implement and enforce human rights or to fail to do so.

Furthermore, the outcomes of the claims-making process tend to be less predictable and more ambiguous than either grassroots SMOs or their elite allies in political parties would prefer. Whether in the form of augmented personal security, voting rights, increased freedom of expression, and other civil liberties or in the form of the minimum wage, social security, and other social entitlements, actual achievements in human rights prove precarious in that they can always be rolled back by further legislation. Doubtless, a number of countries have added new rights to their constitutions. In theory, this would strengthen rights-oriented policymaking. In practice, the jury is out on the question of how constitutional revisions and amendments affect the policymaking of parliaments, the decisions of courts, and the behavior of SMOs. To date, no scholar has undertaken a comprehensive analysis of how revised constitutions affect the ratification and implementation of social policy. Such a future study would contribute to the sociology of human rights.

While globalization has not eliminated the role of the state in implementing, enforcing, and preserving human rights, the attendant advances in communications technology (satellite TV, Internet, personal computers, cell phones, etc.) have not only generated more publicity for human rights abuses, they have also brought greater exposure to non-Western conceptions of human rights. Indeed, cutting-edge human rights thinking emanating from the Global South and often challenging the destructive legacy of European colonialism and the enduring reality of economic and political inequality among nation-states – two issues addressed routinely, if incompletely, by the UN system – often transcends the conventional categories of civil and political rights, economic and social rights, and cultural and environmental rights. Such thinking can inspire us to reflect on our relations not only with other cultures, but also with the earth itself. A renowned theorist and practitioner of ecofeminism and the subsistence perspective, as well as a veteran of the Chipko movement in India, Vandana Shiva (1988, 1997, 2005) has devoted considerable attention to these issues. In light of such contributions, it is clear that persons interested in human rights must not only *learn*, but also *interrogate* the existing categories.

Owing to its strong theoretical bent, sociology offers an array of tools for both *working through* and *moving beyond* the customary categories of human rights. As we shall see, "immanent critique" – extrapolating and refining the existing categories to the point where they are sublimated into new categories – offers a sound basis for undertaking the sociology of human rights. Such an immanent critique permits the introduction of a new set of concepts for use by members of the human rights community. It is the author's hope that these concepts will facilitate not only constructive debate, but also the proposal of new policies, whether in the form of long celebrated civil and political protections for *individuals*, more recently acknowledged economic and social entitlements for *individuals*, or highly contested cultural and environmental entitlements for *groups*. Subject to implementation at the level of the nation-state, such policies may take many forms, depending upon political systems and cultural formations. Far from recommending specific programs, the goal of the book is to inspire readers to participate in *conversations* about how to alleviate human rights abuses and thereby establish the conditions for "more just" societies and nation-states.

Accordingly, the book leaves open the question of what would constitute a just society, nation-state, or global system. It is left to the readers to determine how broadly or narrowly to define the term "justice." For the relevant debate on the meaning of justice, readers are referred to Nobel Laureate economist Amartya Sen's *The Idea of Justice* (2009), which critiques and extrapolates John Rawls's influential *A Theory of Justice* (1999) by arguing that justice – defined as fairness – can be properly understood not through an abstract theory of the "just society," but rather through a comparative analysis of "more" and "less" just institutions, policies, and practices. In effect, this book builds on the *spirit*, if not on the letter, of Sen's analysis by relating justice to human welfare, a concept that cuts across the "spheres" of the economy, the polity, society, culture, and the environment. For example, the book defines poverty not in purely economic terms, but rather in terms of the denial of human welfare. In turn, the denial of human welfare is defined as a multi-causal and multifaceted *human rights problem*.

The Sociological Vision

This book rests on the presupposition that sociology – a discipline devoted to the analysis of inequalities stemming from racism, class structure, sexism, homophobia, xenophobia, and other forms of structural violence – offers a coherent and useful vision of human rights in the contemporary world. Doubtless, it is not the only viable academic perspective available to the human rights community (Cushman 2011). Such adjacent disciplines as political science (particularly the subfields of international relations and comparative politics), anthropology (particularly the subfields focusing on non-Western societies and cultures), and geography (particularly the subfields focusing on humanity, society, and environment) have also contributed greatly to our understanding of human rights. For their part, historians have paid considerable attention to human rights (Moyn 2012). But the sociological perspective merits further elucidation, elaboration, and application for a variety of reasons: the discipline's theoretical strength, methodological pluralism, and facility in addressing inequalities, social problems, power relations, and processes of identity formation. It is common, though certainly not obligatory, for sociologists to embrace the idea of using research and teaching not merely to analyze inequalities and social problems, but also to explore possible state policies to reduce inequalities and resolve social problems. For example, sociologists have always been at the forefront of debates on the welfare state (and proposed reforms to it), healthcare (and its proposed expansion to cover more citizens), education (and possible ways of improving it), and the prison system (and possible alternative forms of deterrence, punishment, and rehabilitation). Such problems as economic insecurity and poverty, preventable diseases and environmental hazards, poor education, and large-scale incarceration not only pose serious threats to the social fabric, but also run counter to prevailing conceptions of the "good society." Accordingly, it has been a smooth transition for many sociologists to proceed from analyzing inequalities and social problems to studying human rights per se.

This book espouses a common, but by no means mandatory, conception of the sociology of human rights as a social scientific enterprise that *illuminates the stakes of human rights debates and conflicts*. To elucidate what is at stake in a given rights struggle is not necessarily to take a side. It is merely to capture the causes, context, and potential consequences of the struggle. In accordance with this conception, the book uses sociological theories to explore:

- the economic, political, social, cultural, and environmental circumstances (called "rights conditions") under which under-represented, exploited, or marginalized groups begin to mobilize to air their grievances;
- the processes by which SMOs and their allies translate grievances into explicit demands (called "rights claims") made of states and other political authorities;
- the political and practical consequences and outcomes (called "rights effects") of rights-oriented policies, instruments, and institutions. These outcomes may also include altered power relations among social actors.

Since the sociological perspective complements those offered by political science, anthropology, and geography, this book pays careful attention to the role of academic disciplines in both *discovering* and *creating* knowledge, an issue normally reserved for such scholarly domains as epistemology, the philosophy of science, the sociology of knowledge, and the history of ideas. Owing to its novelty as an autonomous field, the sociology of human rights has an epistemological component built into it. More precisely, researchers in this new field are compelled to think about language issues: how human rights claims are *framed* in UN treaties and declarations, the platforms of political parties, NGO reports, and SMO pronouncements. They are also forced to ponder philosophical issues: ways of knowing and experiencing human rights; and the possible foundation of human rights (e.g., in *human nature* or in the *accumulated experiences* of humanity). While this book devotes considerable attention to language as a medium for the expression of rights claims, it does not take definitive positions on ontological issues.

This book devotes the bulk of its attention to the contributions of academics to human rights knowledge, not least because academic research informs UN agencies and NGOs. At the same time, the book makes it clear that academia is by no means the sole wellspring of human rights knowledge. Academics form only one constituency of the human rights community. Indeed, human rights knowledge emanates from many sources, including aggrieved populations, SMOs, and the general public. With this in mind, it is important for sociologists to take stock of how social learning contributes to human rights (via complex processes of mediation). In effect, the social learning in question usually emerges when aggrieved or disenchanted parties, community-based organizations, and SMOs lay claim to different types of rights. Under the proper conditions, the knowledge is transmitted to NGOs and UN agencies that serve as intermediaries, placing pressure on national governments – the ultimate arbiters of human rights – to enact changes in policy. The process of translating and communicating social learning on human rights proves extremely complex, contradictory, and open-ended, as it involves a multitude of entities, with variable levels of power and access to resources, as well as different constituencies and ideological perspectives. The complexities and contradictions associated with the advocacy and implementation of human rights constitute sources of debate, frustration, and disappointment for policymakers, and activists alike.

Academic Disciplines and Human Rights Knowledge

Let us return to the role of academic disciplines in the formalization and dissemination of knowledge, both within and beyond the confines of the university system. For the purpose of this discussion, we will leave the humanities, including philosophy (in a sense the progenitor of all of the academic disciplines) and history (which forms subfields in sociology, political science, anthropology, and geography respectively), to the side even though these disciplines have contributed greatly to our understanding of human rights. Thus, we will proceed with the proviso that the humanities disciplines (including comparative literature, classics, art history, music, and communication) – with their own theories, methods, styles of scholarly inquiry, and modes of engagement with the general public – merit consideration in future explorations of academic contributions to the epistemic community built around human rights. Occupying the frontier between the humanities and the social sciences, the discipline of history illuminates the intellectual debates, diplomatic squabbles, and policy disputes that define the trajectory of human rights. Nevertheless, the social sciences as such warrant emphasis here insofar as they contribute, whether directly (by exerting influence on public officials and more particularly on their staffers behind the scenes) or indirectly through discipline-based organizations (like the American Sociological Association, the American Political Science Association, the American Anthropological Association, and the Association of American Geographers), not only to the drafting and ratification of policy at the level of the state, but also to the shaping of public sentiment (via communiqués to and interviews in the mass media). In this light, funding entities (like the National Science Foundation and the Social Science Research Council), and think tanks (like Public Citizen, Demos, the Brookings Institution, the Hoover Institution, the RAND Corporation, and the Heritage Foundation) also play a significant role in the consideration of policy. In sum, there exists a revolving door among universities, think tanks, and government (at the level of staffers).

Alas, we must tread cautiously here. Doubtless, these professional organizations and think tanks represent different constituencies and reflect different ideologies, and hence pursue agendas that may or may not pertain directly to human rights. Nevertheless, one of the goals of the human rights community is to inspire professional organizations and think tanks to pay closer attention to human rights, especially when calling for the review of existing policies and the creation of new policies at the level of the nation-state. It is widely understood that social scientific research is particularly useful in the areas of welfare reform, poverty alleviation, education reform, prison reform, and environmental remediation. The next step is to conceptualize these issues in terms of human rights. One of the goals of the sociology of human rights in general, and of this book in particular, is to assist social scientists, think tank researchers, and policymakers in defining social and ecological problems in terms of human rights.

Let us return to the central question: How do the social scientific disciplines in particular contribute to the creation and classification of knowledge? In essence, the social sciences provide their practitioners – undergraduate and graduate students, junior and senior professors, publishers, members of think tanks, government staffers, and others – with a common training, exposure to prevailing schools of thought, a set of textual references that serve as touchstones, an array of methodological tools (whether quantitative, qualitative, or comparative-historical), and prescribed rituals of professionalization. Taken together, these elements of an epistemic community place a disciplinary stamp on knowledge. For example, since all sociologists in the Western world (and many in the non-Western world) are taught to think of Marx, Durkheim, and Weber as the "founders" of sociology as a discipline, all introductory courses in sociological theory, on both the undergraduate and the graduate levels, pay careful attention to these thinkers and the traditions they inaugurated. To this day, such topics as capitalism and industrialization, consumerism, urbanization, conformity and deviance, crime, bureaucracy and law, modernity and rationalization, the role of the West, and the relationship between the state (as both an agent unto itself and a playing field for contending forces) and civil society figure prominently in the domain of sociology. Far from being arbitrary selections, these topics testify to the manner in which Marx, Durkheim, and Weber unwittingly set the stage for the eventual consideration of human rights. Nevertheless, though employing vastly different theoretical and methodological frameworks, the writings of Marx, Durkheim, and Weber share a reluctance to consider human rights per se as a subject of intellectual analysis (Deflem and Chicoine 2011).

In effect, the Marx–Durkheim–Weber triad, which itself has a definable history in a power struggle within the Western academy (particularly in the US), provides sociology students and professors with a common vocabulary for exploring an array of social problems with profound implications for human rights. Doubtless, political science, anthropology, and geography have their own theoretical touchstones geared for the same purpose, with some overlap among them. For instance, Marx plays a role in anthropology (especially among those who analyze class structure and colonialism) and geography (especially among those who study poverty and under-development), while Durkheim plays an important role in the disciplines of criminology and criminal justice. In offering great insight into the workings of the state and other bureaucracies, Weber appears in the pantheon of political science. Nonetheless, contemporary sociologists have been forced to move considerably beyond the Marx–Durkheim–Weber triad in order to analyze human rights (Deflem and Chicoine 2011).

Though designed to specify how sociology *per se* contributes to the knowledge of human rights, this book embraces the spirit of committed interdisciplinarity – the proposition that the academic disciplines ought to work together not only to diagnose problems, but also to improve the human condition. This can be achieved by calling upon sociologists to join other social scientists in human rights institutes, as well as interdisciplinary programs in peace and justice studies, development studies, women's studies, LGBT (lesbian, gay, bisexual, and transgender) studies, cultural studies, and environmental studies. This objective can also be achieved by gearing academic work toward the realization of human rights (however defined) in the real world.

To that end, the author adopts a holistic approach to research, teaching, and service. In other words, each aspect – publishing articles and delivering conference papers, teaching courses and mentoring students, and working internally to build curricula and externally for academic organizations – informs the other aspects in profound ways. Though based primarily on the author's continuing research on the origins, evolution, and future prospects of the human rights community (consisting of academics, journalists, policymakers, and activists), this book draws additionally on the author's experiences teaching a course titled "The Sociology of Human Rights" at both undergraduate and graduate levels, incorporating human rights into an array of courses (on economic sociology, poverty, globalization, social movements, the sociology of law, and the sociology of peace and justice), building and implementing a curriculum in peace studies at the undergraduate level, serving as the faculty moderator for campus chapters of Amnesty International, working with academic organizations to institutionalize a rights-oriented sociology, and speaking publicly on issues pertaining to human rights, peace, and social justice in the age of globalization.

Analysis and Advocacy in the Sociology of Human Rights

A significant caveat is in order, however. While writing, teaching, and service in the field of human rights often inspire scholars to reflect on normative proposals for a better world, the connection between analysis and advocacy proves complex and challenging even to seasoned practitioners of the sociology of human rights. In other words, many rights-oriented sociologists face the daunting task of observing social scientific protocol (in terms of research design, methodological rigor, and the interpretation of empirical data), while intervening to alleviate the conditions for human rights abuses (including racism, exploitation in the workplace, sexism, homophobia, xenophobia, and related forms of bigotry, bullying, discrimination, exclusion, and violence) in the real world (Frezzo 2011). As an influential collection of essays has shown, scholarship on human rights is not only interdisciplinary, it is also pluralist in theory, method, and substance (Cushman 2011). It follows that sociologists of human rights are not committed to a single scientific or normative perspective.

In fact, reconciling social scientificity with an interest in social justice (however defined) constitutes a significant and permanent challenge to sociologists. While some sociologists (e.g., Blau and Moncada 2009) have pursued the goal of marshaling scholarship for specific social policies and laws, others have made strong arguments in favor separating social scientific research from advocacy (Deflem 2005). In effect, the unfinished debate on analysis versus advocacy recapitulates an earlier debate on the legitimacy and efficacy of the public sociology project in the American Sociological Association (Nichols 2007). More precisely, sociologists who favor connecting their scholarship with advocacy (Blau and Iyall Smith 2006) tend to align themselves with public sociology. In contrast, sociologists who prefer to keep their research separate from advocacy tend to be critical of public sociology (Deflem 2005). As a consequence, it is important to note that there is disagreement on the analysis-advocacy question among sociologists of human rights. It is equally crucial to bear in mind that the sociology of human rights is theoretically, methodologically, and substantively *pluralist* (Cushman 2011). To date, no definitive paradigm has emerged within the field. Since it remains an open question as to whether rights-oriented sociologists ought to be codifying a *paradigm*, this book confines itself to formalizing a *perspective*.

In light of the challenges associated with the analysis-advocacy dispute, this book sets aside the question of public sociology per se. The author proceeds cautiously. On the one hand, the author accepts the argument that the linking of science and human rights holds considerable promise for both domains (Claude 2002). On the other hand, the author recognizes the importance of eschewing the platforms of political parties and the programs of SMOs. While natural and social scientists have a responsibility to operate in the service of human welfare, they have an equal obligation to respect the proper role of activists and policymakers in bringing human welfare to fruition. More to the point, it is the job of activists to push for new policies and laws in the interest of human welfare. Meanwhile, it is the job of government officials to ratify and implement measures to improve human welfare. Thus, instead of defending a specific platform or program for the institutionalization of human rights by governments, this book highlights ways for sociologists (whether students or professors) to observe the prevailing scholarly standards and professional practices, while addressing the issues and events of the day. The tools of sociology can elucidate what is at stake – in terms of political power, access to social life, availability of social programs, protection of cultural traditions, control over natural resources, and preservation of the natural environment – in a given rights struggle. Such insights are useful to all interested parties, including the claimants and their allies, policymakers, and the general public.

Universalism

Doubtless, there exist innumerable ways of broaching the question of how and to what extent to incorporate a normative vision into social scientific work. Without precluding other approaches to the relationship between scientific research and human values – an issue that cannot be resolved definitively – this book confines itself to marshaling sociological analysis in support of three rights bundles or normative proposals (for longevity, the full development of the person, and peace). It is worth noting that this book *adapts* the notion of a "bundle of rights" from the academic domain of property law (Klein and Robinson 2011). Whereas scholars in property law use the term "bundle of rights" to capture the interrelated rights to use, own, lease, and permit or deny access to a parcel of land, sociologists of human rights use the term to denote any set of rights that are postulated as being inextricable from one another. The argument is that, in traversing the conventional categories of human rights, the aforementioned bundles capture three universal aspirations: the desire to lead a long, healthy life (and to see one's family, friends, colleagues, and fellow members of the community or nation do the same); the desire to acquire sufficient information, education, training, and opportunities to discover and nurture one's identity, choose one's vocation, and avail oneself of fulfilling leisure activities; and, finally, the desire to live without the fear of war, forced migration, street crime, bullying, and domestic violence. Notwithstanding their universality, the aspirations for longevity, the full development of the person, and peace present themselves differently according to cultural context. This is an excellent example of how the recurring issue of universalism versus cultural pluralism plays out in the real world. As we shall see, this highly contentious issue has a great bearing on the social scientific study of human rights (Pearce 2001; Donnelly 2003).

Following the work of anthropologists in the field of human rights, the sociological approach pays careful attention to the need to balance pretensions to universality with cultural sensitivity (Goodale 2006). If we are to make lasting progress in implementing human rights on a global scale, we will need to reconcile universalism (understood as the desire to establish a globally binding framework for human rights) with cultural pluralism (understood as the desire to protect the world's many cultures). To that end, we must acknowledge that human rights thinking springs from diverse sources: modern and contemporary; Western and non-Western; secular and religious; and spanning a good portion of the political spectrum. Rights thinking changes across historical time and geographic space. The concept of rights bundling offers important clues about how to accommodate both universalism and cultural pluralism in the globalization era. Accordingly, this book aims to point the way to a resolution of a persistent problem – namely, the assumption that the supposedly Western provenance of human rights precludes the doctrine from being applied in non-Western cultural settings. Interestingly enough, this argument is sometimes found among critics of Eurocentrism, who unwittingly give undue credence to the innovativeness of the West. The answer is to capture the uses and abuses of both Western and non-Western conceptions of human rights.

To that end, this book argues that non-Western cultures have always contributed to human rights thinking (before the advent of the "West" as a social construct, during the heyday of the European Enlightenment, with the founding and expansion of the UN system, and through the current period, with mass mobilizations in various countries) (Ishay 2008). The book also argues that universalism need not be Eurocentric (Amin 2010). Indeed, this book asks and answers the (rhetorical) question: Why should we leave universalism to advocates of Eurocentrism? To put it bluntly, there is absolutely no reason to do so. Nevertheless, we must envisage universalism not as a *fait accompli*, but rather as a *project* to be pursued on an ongoing basis (Pearce 2001; Donnelly 2003). As we shall discover, the project of building a genuine universalism entails an open-ended dialogue across civilizations.

To imagine, reflect upon, and debate rights bundles – in pursuit of a genuinely global, non-Eurocentric, and defensible universalism – amounts to considerably more than an intellectual exercise. It is also a way of orienting one's practical interventions in the real world. In sum, the advancement of rights bundles – a practice that this book aims to instill in its readers – constitutes one way of using sociology to intercede in the events of the day: interstate warfare, civil strife, poverty, inequality, exploitation, cultural exclusion, environmental degradation, and the other problems that figure prominently in nightly newscasts. It goes without saying that scholars and students may have their own ways of gearing sociological research and acumen for the benefit of the real world. Some might be more reticent, while others might be more audacious in intervening in the name of human rights. It is reasonable to expect a spectrum of approaches to the issue.

Human Rights, Service-Learning, and Civic Engagement

In any case, this book applauds the growing interest across the US university system in service-learning and civic engagement – the marshaling of academic expertise for the public good, coupled with the preparation of students for active citizenship in the age of globalization. Service-learning courses require students to supplement their reading, classroom discussions, and written assignments with volunteer work in the community. Students work for soup kitchens, urban gardens, clinics and hospitals, eldercare facilities, community centers, children's clubs, support groups for LGBT persons, and other organizations. The pedagogical justification for such courses is that students learn the academic material in a more profound and lasting way by putting it into practice through community service. On the one hand, students apply the theories, concepts, and substantive material that they have learned in the classroom to the real-world issues confronting their community groups. On the other hand, students bring their experiences with their community groups back to the classroom. Needless to say, service-learning tends to work best for social science courses that have a direct bearing on social problems and policy debates. Nevertheless, innovative professors across the US have devised service-learning courses for such disciplines as history, philosophy, art, and music – often by providing instruction to the public (especially schoolchildren) in these areas. This is a very encouraging event for the US university system as a locus of human rights education and praxis.

It is thoroughly feasible to build a concern for human rights into core curricula and service-learning programs at all levels. Yet it is crucial to distinguish a "concern" for human rights from the defense of political party platforms or SMO programs. With this distinction in mind, this book embraces the spirit of human rights education, while refraining from delineating a singular pathway to the realization of human rights. In fact, one of the purposes of human rights education is to demonstrate to learners that there are *multiple* pathways to the expansion of human rights on a global scale. As a consequence, human rights education tends to stay close to the *existing canon*.

Though not its primary purpose, this book points to ways of incorporating human rights education into the training of students seeking bachelor's, master's, and doctoral degrees in the social sciences and such pre-professional fields as social work, clinical psychology, and nursing. This goal is consistent with the mission of the Human

Rights Education Associates – an NGO that uses its website, listserv, online courses, and fieldwork to provide resources and instruction in the theory and practice of human rights (http://www.hrea. org/index.php?base_id=273&language_id=1). The renowned human rights NGO Amnesty International, to which references are made throughout this book, has incorporated human rights education in its mission. Arguably, human rights education serves as the best means of training students for global citizenship, not least because it inspires students to think through the debates on global versus local governance, universalism versus cultural specificity, public versus private goods, the role of the market, the goals of social programs, the importance of protecting cultural and environmental diversity, and, ultimately, what may be plausibly expected from government (and from inhabitants of civil society). Moreover, students' service-learning work may motivate them to maintain lasting contact with rights-oriented NGOs and community groups that address poverty, exclusion, urban decay, domestic abuse, bullying, discrimination, environmental degradation, and other problems. At the very least, service-learning trains students not only to seek practical applications for their classroom learning, but also to work with persons from diverse backgrounds in the pursuit of common objectives.

Fittingly, service-learning and civic engagement have found broad support not only in universities and colleges, but also in academic organizations, including those that represent the social scientific disciplines. Needless to say, all academic organizations have ethical standards built into their charters. These concern not only the conduct of research, but also the professional obligation to assist communities, societies, and humanity as a whole. In principle, these standards can be translated very easily into human rights concerns. To take a particularly crucial example, the right not only to enjoy the benefits of science and technology, but also to be protected from the excesses of scientific research and technological advancement – expressed in Article 15 of the International Covenant on Economic, Social, and Cultural Rights (1966) – forms the basis of the outreach of the American Association for the Advancement of Science (AAAS). Numerous social scientific disciplines, including sociology, anthropology, and geography, have joined their counterparts in the natural sciences in the AAAS Science and Human Rights Program. For a scholarly analysis of the implications of Article 15, readers are encouraged to consult Richard Claude's *Science in the Service of Human Rights* (2002). By definition, such programs go to great lengths to maintain scientific protocol and rigor, while promoting research on social problems, environmental degradation, physical and psychological health, crime, interstate warfare and civil strife, humanitarian disasters, and other issues associated with human welfare.

Like their counterparts in other academic disciplines, rights-oriented sociologists tend to pay careful attention to the implications of their research for the general public. It is worth pointing to forays into human rights undertaken by academic organizations that involve sociologists. To take the most relevant example, the ASA – the professional organization for sociologists across the US, the sponsor of the largest annual sociology conference, and the publisher of several peer-reviewed journals – founded a Section on Human Rights in 2008 (http://www.asanet.org/sections/humanrights.cfm). For its part, the International Sociological Association (ISA) – the professional organization for sociologists across the globe – established a Thematic Group on Human Rights and Global Justice in 2006 (http://www.isa-sociology.org/tg03.htm). The ASA and ISA groups have contributed greatly to the institutionalization of the sociology of human rights as a distinct academic field. In various ways, this book builds on the author's experiences not only as an officer in the ASA Section on Human Rights and as a session organizer for the ISA Thematic Group on Human Rights and Global Justice, but also as a member of the Council and Steering Committee of the Science and Human Rights Coalition of the AAAS, a project that brings together social and natural scientists from across the US in the mobilization of scientific expertise for the advancement of human rights (http://srhrl.aaas.org/coalition/index.shtml). To conclude, this book is designed not only to spread the insights of rights-oriented sociology to students, scholars, policymakers, activists, and members of the general public, but also to invite readers to participate actively in debates on human rights. Phrased differently, this book captures the insights of sociology in an effort to assist readers in joining the epistemic community built around human rights.

Introduction:
Thinking Sociologically
about Human Rights

This book introduces undergraduate and graduate students, scholars, policymakers, and activists to the theories and substantive issues of the sociology of human rights – a nascent but rapidly growing field in academia. Whereas philosophers, legal scholars, and political scientists have, for some time, devoted considerable attention to human rights, it is only recently that a significant number of sociologists have begun to use their disciplinary lens to examine the social underpinnings and implications of human rights. For this reason, the emerging field remains pluralist in theory, methods, and substantive orientation (Cushman 2011). From the outset, the new domain had a pronounced theoretical inclination. In the mid-1990s, Turner (1993) grounded human rights in a sociological theory of the body, while Waters (1996) advanced a social constructionist theory of human rights. Later, Sjoberg et al. (2001) set the tone for further research by using sociological tools to illuminate both the language and the practices of human rights in the contemporary world.

In another early intervention, Pearce (2001) emphasized the role of African perspectives in shaping human rights, and urged sociologists not to hypostatize the opposition between "Western" and "non-Western" conceptions of human rights. Finally, Hajjar (2005) urged sociologists to consider not only the debates and conflicts surrounding the drafting, implementation, and enforcement of international law by nation-states, but also the role of popular mobilizations in generating rights claims. Soon after, the new domain found expression in the Thematic Group on Human Rights and Global Justice in the International Sociological Association in 2006 and the Section on Human Rights in the American Sociological Association in 2008. With a view to complementing the contributions of their colleagues from other disciplines, sociologists aim to elucidate the economic, political, social, and cultural forces that impact the construction,

1

interpretation, implementation, and enforcement of human rights norms, policies, and laws. Far from treating human rights as immutable properties of persons, sociologists conceptualize human rights as highly contested claims that vary across historical time and geographic space.

At the outset, the following question emerges: How have human rights accumulated over time? In essence, sociologists seek a middle ground between the Enlightenment assertion of the inevitability of progress and postmodern skepticism about the possibility of advancement. On the one hand, it is clear that rights have accumulated both on a global scale and within nation-states since the publication of the US Declaration of Independence (1776) and the French Declaration of the Rights of Man and of the Citizen (1789) – two signal documents cited by scholars and policymakers (Lauren 2003). On the other hand, it is equally evident not only that the accumulation of rights has been anything but a linear process guided by Nature or by some other trans-historical force, but also that significant contributions to the corpus of human rights have come from non-Western cultures (both from the ancient world – before the codification of the "West" as a social construct – and from the modern world) (Lauren 2003).

Not only does the modern concept of human rights have antecedents in ancient religious traditions emphasizing dignity – long before the advent of Europe as a self-conscious entity – it has also been influenced by contributions from peoples formerly conquered and dominated by Europe (Lauren 2003; Ishay 2008). As a consequence, social scientists' attentiveness to the *historicity* of human rights is closely connected to their *critique of Eurocentrism* – a vision that installs Europe as the model for the rest of the world, thereby underestimating the role of non-European peoples (for example, in the quest for national self-determination in former colonies) in shaping human rights doctrine (Blaut 1993; Nandy 1995; Amin 2010). Indeed, as a renowned scholar has noted: "Third World diplomats made pivotal contributions to some of the most significant events in the UN human rights project. Their arguments shifted debates that determined the universality of rights. Their votes shaped the two most authoritative instruments in human rights law, the International Covenants" (Burke 2010: 1–2).

In sum, the human rights canon – though subject to critique from post-colonial scholars – does reflect the influence of Third World movements, governments, and academics in the post-Second World War period. Far from being a mere historical detail, this insight has a significant bearing on the quest for a genuinely global, non-Eurocentric, and defensible form of universalism – the consideration of which constitutes one of the major functions of this book. For the sake of precision, it is worth noting that the term "Third World," which was popularized in the 1950s as a way of distinguishing recently decolonized nations from the "First World" (i.e., the US, Western Europe, Japan, and other wealthy nations) and the "Second World" (i.e., the Soviet Union and its satellites in Eastern Europe) – has been replaced in much of the literature by the term "Global South." When analyzing conceptions of human rights during the post-1945 period, this book employs the term "Third World"; when examining notions of human rights in the contemporary period, this book uses the term "Global South."

By training and inclination, sociologists tend to emphasize the *social* character of human rights. While it may well be the case that rights are grounded in human physiology and/or the intrinsic human capacity for sociability – a philosophical question that recurs in the sociological literature and harbors potential ramifications for the possibility of universalism – it is clear that human rights are achieved not only through the efforts of enlightened politicians and jurists, but also through the organized struggles of ordinary people. In other words, aggrieved parties, social movement organizations (SMOs), and their non-governmental organization (NGO) allies participate in the epistemic community built around human rights. In this light, it is worth mentioning that the US has provided innumerable examples of large-scale mobilizations in the name of human rights. Attentive to the struggles of people of color, workers, women, the LGBT (lesbian, gay, bisexual, and transgender) community, immigrants, and persons living with disabilities, sociologists are particularly interested in how human rights – once achieved on the level of the nation-state – empower aggrieved parties vis-à-vis other groups and the state.

Throughout the book, reference is made to the role of movements in advancing rights claims. At the same time, the book emphasizes that movements do not always get what they want; and the actual outcomes of struggles tend to be ambiguous and precarious in terms of lasting policies at the state level. Thus, it is difficult not only to assert that a specific movement "produced" a given piece of legislation (since there are levels of mediation involved), but also to predict whether a given policy will endure (since all policies can be modified or repealed with changes in alliances, political climate, and even economic circumstances). Accordingly, sociologists of human rights must remain circumspect in evaluating the consequences and outcomes – in terms of enduring state policies and altered power relations – of rights-oriented struggles. In this light, the literature on social movement consequences and outcomes proves particularly useful (Giugni 1998; Amenta et al. 2010).

Whether operating within institutes on human rights, programs in peace and justice studies, in their home departments, or independently, social scientists have increasingly recognized the importance of human rights not only for the legal system, but also for public policymaking, social movements, the transmission of norms across societies, the preservation of cultural life, and the protection of the natural environment. In delineating a sociological perspective on human rights (defined as a set of protections and entitlements that regulate relations among such social actors as transnational corporations, national and local governments, communities, families, and individuals), this book complements the contributions of political scientists, anthropologists, and geographers, all of whom have placed their disciplinary imprints on the analysis of human rights.

Fundamental Questions

En route to demonstrating the utility of the sociological perspective on human rights, this book explores two fundamental questions. First, what do sociologists have to offer to scholarship and practice in the domain of human rights? The short answer is that sociologists bring a fresh perspective to the analysis of the origins, evolution, and the possible future of human rights norms, laws, treaties, institutions, and practices. More precisely, sociologists, especially those with interests in political economy/development, social movements, politics and the inner workings of states, and law, are well equipped to analyze *rights conditions* (circumstances that cause popular forces to express grievances), *rights claims* (competing interpretations of the human rights canon devised and propagated by social actors), *rights effects* (ways in which social actors are empowered and/or constrained when political authorities grant rights through policies and laws), and *rights bundles* (parcels of interconnected rights proposed and defended by critics of the existing order). The concept of "rights bundles" is transplanted from the field of real estate law (Klein and Robinson 2011), in which it denotes the interrelated rights attached to a parcel of land. Needless to say, these four concepts – rights conditions, rights claims, rights effects, and rights bundles – will be defined in greater detail as the book progresses.

For the sake of clarity, it is safe to say that political economy/ development sociology, with its concentration on the workings of contemporary capitalism, proves well equipped to analyze rights conditions (with the proviso that a cultural approach might also be useful in this regard). Social movement research, with its attentiveness to organizational structure, strategy and tactics, and framing in SMOs, proves useful for the examination of rights claims. Political sociology, with its sensitivity to power blocs, political parties, and legislative processes, proves well suited for the exploration of rights effects. While political economy/development sociology, social movement research, and political sociology – as prominent fields with their own substantive concerns – are not obligated to consider human rights, they can be mobilized for such a purpose. Moreover, when woven together, the three approaches permit the formulation of normative proposals in the form of rights bundles. Accordingly, the current work builds on latent tendencies within political economy/development sociology, social movement research, and political sociology in order to highlight human rights concerns.

Though recurring throughout the book, concrete examples of rights bundles, designed to meet the requirements of the chaotic age of globalization by addressing such human rights issues as economic inequality and poverty, cultural exclusion, and environmental degradation, will be examined in particular detail in chapter 6. Readers will be invited to generate their own rights bundles, based not only upon their own assessments of local, national, and global problems, but also upon their own values. Such invitations rest on the presupposition that participation in the epistemic community should be considered a human right, irrespective of one's education, vocation, social status, citizenship, or racial, ethnic, gender, or sexual identity.

The second question is as follows: What does the interdisciplinary domain of human rights have to offer to the discipline of sociology? In response to the work of UN agencies, NGOs, SMOs, and community groups, sociologists have increasingly conceptualized poverty, social inequalities (stemming from institutional racism, sexism, homophobia, and xenophobia), cultural exclusion, and environmental degradation not only as social problems, but also as *human rights abuses* (i.e., practices and power structures that contravene emerging norms on economic, social, cultural, and environmental rights). Accordingly, sociologists have built on interdisciplinary studies of how norms, including the intertwined discourses of human rights, multiculturalism/cultural pluralism, and environmental justice, shape global affairs (Khagram et al. 2002). In the process, they have demonstrated that norms never operate in a vacuum. While it remains to be seen if sociology as a whole will take a human rights turn, it is clear that interest in the subject has grown considerably across the discipline, especially in the fields of social movement research, political sociology, the sociology of law, and social theory (Cushman 2011; Brunsma et al. 2012).

An Invitation to Human Rights

Deriving from the Latin word *invitatio*, denoting not only the act of being pleasant toward and providing entertainment for someone, but also the idea of challenging or inciting someone to pursue a noble objective with vigor and enthusiasm, the English word "invitation," bearing as it does the traces of its etymology and passage through other languages, connotes an amiable exhortation to pursue a worthy endeavor. By custom in the Western world, invitations, whether to private functions or public events, are extended to *restricted* audiences. Naturally, the size of an invitation list is normally determined by a number of factors, including membership in a voluntary organization, employment at a company, participation in a social network, or residency in a given neighborhood. In the non-Western world, invitations can take vastly different forms. Thus, even a seemingly basic concept like that of "invitation" must be filtered through diverse cultural frameworks. With the imperative to address the tension between universalism and cultural pluralism in mind, the invitation to participate in a collective dialogue on the nature, scope, and applicability of human rights (in the form of ideas, norms, policies, laws, institutions, and practices) is extended to an *expansive* audience – indeed, to an audience of 7 billion persons, spread across 193 sovereign nation-states, participating in a spectrum of cultural rituals, speaking thousands of languages, belonging to a vast number of religious and spiritual traditions, and residing in an array of ecosystems.

In light of its subject matter, namely the protections (usually called civil and political rights) and entitlements (usually called economic and social rights) that ought to be enjoyed by all humans without regard to race, class, gender, sexual orientation, nationality, religious preference, disability, or other personal characteristics, this book constitutes an open-ended invitation to participate in a sustained, cross-cultural conversation on the successes and failures, promises and limitations of human rights doctrines, policies, institutions, and practices. Accordingly, the central message of this book is that the sociological perspective – understood as a complement to the perspectives offered by neighboring social science disciplines (especially political science, anthropology, and geography) – offers unique insights into a number of disputes on and struggles over human rights. At the same time, insofar as they testify to the significance of knowledge (whether gathered through scholarship or through social learning) in molding the behavior of social actors, rights-oriented disputes and struggles shed light on SMO-state relations, the processes of mediation between popular mobilizations and policy outcomes, and the role of NGOs and UN agencies in influencing the conduct of national governments. It follows that the sociological analysis of human rights harbors the potential to make a substantial contribution to the growing literature on global governance in the contemporary period (Wilkinson 2005).

A Dilemma in Human Rights

With a view to illuminating the interconnectedness of human rights on a global scale – a reality that globalization has brought to the foreground with greater publicity for human rights *abuses* and increasing discussion of human rights *remedies* – this book grapples with a cardinal dilemma. On the one hand, human rights – understood as the "attributes" or "property" of all 7 billion human beings irrespective of race, class, gender, sexual orientation, nationality, culture, religious affiliation or non-affiliation, age, ability or disability, and other identity characteristics – are, by definition, *global*. This is reflected not only in the spate of treaties and declarations associated with the UN, which taken together serve as the *human rights canon*, but also, and perhaps more importantly, in the work of NGOs, SMOs, community groups, and individuals that push for the expansion, monitoring, and enforcement of human rights on a global scale.

On the other hand, notwithstanding the increasing economic, political, social, and cultural integration associated with globalization, the world remains divided into 193 nation-states, each defined as a separate political-legal jurisdiction endowed with sovereignty. As a consequence, there exist 193 frameworks for conceptualizing, enacting, and enforcing human rights legislation (or failing to do so). Despite intensified interactions among nation-states and a greater role for transnational corporations, especially through the liberalization of trade policies and the proliferation of consumerism, the nation-state has maintained considerable authority and influence not only as the monopolist of the legitimate use of coercive power, but also as the arbiter of justice (through civil and criminal courts) and the provider of protections (often in the form of civil and political rights) and entitlements (often in the form of economic and social rights). Although anchored in its 193 member states, along with an array of NGOs that enjoy UN consultative status, the UN exerts considerable influence on state policymakers, the nation-state remains the most important agent in either implementing or failing to enact, respecting or violating human rights. In essence, when aggrieved parties and their allies in NGOs and UN agencies militate for the implementation of human rights, they are appealing to *nation-states* for new laws and policies (whether civil and political, economic and social, or cultural and environmental).

To further complicate matters, human rights norms, even when seemingly part of a broad consensus of policymakers and advocates, must be filtered through a multiplicity of cultures, each offering a different matrix for interpreting the human rights canon and for formulating rights claims (Khagram et al. 2002). Thus, any conceivable universalism would need to provide for considerable cultural pluralism – a permanent problem with which all members of the human rights community must contend (Pearce 2001). As we shall see, the universalism-cultural pluralism problem instantiates itself in innumerable ways both within and among nation-states.

The Human Rights Community

Though employed frequently by UN, NGO, and government officials, the concept of the "human rights community" merits further elucidation, not least because this book invites its readers not only to observe the undertakings of experts in the theory and practice of human rights, but also to become active participants in debates on what is imaginable, feasible, and desirable in terms of human rights, state policies, and global governance in a contemporary period marked by rapid economic integration and the attendant flows of capital, commodities, information, cultural artifacts, and flesh-and-blood human beings across national frontiers (Wilkinson 2005). It is difficult, if not impossible, to examine the prospects for and the limitations of human rights in abstraction from either the emancipatory potential or the exacerbated inequalities associated with globalization. In other words, globalization cuts both ways; and human rights can be molded to fit the requirements of conflicting power blocs and constituencies.

In this light, the operative assumption of the book is as follows: though marked by power-differentials (e.g., between the Global North and the Global South, between state actors and non-state actors, between elites and non-elites, and between those who can attend international conferences sponsored by universities, the UN, and governments and those who cannot do so), the human rights community proves more varied and uneven than conventional conceptualizations would suggest. Thus, it is crucial for scholarship and policymaking alike to formally acknowledge the reality of diversity and inequality. Moreover, to offer a normative judgment, ordinary people – especially but not exclusively activists – ought to lay claim to membership in the human rights community irrespective of their level of expertise. Indeed, there is an implicit, but insufficiently acknowledged, consensus that membership in this community, like access to information in general, constitutes a fundamental human right. As we shall see, this right is closely connected to the right to education (en route to the full development of the person) and the right to democracy (or, at the very least, to popular participation in decision-making processes). Though education and democracy remain subject to different interpretations in the world's 193 nation-states and thousands of cultural frameworks, the importance of information on human rights and participation in decision-making processes is recognized nearly universally. This realization offers a sound starting point.

Building on the concept of an "epistemic community" – a notion that figures prominently in the literature on international organizations and cooperation among nation-states, both within and beyond the discipline of political science – we may acquire a better sense of how debates on human rights unfold in the spaces among universities, UN agencies, NGOs, and governments. As a noted analyst of policy coordination among nation-states (both through intergovernmental organizations (IGOs) and independently of them) has demonstrated:

> Although an epistemic community may consist of professionals from a variety of disciplines and backgrounds, they have (1) a shared set of normative and principled beliefs, which provide a value-based rationale for the social action of community members; (2) shared causal beliefs, which are derived from their analyses of practices leading or contributing to a

central set of problems in their domain and which then serve as the basis for elucidating multiple linkages between possible policy actions and desired outcomes; (3) shared notions of validity – that is inter-subjective, internally defined criteria for weighing and validating knowledge in the domain of expertise; and (4) a common policy enterprise – that is, a set of common practices associated with a set of problems to which their professional competence is directed, presumably out of the conviction that human welfare will be enhanced as a consequence. (Haas 1992: 3)

Having identified four essential components of an epistemic community – common values and objectives (motivated by an underlying conception of human welfare), a common understanding of how social scientific research contributes to policy outcomes, a shared comprehension of what constitutes valid knowledge in social science, and a shared interest in successful policy outcomes (especially at the state level) – Haas has offered a compelling explanation of the workings of the human rights community. It is worth noting, however, that the human rights community inevitably incorporates the *social learning* of aggrieved parties and ordinary people not only in disadvantaged constituencies and communities in the Global North, but also in the vast and diverse populations of the Global South. Across the world, disadvantaged groups – though underrepresented in academic and policymaking circles – make sense of their own experiences, communicate through the mediation of their own leaders and intellectuals, and thereby influence the evolution of rights thinking.

For example, the social learning of African Americans – forged under conditions of segregation, exploitation, and discrimination – had a decisive impact on the conceptualization of civil rights in the US. Similarly, the social learning of indigenous and peasant communities in Latin America – reflective of centuries of colonialism, cultural exclusion, and unjust land distribution – has found recognition not only in a few recent national constitutions in the region, but also in the philosophical and ideological frameworks of SMOs in the Global North (e.g., in the Occupy Wall Street and allied "occupy" movements, along with the anti-austerity and pro-global justice mobilizations that preceded it). Witness the emphases on "horizontal" – as opposed to hierarchical – forms of organization, direct democratic decision-making processes, and occupations of land, public spaces, and factories, which have spread from Latin America to the US and the European Union (through the Zapatista Solidarity Network, the World Social Forum, among other agents) (Leite 2005). Accordingly, in treating the nexus of diverse parties interested in human rights as an epistemic community, this book adds a serious and sustained consideration of the contributions of *non-elites* – especially in the non-Western world – to ongoing debates on the nature, scope, and applicability of the human rights canon (Gordon 2004). This addendum to the definition of epistemic community offered by Haas derives as much from a social scientific imperative (to analyze the workings of human rights) as it does from a normative impulse (to deploy human rights in improving the world).

The Human Rights Canon

Though carrying a religious valence (from its use by Catholic, East Orthodox, and other Christian churches to denote the collection of authoritative texts and teachings that forms the basis of religious teachings, laws, and customs), the term "canon" is used by the humanities disciplines (especially classics and the various national literatures) in the university systems of the West to designate the standard works and themes in which all scholars and students should be conversant. While the sociology of human rights is too young to have its own canonical texts, the field is well equipped to elucidate the function of the human rights canon in the corresponding epistemic community. It is crucial to recognize that "what bonds members of an epistemic community is their shared belief or faith in the verity and applicability of specific forms of knowledge or specific truths" (Haas 1992: 3, ff. 4). When applied to the case of the human rights community, this statement points to the pivotal role of the canon – understood as the encapsulation in the form of UN treaties, declarations, and commentaries written thereupon (by scholars and policymakers) of *accumulated knowledge* in the domain of human rights – in providing common reference points for a diverse array of social actors (including both elite and grassroots agents).

In effect, the canon is *more than* a heuristic device for sketching the landscape of human rights violations and remedies and *less than* a scientific paradigm for solving puzzles in human rights. Falling equidistant between these two poles, the canon provides the syntax and semantics for deliberation and contestation on which rights individuals and collectivities have and how such rights translate into state policy. Thus, claimants – whether the aggrieved groups themselves, their SMO and NGO representatives, members of sympathetic political parties, or supportive UN officials – undertake *exegeses* of canonical texts in the service of their perspectives and interests. Naturally, some groups endeavor to circumscribe the human rights canon, while others attempt to extrapolate it – a tendency that has its roots in the offshoots of the European Enlightenment. Some entities advocate strict adherence to the original texts, while others espouse both the transformation of existing documents and the drafting of new ones – a process that exhibits similarities with both the scholarly analysis of sacred texts in religious institutions and the rigorous inter-pretation of constitutions in legal communities.

In sum, this book adds two elements to the concept of epistemic community advanced by Haas: first, an acknowledgement of the participation of popular forces – in addition to scientific experts, policymakers, and elites – in the determination of what counts as knowledge; and second, the illumination of the crucial position of the canon in fomenting vigorous debate on beliefs (albeit within strictly defined parameters). An addendum to the second element comes in the recognition of how exegesis – the critical interpretation of texts (as evidenced in the humanities fields of religion, classics, and compara-tive literature) – contributes the resolution of disputes. With this in mind, let us turn our attention to the major documents of the human rights canon.

Major Documents in the Human Rights Canon

To reiterate, this book makes frequent allusions to the *human rights canon* – a collection of documents that serve, despite their intrinsic limitations, as reference points for scholars, policymakers, UN agen-cies, NGOs, SMOs, and others engaged in debates on the successes and failures, the uses and misapplications, and the history and future of human rights. By custom, three documents serve as the primary touchstones in the human rights canon: the 1948 Universal Declaration of Human Rights (UDHR), the 1966 International Covenant on Civil and Political Rights (ICCPR), and the 1966 International Covenant on Economic, Social, and Cultural Rights (ICESCR). Though cut from the same cloth, the two covenants were designed to advance two different categories of rights – protections or "negative rights" for individuals in the first case and entitlements or "positive rights" for individuals in the second case. Taken together, these documents were conceived by their framers as the three pillars of the putative' International Bill of Human Rights (IBHR) – an informal name used by UN officials to designate the doctrinal or even constitutional foundation of an *imagined* interstate system (in which a modicum of universalism would prevail).

What happened? In essence, UN officials hoped that the IBHR would serve as a legal reference point and moral compass for forces seeking to advance the cause of human rights across the world – especially in regions that had suffered under the yoke of European colonialism. Though the historical narrative falls outside of this book's purview, suffice it to say that the IBHR project was obstructed by the contradictions of decolonization, the strategic interests of the US and other great powers, and the entanglements of the Cold War. In effect, the Cold War antagonism between the US and the USSR, characterized by the diversion of state funds from social programs to military expenditures, the growth of military-industrial complexes, the stockpiling of nuclear weapons, and the prosecution of "proxy wars" in the Third World, inflected the human rights agenda from the breakdown of the wartime alliance circa 1947/1948 through to the collapse of the Soviet Union in 1991. In other words, the Cold War exerted considerable influence on the interpretation not only of the major documents in the human rights canon, especially the ICCPR (favored by the US and the Western powers) and the ICESCR (favored by the USSR and the Eastern Bloc), but also of the rights to national self-determination and development (with repeated interventions in poor countries on the part of the competing superpowers). In short, the Cold War limited the UN's ability to promote a more uniform implementation of human rights on a worldwide scale.

As a consequence, scholars and policymakers alike have tended to treat the three documents separately (albeit with the understanding that the two covenants – though dedicated to different categories of rights for individuals – overlap considerably). In short, the failure of the IBHR to take root both *reflected* and *affected* the codification of the three-generations framework. In other words, an incipient concep-tion of the three generations had manifested itself already with the ratification of the UDHR in 1948; and by the time the two covenants were ratified in 1966, this framework had been spelled out more clearly. One of the objectives of this book is to work through the three-generations framework to the end of restoring a holistic vision of human rights that has been present in the rights-oriented epistemic community from the outset, but received greater attention in the age of globalization (for reasons that will be explained later).

Commissioned by the General Assembly of the UN, the UDHR, the ICCPR, and the ICESCR can be interpreted as attempts not only to learn the lessons of a series of historical events, including the First World War, the failure of the League of Nations to check the growth of nationalism and militarism, the Great Depression, the Second World War, and the Holocaust, but also to prepare the ground for decolonization, nation-building, and development in the non-Western world (Glendon 2002). Reading these documents in the present day, we can get a visceral sense of the three dilemmas confronting the UN at its inception in 1945: how to regulate the competition between the US and the Soviet Union, which produced a nuclear arms race and an array of proxy wars that posed a grave threat to the security of the world; how to bridge the gap between the wealthy, powerful nation-states situated primarily in the Northern Hemisphere and the poor, weak nation-states and colonies located primarily in the Southern Hemisphere; and, finally, how to balance the demand for human rights with the requirements of national sovereignty and cultural pluralism. While the first dilemma disappeared with the collapse of the Soviet Union and concomitant end of the Cold War circa 1991, the second and third dilemmas still weigh heavily on the General Assembly, the Security Council, and the agencies of the UN. Interestingly enough, all sides in these debates – the dispute on the North–South divide and the dispute on the limits of national sovereignty and the prospects for cultural pluralism – lay claim to the doctrine of human rights. This testifies to the flexibility and durability of the human rights canon.

As the main components of the human rights canon, the aforementioned documents merit further consideration by sociologists, not least because they bear the traces of the *social conditions* under which they were produced and implemented. For example, it is significant that the UDHR was issued in the post-Second World War context not only of emerging movements of African Americans and women in the US – the main sponsor and host of the UN – but also of growing decolonization movements in the non-Western world (Anderson 2003). Although the implementation of major documents has been incomplete and uneven, we should not be dissuaded from analyzing them *sociologically*. In other words, we should feel free to explore the social underpinnings and impacts of these documents – a task for which this book prepares readers. Doubtless, the signatories – nation-states pursuing conflicting strategic objectives and espousing competing ideologies – have manifested variable levels of commitment to the UDHR, the ICCPR, and the ICESCR. Indeed, as the annual reports of Amnesty International, Human Rights Watch, and other rights-oriented NGOs (charged with the task of monitoring compliance) have demonstrated, these documents have not compelled nation-states (or the social actors within them) to respect human rights as deeply or consistently as their framers had wished. This is a recurring source of disappointment for scholars and practitioners in the domain of human rights.

Arguably, none of the nation-states that were decisive in implementing the post-1945 human rights regime have lived up fully to their own stated values. Though some nation-states fare better than others in conventional evaluations, no nation-state has a perfect record. Activists, policymakers, and scholars routinely consult the annual reports of Amnesty International on the human rights records of all nation-states (http://www.amnesty.org/en/human-rights/human-rights-by-country). In light of the incomplete implementation and imperfect enforcement of human rights, the question arises: Should we treat the UDHR, the ICCPR, and the ICESCR as mere pieces of paper? Or have these documents served an important purpose despite the limitations of nation-states? Far from being mere abstractions, these documents, bolstered by the authority of the UN, eventually became reference points for NGOs, SMOs, community groups, and individual activists seeking not only to improve the lives of poor, excluded, and otherwise vulnerable humans, but also to alter power arrangements both within and among nation-states. In effect, these documents have inspired popular forces to articulate their grievances in terms of human rights – a process that is explained in considerable detail in this book. It goes without saying, however, that many grievances, even when convincingly articulated as human rights, never come to fruition in the form of policy enacted by states. Though addressed only sparingly in the extant literature, the complexity and ambiguity of the relationship between movements claiming rights and the realization of rights through social policy at the state level ought to figure prominently in the research agenda of the sociology of human rights. Clearly, this issue forms a major point of convergence between social movement research and political sociology. In the conclusion of the book, the issue appears among the list of priorities for future inquiry.

Human Rights, Social Policy, and Law

Though auspicious for mass mobilizations (whether in terms of ideological orientation, platform building, or claims-making), the construction and propagation of human rights norms – often in reference to major declarations and treaties as moral or political compasses – has always been fraught with contradictions, shortcomings, and setbacks (Khagram et al. 2002). This is par for the course not only because of the complexities of exegesis, but also because of the difficulty of predicting how sympathetic policymakers and elites might respond to the rights claims of SMOs. Moreover, it can be difficult, if not impossible, to demonstrate conclusively – that is, in a truly *social scientific* fashion – that a given movement or coalition has produced specific human rights legislation or favorable public policy. For example, it would be challenging to prove definitively that popular forces, including the unemployed, the marginally employed, and low-wage workers, *precipitated* the flurry of legislation (in the area of economic and social rights) that comprised the New Deal in the US. Clearly, the administration of Franklin Delano Roosevelt in particular and the Democratic Party in general were concerned not only about the potential for popular unrest, but also about the threats that the Great Depression posed for the existing economic system (Levine 1988). Thus, make-work projects like the Civilian Conservation Corps (1933–42) and the Works Progress Administration (1935–41) – directed as they were at the problem of unemployment/under-consumption – were rightly seen as addressing the needs of workers and employers simultaneously, and hence found support in a popular-elite coalition (Levine 1988).

Similarly, it would be difficult to demonstrate conclusively that the US civil rights movement, with its competing SMOs (each with a different set of objectives, strategies, tactics, and framing techniques) and complex web of allies (including policymakers and elites), *produced* the Civil Rights Act of 1964 or the Voting Rights Act of 1965. Clearly, the administration of Lyndon Baines Johnson in particular and the Democratic Party in general had numerous reasons for supporting the abrogation of Jim Crow laws, the desegregation of public facilities and social spaces, and the institutionalization of civil and political rights for African Americans and other racial minorities in the South. In sum, the cases of New Deal policies and civil rights legislation point to the need for multi-causal explanations. As the emerging literature on social movement consequences and outcomes shows, the enactment of policy involves the complex interplay of an array of forces both beyond and within the state (Giugni 1998; Amenta et al. 2010). This insight serves as an important proviso for sociologists of human rights.

Let us return to the role of the human rights canon as a touchstone for a multitude of agents. Throughout the book, the author refers to the UDHR, the ICCPR, the ICESCR, and other documents not as sacred texts or definitive statements, but rather as *markers* of disputes and contestation over human rights. Accordingly, this book rejects both the *idealist* contention that aspirational documents are decisive in guiding the behavior of social actors and the *realist* assertion that such texts are irrelevant to the conduct of social actors. In charting a middle course between these two poles, the author interprets treaties, declarations, and pronouncements not only as reflections of past debates and struggles, but also as stepping stones to new discussions and conflicts on the meaning and policy implications of human rights in the present day. To analyze the human rights canon *sociologically* is to move beyond textual analysis in order to explicate the claimants, constituencies, and power-blocs underlying competing interpretations of the ICCPR, the ICESCR, and other major texts. From there, it is possible to examine the circumstances under which given interpretations of the major textual reference points "stick" (or fail to do so).

For a given interpretation to "stick," it must resonate with a substantial contingent in the rights-oriented epistemic community. In principle, a cluster of aggrieved parties, SMOs, and/or NGOs would need to convince sympathetic state policymakers (through the mediation of political parties) to take seriously the idea of using the political, moral, and ideological force of the ICESCR as a justification for the enactment and implementation of state-level policy. In effect, the ICESCR – serving as the encapsulation of the accumulated wisdom of the human rights community – would provide the inspiration for social programs (e.g., to alleviate economic inequality and poverty). In short, it is not sufficient merely for a coalition to offer a plausible interpretation of the text. It is necessary for the coalition to attract support for said interpretation among state policymakers. These policymakers, in turn, must undertake a complex process of *translation* in applying the insights of an international declaration to specific national conditions. As we shall see, the process of translation – applying the insights of a major text in the human rights canon to the policy needs of a given nation-state – figures prominently among subjects for the sociologists of human rights to consider.

In shedding light on the human rights canon, its function as a reference point for NGOs and SMOs, and its possible influences on social policy and law, the sociological perspective approaches the organizational and institutional achievements of the post-1945 period with critical detachment. Clearly, the UN system and the corresponding network of NGOs have increased awareness among policymakers and the general public alike of human rights issues. Moreover, there is evidence that human rights norms, laws, and policies have altered not only the workings of the interstate system, but also the internal dynamics of nation-states (in terms of how political parties interact with popular forces) (Khagram et al. 2002). Finally, it is apparent that an increasing number of SMOs are articulating their demands in the syntax and semantics of human rights, whether for internal reasons or under the influence of NGOs and other entities providing logistical and material support, publicity, and other benefits. Nevertheless, a certain degree of circumspection regarding the possible trend remains appropriate. While it may be tempting to conceptualize such breakthroughs as the UN system and the proliferation of rights-oriented NGOs in terms of "human rights revolutions" – a notion that appears frequently in the publications of the UN and major NGOs – the sociological perspective would suggest that the jury is out not only on the profundity of the rupture with the past, but also on the successes and failures of a series of human rights agendas. Accordingly, this book argues that the human rights agenda – understood as a compromise among competing forces – merits investigation insofar as it both *reflects* and *affects* power relations among a range of social actors. In this light, let us turn our attention to the major contributions of the book.

Special Features of the Book

Designed to introduce readers of varying degrees of experience and expertise to the origins, applications, and implications of the sociological perspective on human rights, this book contains six special features. These features are given deeper definitions in chapter 1. First, the book defines the *sociology of human rights* as the use of sociological theories and methods to explain (a) the conditions – whether economic, political, social, cultural, environmental, or otherwise – under which aggrieved parties and their allies formulate rights claims, (b) the manner in which rights-oriented policies are implemented by national governments, and (c) the political effects of human rights legislation – whether in the form of changing power relations among a range of social actors or in the form of new policies and institutions created by government authorities. Second, the book delineates the concept of *rights conditions,* understood as circumstances inspiring or forcing under-represented or maltreated populations to express their grievances. Third, the book elaborates the concept of *rights claims,* understood as appeals for protections and entitlements that aggrieved parties make to political authorities. Fourth, the book develops the concept of *rights effects,* understood as palpable changes in power structures and social relations that emerge when aggrieved parties actualize new rights through policy, law, or custom. Fifth, the book explains the concept of *rights bundles,* understood as packets of organically connected rights that exceed the conventional categories. Sixth, the book offers a critical reworking of what was once the prevailing classification schema in the field of the human rights: a framework that specifies first-generation civil and political rights designed to ensure liberty; second-generation economic and social rights designed to ensure equality; and third-generation collective rights – especially in the areas of culture and environment – designed to ensure solidarity. Since it points to one of the major theses of the book, the sixth feature demands a brief comment here. Rather than summarily rejecting the three-generations framework, the book *works through it* in order to demonstrate its uses and limitations for research, teaching, service, and advocacy. Such a gesture has both a *historical* and a *theoretical* justification.

Though the three-generations framework remains a useful analytic, pedagogical, and political tool, it should be seen primarily as a *device* – a means of framing issues for further exploration by scholars, policymakers, activists, and other participants in the epistemic community built around human rights. Thus, the three categories – civil and political rights for individuals, economic and social rights for individuals, and cultural and environmental rights for groups – are treated as *theoretical abstractions.* As such, the categories are used by various parties in the human rights community – but especially by academic researchers – to analyze real-world puzzles. Puzzle solving, in turn, constitutes the essential task of the sciences (whether natural or social) in general. By definition, the sociology of human rights in particular – understood as a complement to the political science, anthropology, and geography of human rights – concerns itself with setting up and solving puzzles involving not only the *denial* of *actualized* rights to, but also the *claiming* of *potential* rights by, aggrieved parties across the world. In other words, the puzzles analyzed by rights-oriented sociologists may pertain either to the failure on the part of governments and their agents to respect the rights that appear in the human rights canon or to the demands for rights (translated into state policies, political institutions, and legal practices) made by popular forces and their allies.

What constitutes a rights puzzle? In principle, any complex social problem that has a bearing on actualized or proposed human rights (as manifested either in the human rights canon or in critiques thereof) can be formalized by sociologists (or other social scientists) as a *rights puzzle* – a multifaceted issue, with implications for human rights, that challenges or even confounds researchers. For the purposes of this book, rights puzzles include such enduring social problems as poverty, inequality, exploitation, and discrimination on the basis of identity, cultural destruction, and environmental devastation. How do sociologists solve rights puzzles? Drawing on sociological theories and methods, researchers: (a) describe why a given social problem should be conceptualized as a rights puzzle, (b) explain why the problem defies conventional solutions, and (c) show how state policies, if implemented successfully and enforced consistently, would solve the problem. To address the example that figures most prominently in this book, poverty constitutes a rights puzzle not only because it has proven difficult to solve through social programs, but also because it cuts across the economy, the polity, culture, and the environment. Thus, a solution to the poverty puzzle would entail state policies that take a range of non-economic factors into consideration.

As we have seen, the fundamental task of the sociology of human rights is to address rights puzzles. In effect, this entails critically working through the three generations of human rights in order to arrive at more felicitous and productive ways of thinking about and acting upon the precepts of human rights. Why is this necessary? In the real world, such rights puzzles as poverty, inequality, exploitation, discrimination on the basis of identity, the destruction of cultures, and environmental degradation routinely demand solutions that cut across the three generations of human rights. Since the puzzles are invariably attributable to multiple causes, they necessitate complex remedies in the form of rights bundles. Accordingly, the book is designed to inspire readers to reflect on the rights bundles proposed in chapter 6: longevity (or the right to lead a long, healthy life), which entails proper nutrition and healthcare, as well as a nurturing environment; the full development of the person (or the right to develop one's talents and cultivate one's identity), which necessitates a proper education, vocational training, work opportunities, leisure time, and lifestyle options; and peace (or the right to be protected from interstate war, civil conflict, bullying, and domestic abuse), which implies civilian defense, enlightened policing and alternatives to incarceration, institutions of non-violent conflict resolution, and educational programs. Readers are also encouraged to advance rights bundles of their own (according to their own precepts and visions of a better world). To encourage readers to propose their own rights bundles is to celebrate popular participation in pursuing a new human rights agenda. On the one hand, defensible rights bundles must be bolstered by the specific needs and aspirations of aggrieved societies, groups, and communities. On the other hand, such bundles must be forged in the spirit of universalism. This presents us with an exciting challenge.

1 Defining the Sociology of Human Rights

This book offers a detailed introduction to the sociology of human rights, which is a growing field in academia, especially in the US, but also elsewhere in the world. Premised on the idea that sociology, defined as the scientific analysis of power relations among human beings in their economic, political, social, cultural, and environmental lives, complements the insights of political science, anthropology, geography, and other disciplines, this book begins with the following question: How do sociologists explore the set of protections and entitlements known as human rights? By training and inclination, sociologists are interested in the three major aspects of the human rights "cycle": first, the circumstances or rights conditions under which social movement organizations (SMOs) and their non-governmental organization (NGO) affiliates translate grievances (e.g., complaints about abuse, inequality, exploitation, exclusion, and other social and environmental problems) into rights claims (or appeals to political authorities for redress); second, the fashion in which rights claims, once filtered through political and legal systems, are implemented in the form of policies, laws, and institutions; and third, how the enactment of new policies and laws at the level of the nation-state alters power relations among social actors, outcomes known as rights effects. Thus, human rights are conceived not only as regulative ideas, noble aspirations, and pieces of paper, but also as concrete measures – in the form of policies, laws, and institutions – that shape the interactions among governments, transnational corporations, organizations, groups, and persons.

Moving beyond intellectual history and the sociology of knowledge, this approach elucidates not only the embeddedness of ideas, policies, laws, institutions, and practices in webs of power relations, but also the resulting "fits" (or moments of convergence) between particular notions of rights and specific power structures. As we shall discover, sociology proves well equipped to elucidate these fits for use by members of the epistemic community. For example, the US civil rights movement – understood as a collection of SMOs (including the Southern Christian Leadership Conference and the Student Nonviolent Coordinating Committee) that collaborated and competed with one another in challenging Jim Crow laws and other forms of institutional racism in the South – participated in a process that eventually produced the Civil Rights Act of 1964 and the Voting Rights Act of 1965. Using marches, sit-ins, freedom rides, and other direct action tactics, such SMOs challenged the racist laws and practices that preserved segregation, disenfranchisement, job and housing discrimination, and other human rights abuses across the South. Notwithstanding differences in philosophy, strategy, objectives, organizational structure, membership, and constituency, such SMOs participated in the push for *national* legislation to institutionalize such civil and political rights as the right to use public spaces, the right to equal access to education, and the right to vote for African Americans. It is difficult to ascertain how much influence such SMOs and their elite allies exerted on Congress. As the literature on social movement outcomes suggests, more research is required to determine the degree to which such SMOs swayed policymakers (Giugni 1998; Amenta et al. 2010). Nevertheless, it is clear that the new legislation occasioned a fit between popular forces (aggrieved parties) and fractions of the federal government (especially in the Democratic Party). Once implemented, the Civil Rights Act and the Voting Rights Act helped to alter power relations by providing for greater personal security and freedom, educational and career opportunities, and voting rights for African Americans.

The Sociological Perspective

In distinguishing the sociological perspective from the perspectives of political science, legal studies, and other disciplines, prominent figures in the nascent field have noted:

> Where sociology does not presuppose the relevance or inevitability of the state, human rights instruments and the formal human rights regime comprise only one small part of the larger whole. The human rights enterprise represents this whole, where grassroots struggles outside of and potentially against the formal state arena are seen as equally relevant to interpreting, critiquing, and realizing human rights in practice. The human rights enterprise should, again, be seen as the sum total of *all*

struggles to define and realize universal dignity and "right." (Armaline et al. 2011: 3)

As Armaline et al. have argued, sociology is by definition interested in the *totality* of debates, disputes, contests, and struggles concerning human rights worldviews and ideas, policies and laws, institutions and organizations, and practices – an inclusive category that they have termed the "human rights enterprise." In delineating the category, the authors compensate for the tendency on the part of segments of the epistemic community to overlook the contributions of popular forces to human rights thought and practice. As a consequence, they offer a "bottom-up" approach to human rights.

As another set of prominent scholars have demonstrated, the emerging field of rights-oriented sociology stands to receive contributions from every research cluster of the American Sociological Association: from such obvious candidates as the Section on Sociological Practice and Public Sociology (with its emphasis on utilizing sociological tools for the betterment of society) and the Section on Peace, War, and Social Conflict (with its focus on causes, effects, and possible solutions to warfare and civil strife) to such surprising candidates as the Section on Evolution, Biology, and Society and the Section on Mathematical Sociology (Brunsma et al. 2012). The field also stands to *make* contributions to the discipline as a whole (Brunsma et al. 2012). Indeed, as Brunsma et al. have argued, the sociological approach to human rights harbors the potential to reorient the discipline toward the use of rigorous social scientific methods (whether qualitative, comparative-historical, or quantitative) for the elucidation and resolution of human rights problems. While it remains to be seen whether rights-oriented sociology will precipitate an "epistemological revolution" in the wider discipline, it is clear that the emerging field holds considerable promise for generating research.

As the foregoing analyses suggest, sociologists explore the origins, evolution, outcomes, and implications of struggles over the following: civil and political rights (including the right to the security of person, the right to vote, freedom of religion, and the rights to association, assembly, speech, and petition) for individuals; economic and social rights (including the rights to a decent job, unemployment insurance, social security, and healthcare) for individuals; cultural rights (including the rights of indigenous peoples to inhabit their ancestral lands and preserve their identities, lifeways, and languages) for collectivities; and environmental rights (including the rights to clean air and water, arable land, accessible and sustainable commons, and preserved forests) for collectivities.

Using the sociological lens to examine the broad spectrum of human rights, three points become apparent. First, civil and political rights are the most widely understood and accepted, while there remains considerable debate on the existence, nature, and scope not only of economic and social rights, but also of cultural rights and environmental rights. This is especially true in the US, since the Constitution places great emphasis on civil and political rights but pays less attention to other forms of rights. Second, while it is useful for analytic, pedagogical, and political purposes to place human rights in distinct categories (understood as theoretical abstractions), it is evident that different types of rights overlap with one another in the real world. Third, notwithstanding efforts to pursue an expansive project of human emancipation that would gradually include more maltreated or disaffected constituencies and dissolve enduring inequalities, it is clear that rights claims, however noble, justifiable, and plausible they may be, often come into conflict with one another in entanglements of power relations, competing interests, coalitional politics, and ambiguous or even contradictory legislation. As a consequence, sociologists are forced to sift through conflicts surrounding the theories, institutions, policies, and practices of human rights. In fact, one of the central purposes of the sociological study of human rights is precisely to illuminate the probable causes of and possible remedies for competing rights claims.

This book offers a particular approach to research and teaching in the sociology of human rights that draws on political economy/ development sociology (with its capacity to elucidate the conditions that give rise to grievances), social movement research (with its ability to explain how the organizational structures, strategies, tactics and framing techniques of SMOs influence rights claims), and political sociology (with its attentiveness to the role of rights-oriented policies in altering power relations) in formalizing a set of theories and concepts. Accordingly, this chapter pursues three interrelated objectives. First, it offers a preliminary definition of human rights as a set of protections and entitlements conferred, at least in principle, upon all 7 billion members of the human species regardless of race, class, gender, sexual orientation, cultural background, religious affiliation, national origin, or geographic location. Second, this chapter paints a picture of how the field analyzes the social conditions under which different types of rights (e.g., civil and political, economic and social, cultural and environmental) are reinterpreted or invented by the epistemic community, claimed by SMOs and NGOs, and either granted or denied by governments and other authorities.

Third, this chapter introduces some of the building blocks of the sociology of human rights, including the concepts of *rights conditions* (i.e., the economic, political, social, and cultural circumstances under which grievances are formulated in reference to the human rights canon), *rights claims* (i.e., the specific demands for protections and entitlements that aggrieved parties make on political authorities), *rights effects* (i.e., changes in power relations stemming from the achievement of rights by new constituencies), and *rights bundles* (i.e., packets of interlinked rights that transcend the conventional classifications). In sum, this chapter provides readers with an understanding of the scholarly, political, and practical uses of the sociological perspective on human rights.

What Are Human Rights?

We find ourselves in a position to examine the most fundamental question in this emerging domain of academic research, teaching, and service: How do sociologists – whether in concert or contradistinction with other academics – define human rights? Building on the work of philosophers, legal scholars, and political scientists, sociologists define human rights as a set of protections and entitlements possessed by all members of the human community regardless of race, class, gender, sexual orientation, cultural background, national origin, or other forms of identity or social standing. To a certain extent, sociologists distinguish themselves from their counterparts in philosophy, legal studies, and political science by focusing on the *social character* of both protections and entitlements, a tendency shared by those anthropologists and geographers who analyze human rights. In essence, this implies that the meanings, powers, duties, and constraints associated with human rights are embedded in society. For the moment, we may bracket the unsettled question of whether rights – protections and entitlements alike – should been seen as having a foundation in *human nature* or, alternatively, whether rights should be seen as *social constructs* (Turner 2006; Gregg 2012). In either case, it is clear that our conceptions of human rights not only vary across historical time and geographic space, but also prove subject to the mediation of culture. Accordingly, the issue of culture – especially amidst the contradictory pulls of homogenization and particularization in the era of globalization – figures prominently in this book (Vrdoljak 2013). Even the most "grounded" and "universal" human rights (e.g., the first-generation rights to life and the security of person) find expression only in particular cultural frameworks. In other words, what it means to live as a secure person varies greatly from one cultural formation to another.

As we might expect, sociologists disagree on how to address ontological and epistemological questions (including the question of human nature and what science can tell us about it). Notwithstanding potential divergences on the issue of human nature versus social construction, sociologists tend to agree on the possibility and desirability of cross-cultural communication on values and institutions. Whatever our intrinsic commonalties as humans may be, we have the capacity to build on shared perceptions and experiences in making the world a more peaceful, equal, culturally inclusive, and ecologically sustainable place for everyone. In other words, sociologists tend to believe that human beings may choose to work together in the pursuit of a common framework or set of norms irrespective of whether or not rights are grounded in human physiology and/or an intrinsic capacity for empathy, sociability, cooperation, and solidarity. While it is distinctly possible that a genuinely global universalism would be easier to achieve if rights were founded on a knowable, representable, and continuous human nature, it remains plausible that a form of universalism could be *constructed* on the basis of common experiences, negotiated values, regulated interactions, and shared institutions (Donnelly 2003). What matters here is the realization that universalism – the idea that a set of human rights should be institutionalized on a global scale – entails dialogue and negotiation among intergovernmental organizations (especially the UN, with its array of specialized agencies), national governments (especially those possessing great economic, diplomatic, military, and ideological power), NGOs, SMOs, and community-based organizations. Ideally, this process of dialogue and negotiation would open spaces not only for poor and weak countries, but also for marginalized populations across the world. With this in mind, we may return to the larger question of how to define human rights in sociological perspective.

Negative Rights/Civil and Political Rights

The first part of the larger question is as follows: What types of *protections* do human beings have? In theory, all humans must be protected from abuse, humiliation, exploitation, and exclusion perpetrated by governments, organizations, small groups, and individuals. Known as negative rights – rights that protect individuals from abuses perpetrated by one another and by the state – these rights include the rights to life, bodily integrity, dignity, due process of law, association, assembly, free speech, religious affiliation (or non-affiliation), and representation in government (Blau and Moncada 2009). In principle, it is the responsibility of governments at the national and local levels to guarantee negative rights to all persons. In practice, ensuring negative rights means that governments must check their own powers, primarily through the judiciary, but sometimes through the executive branch. For example, the US Department of Justice investigates civil rights violations perpetrated by federal, state, or local authorities, an issue that has presented itself periodically since the ratification of the Civil Rights Act in 1964 and the Voting Rights Act in 1965.

To take a current example, as the prevailing interpretation of the Constitution suggests, the US government serves as the principal guarantor of the right to privacy. Citizens across the political spectrum define privacy as a prominent negative right that prohibits undue state intrusion in the individual's personal life. In pursuit of expanded security objectives (directed at the terrorist tactics of non-state actors that oppose US foreign policy), the same government has established a program for monitoring the private e-mail messages, texts, and phone calls of its citizens. In this light, the recent debate on the US National Security Agency's programs monitoring the personal communications of citizens can be seen as an exhibition not only of the complex role of the government, but also of the tension between two negative rights: the right to privacy and the right to personal security. Since 2001, the American public has found itself in an ongoing debate on possible trade-offs between the right to privacy and the right to personal security.

Bracketing the question of the constitutionality, legality, legitimacy, and efficacy of such programs – a matter that requires debate on the part of the general public, advocacy groups, the three branches of government, political scientists, and legal scholars alike – this example demonstrates the complexities, ambiguities, and contradictions associated with the conferral and enforcement of negative rights by states. Considered together, the aforementioned negative rights, entirely civil and political in character, ensure not only a person's life, privacy, safety, security, dignity, personality, and conscience, but also his or her participation in public life and freedom from excessive interference on the part of the state in personal matters.

Owing to the language of the Constitution and the political culture, Americans tend to be familiar with and enthusiastic about negative rights. In fact, many Americans assume that negative rights encompass the full range of human rights, an assumption that accords with the tradition of possessive individualism. As a consequence of their social scientific training and the critical detachment that goes along with it, sociologists take issue with this contention. Although negative rights can take us very far, they cannot ensure the fulfillment of the needs for food and water, shelter, clothing, healthcare, and an education. Accordingly, we must examine a number of positive rights or entitlements, including the economic and social rights that are reflected in the social programs associated with welfare states in the US, the European Union, and elsewhere in the Global North, along with the social policies that were implemented, albeit in a more modest way, in development states in the Global South (Esping-Andersen 1990). This is an excellent example of how the sociology of human rights draws on the achievements of political sociology. In a sense, the analysis of economic and social rights – ranging from education and healthcare to employment and anti-poverty programs – converges with the literature on the welfare and development states that once dotted the global landscape. Welfare and development states have recently seen the implementation of market-oriented policies and corresponding budget cuts. In the US, social provisioning has been subject to significant cuts from the Reagan presidency, through the Clinton presidency (which signed the 1996 Welfare Reform Act, the putative "end of welfare as we knew it"), to the present day (Piven and Cloward 1998). More recently, the "Great Recession" has occasioned a wave of protests against economic inequality not only in the US (in the form of the Occupy Wall Street movement), but also in the European Union (particularly in such "peripheral" countries as Spain and Greece). Paradoxically, it is precisely the so-called "retreat of the state" from social programs – a process that has manifested itself across the world – that has opened a space for the discussion of economic and social rights. Such a discussion, in turn, points to the need to excavate past debates on and struggles over social programs in nation-states across the world.

Positive Rights/Economic and Social Rights

This brings us to the second part of the larger question: What kinds of *entitlements* do human beings have? In theory, all humans are entitled to economic structures and social programs that provide them with access to the means of subsistence, permit them to develop physically and mentally, facilitate their entrance into trades and professions, provide them with upward social mobility, give them leisure time, and insulate them from an array of catastrophes (including economic recessions and depressions, human-induced calamities, and natural disasters). Known as positive rights (i.e., rights that entail active intervention and policymaking on the part of governments to compensate for previously existing social inequalities, to assist persons as they make their way from childhood to old age, to aid the most vulnerable members of society, and to mitigate the effects of crises), these entitlements include food, clothing, housing, healthcare, an education, employment, unemployment and disability insurance, social security, a minimum wage, and a basic standard of living (Blau and Moncada 2009).

A conversation on the possibility and desirability of enacting economic and social rights entails some reflection on the history of the welfare state in the US – a narrative that has been obscured amidst bipartisan support for budget cuts in the globalization era (Skocpol 1995; Amenta 1998). In the interest of space, it suffices to tell the story in an abbreviated fashion. It is worth noting, however, that the voluminous literature on the origins and evolution of the US welfare state – understood as part of an international process of using state power to manage the workings of capitalism through boom and bust phases (through what Keynesian economists called "counter-cyclical demand management") – provides many puzzles for the sociology of human rights. Accordingly, this book features as one of its proposals for future research the examination of the US welfare state, with its actualized and retracted, proposed and rejected, insufficiently debated economic and social rights, as an important subject for the sociology of human rights as such. Such a research plank would draw in instructive ways on three major theoretical sources of the sociology of human rights: political economy/development sociology, social movement research, and political sociology. More precisely, it would illuminate the conditions (e.g., widespread unemployment during the Great Depression) under which popular-elite coalitions advanced claims for economic and social rights, the ways in which such claims were actualized in state policies, and the effects of such policies on social classes and businesses. In sum, the concepts of rights conditions, rights claims, and rights effects would come in handy in the analysis of the US welfare state.

Let us turn to the historical narrative. Amidst the Great Depression of the 1930s, a number of positive rights were implemented with the relief, recovery, and reform programs that comprised the New Deal (Levine 1988). While President Franklin Delano Roosevelt conceptualized such programs in terms of human rights and eventually proposed a "Second Bill of Rights" that would build social programs into the Constitution, it has been customary, especially in the last 30 years, for politicians and their constituencies to question the acceptability of many social programs. As a consequence, the issue of which economic and social rights Americans may plausibly claim remains unsettled. In light of ongoing debates in the US (especially between the Democratic and Republican parties), the European Union (especially among labor, social democratic, socialist, and green parties and their opponents on the right), and elsewhere in the Global North on the legitimacy and viability of the welfare state, it remains to be seen whether economic and social rights can or should be preserved amidst recurring budget crises. Such crises often produce difficult trade-offs. This book does not speculate on the future of the welfare state, a problem that has been explored in rich detail by political sociologists, economic sociologists, and researchers in comparative politics (Pierson et al. 2013). But the book does refer to research that defines social programs in terms of human rights. Far from being an academic innovation, the idea of a "social rights state" has deep roots in policymaking circles in the European Union.

Well-documented in social scientific research and much celebrated in popular culture, a spirit of possessive individualism and self-reliance, based in part on the mythology of "winning the West" and building "homes on the range," has pervaded US society since its inception. Notwithstanding the array of economic and social rights that found expression in the New Deal in the 1930s and the subsequent expansion of the social safety net through the Great Society programs of the 1960s, Americans tend to be deeply suspicious of positive rights. Americans normally think about social programs not as rights per se, but rather as privileges that may be revoked with changing economic circumstances. Why is this the case? Since positive rights entail the enactment of policies by lawmakers at the federal, state, and local levels to alleviate enduring social inequalities or rectify historical injustices, they are always subject to changing political tides and ideological consensuses. This means that policymakers have the capacity to either expand or reduce the positive rights that are available to the population.

To further complicate matters, there exists no consensus on positive rights either within or between the major political parties – the Democrats on the left and the Republicans on the right – in the US. Since the postwar period, Democrats have been more likely than their Republican counterparts to support economic and social rights. But this tendency is far from absolute. Moreover, as the Welfare Reform Act of 1996 and its offshoots have shown, the Democratic Party has tended to support the reduction of social programs in the name of market-oriented solutions. This is the context in which the debate on the Patient Protection and Affordable Care Act has unfolded. Many supporters of the legislation are reluctant to characterize healthcare as a human right. In short, there is considerable debate on the nature, scope, and applications of positive rights in US policymaking circles. Explaining what is at stake in such debates is one of the primary functions of the sociology of human rights.

Cultural and Environmental Rights

It is worth mentioning that many scholars, policymakers, and activists include in the category of positive rights such cultural entitlements as the rights of indigenous peoples to inhabit their ancestral lands and maintain their identities, lifeways, and practices and such environmental entitlements as the rights to clean air and water, arable land, and a sustainable commons. By convention, cultural and environmental rights are categorized as positive rights for three reasons. First, these rights reflect the most cutting-edge thinking in the human rights community, largely as a consequence of the growing influence of popular forces in the Global South. For example, the Landless Rural Workers' Movement in Brazil, the Zapatista movement in Mexico, along with the community-based organizations, SMOs, and NGOs that convene at the World Social Forum share the tendency to connect land claims not only to the affirmation of particular identities, but also to the spirit of universalism. In the process, they have shown possible ways not only of thinking beyond the conventional categories of human rights, but also of embracing both universalism and cultural pluralism (Pearce 2001). Let us focus briefly on the most renowned of the three examples. Serving since 2001 as an arena for non-violent, non-party organizations to exchange information about philosophy, strategy, and tactics in the struggle against neoliberal globalization, the World Social Forum proposes rights bundles "to ensure that globalization in solidarity will prevail as a new stage in world history. This will respect universal human rights, and those of all citizens – men and women – of all nations and the environment and will rest on democratic international systems and institutions at the service of social justice, equality and the sovereignty of peoples" (World Social Forum 2013).

Second, cultural and environmental rights, having been de-emphasized, ignored, and denied across the world, can be brought to fruition only with the enactment of innovative legislation on the part of states (e.g., to protect and promote threatened cultural practices, redistribute unused land for farming and building communities, restore waterways for fishing, and preserve forests for hunting, gathering, and other subsistence and medicinal practices). Third, cultural and environmental rights are, by definition, accorded not to individuals, but rather to *groups* (whose members are defined by claims to specific identities) and *communities* (whose members are defined by their residency). Thus, cultural and environmental rights are fundamentally different in character from the two sets of rights that are granted to individuals – civil/political rights and economic/social rights.

What does this tell us about the customary ways of classifying human rights? At this point, we can draw three conclusions about the conventional categories that structured human rights thinking from the postwar period though the late 1980s. First, negative rights (understood as protections that the state must provide its citizens) are civil and political in nature, while positive rights (understood as entitlements that the state must provide its citizens) may be economic and social, cultural, or environmental in nature. Second, while drawing a distinction among different types of rights proves useful for research, teaching, and political action or advocacy, it must be acknowledged that negative and positive rights overlap with one another in the real world. Third, while there is little debate over the legitimacy of negative/civil and political rights, there is considerable debate and even controversy on the legitimacy of positive/economic and social, cultural and environmental rights. For these reasons, we must think through the standard classification schemas in order to arrive at an approach that works better in the globalization era.

Rights Bundling

Far from being merely ideological or intellectual in character, these debates reflect complex and contradictory relations among competing power blocs and constituencies. Accordingly, one of the major purposes of this book is to inspire students, scholars, policymakers, and the general public to work through – and perhaps move beyond – the conventional categories in order to better understand debates among agencies of the UN, such prominent NGOs as Amnesty International, Human Rights Watch, and Oxfam International, and SMOs across the global landscape. In both collaborating and competing with one another to define the agenda for human rights, UN agencies, NGOs, and SMOs form a nexus – a force field in which old rights are reinterpreted and new rights are invented. Accordingly, the UN–NGO–SMO nexus, replete with contradictions and ambiguities, holds considerable import for sociologists of human rights. In effect, the nexus determines how the human rights canon – with its central touchstones, the Universal Declaration of Human Rights (UDHR) the International Covenant on Civil and Political Rights (ICCPR), and the International Covenant on Economic, Social, and Cultural Rights (ICESCR) – are interpreted and applied in response to globalization-related problems.

In this light, the case of Oxfam International, a renowned and effective NGO based in the UK, proves particularly instructive for our purposes. In adopting a "rights-based approach" to the complex problem of global poverty, Oxfam International affirms five universal rights: the right to have "a livelihood," which implies decent working conditions, access to natural resources, and a sustainable ecosystem; the right to such "basic services" as clean water, public hygiene, and education; the right to "be safe from harm," which entails protection from the risk of natural disasters; the right to "be heard," which necessitates popular participation in debates and decision-making processes; and, finally, the right to "be treated as equal," which necessitates measures to ensure that ethnic, racial, and religious minorities, women, and persons with disabilities enjoy equal access to jobs, resources, and information (http://www.oxfam.org/en/about/why). Taken together, these rights address the causes and effects of poverty. With multiple causes and manifold effects, the poverty puzzle calls for the proclamation and implementation of a rights bundle.

What else can we conclude about these interlinked rights? Clearly, the five rights affirmed by Oxfam International transcend the distinction between negative/civil and political rights and positive/ economic and social, cultural, and environmental rights. In advancing these rights, Oxfam International argues that the remediation of poverty, far from being merely an economic matter, necessitates consideration of political, social, cultural, and environmental factors. In analyzing cases like that of Oxfam International, a prominent NGO that illustrates the workings of the UN–NGO–SMO nexus, with its connections to UN agencies at the "top" and movements on the "bottom," sociologists aim to explicate the real-world interconnections among different types of rights. With a view to illuminating how NGOs and other types of organizations bundle together ostensibly distinct forms of rights, we will return to the example of Oxfam – and explore others like it – elsewhere in the book.

What is the Sociology of Human Rights?

In a sense, the issue of human rights cuts to the heart of sociology as a discipline. Founded in European, particularly French and German, universities in the nineteenth century, the discipline of sociology took its name from the Latin word *socius*, meaning "companion" and the Greek word *logos*, meaning "knowledge." Implicit in the name of the nascent discipline was the idea of a human companion to scientific knowledge; and science, in turn, was seen as the preferred way of understanding the natural world, the social world, and the complex relationship between the two worlds. Amidst industrialization, urbanization, and other profound yet unsettling transformations, the discipline quickly crystallized as the *science of society*, a notion attributed to the celebrated humanist philosopher Auguste Comte, who proposed "Love as the principle and order as the basis; progress as the goal." (Interestingly enough, the spirit of Comte's humanist and progressivist philosophy would later be reflected in the slogan on the Brazilian flag.) There is much debate on how Comte and the other pioneers of the discipline conceptualized "science," for example, the question of whether or to what extent sociology should adopt the methods of the natural sciences and aspire to value neutrality. Nonetheless, it is clear that the founders envisaged sociology as a *systematic* line of inquiry. To one degree or another, scientificity proved significant for the early sociologists.

Although the early sociologists, including the putative founders, Karl Marx, Emile Durkheim, and Max Weber, showed great interest in laws, norms, and ideological constructs, they paid scant attention to human rights per se (Deflem and Chicoine 2011). In fact, it was not until the mid-1990s that the sociology of human rights was formalized as a distinct field of research and teaching in the university systems of North America and Europe (Frezzo 2011). Hence the question arises: Why was sociology hesitant to undertake the systematic study of human rights? As one of the pioneers of the new field has contended, the competing legacies of positivism (i.e., the belief that sociology should borrow the methods of natural science and maintain strict value-neutrality) and cultural relativism (i.e., the belief that values have significance only in the cultural contexts that create them) prevented many sociologists from noticing the human rights revolution of the twentieth century, a process that produced not only an array of treaties and declarations, but also the UN and its agencies, a large number of NGOs, and other institutions (Turner 2006). While it would be overstating the case to assert that most sociologists were either positivists or relativists, it seems likely that the *legacies* of these contradictory traditions inhibited the emergence of an explicitly rights-oriented sociology. In effect, there was a time lag between the codification of the human rights canon (amidst the founding of the rights-oriented epistemic community) and the creation of a branch of sociology devoted to the analysis of human rights. In the meantime, other social sciences, in particular political science (especially the branches of international relations and comparative politics) and anthropology (especially the branch devoted to the study of cultural norms and practices), made forays into the analysis of the workings of human rights.

Which factors prompted sociologists to join their counterparts in political science, anthropology, and other disciplines in addressing human rights in a systematic fashion? The story is complex, but worth telling. The 1990s occasioned not only the end of the Cold War and the reincorporation of the erstwhile socialist states (including Bulgaria, Czechoslovakia, East Germany, Hungary, Poland, Romania, the former republics of the Soviet Union, and the states of ex-Yugoslavia) into the capitalist world economy, but also a proliferation of popular protests – first in the Global South and later in the Global North – against the neoliberal policies advocated by the International Monetary Fund (IMF), the World Bank (WB), and the World Trade Organization (WTO), and implemented by compliant governments across the world (McMichael 2012). Designed to balance budgets, control inflation, stabilize currencies, and facilitate the operation of transnational corporations, the neoliberal platform had five planks:

fiscal austerity (cuts to social programs), deregulation (lifting of labor, safety, and environmental regulations), privatization (sale of state-owned enterprises), financial liberalization (lifting of controls on the flow of capital across national boundaries), and free trade (elimination of tariffs on imports and subsidies on exports). Associated with globalization and the post-Fordist work regime (in which transnational corporations outsourced industry from high-wage zones in the Global North to low-wage zones in the Global South), neoliberalism involved the "retreat of the state" from social programs and the celebration of "market rationality" (Bandelj and Sowers 2010: 177–84). Over time, SMOs, especially in Latin America, began to resist neoliberalism while invoking the master-frame of human rights (Smith 2007). In the process of challenging neoliberal policies in the name of justice, democracy, cultural pluralism, and environmental sustainability, certain SMOs and their NGO allies effectively *reinterpreted* old rights and *invented* new rights, a trend that caught the attention of scholars interested in political economy/development sociology, social movement research, and political sociology. In effect, there was a "backflow" of human rights ideas from the streets, factories, fields, and universities of the Global South to the corridors of academia in the Global North. Needless to say, this backflow was made possible by one of the most prominent features of globalization: the proliferation of advanced communications technologies across the Global South. As a recent example of this "backflow," activists in the Occupy Wall Street movement borrowed the principle of "horizontality" and the practice of direct democracy from the Zapatistas in Mexico and certain SMOs in the World Social Forum, based in Brazil.

Sociological Angles on Human Rights

Though far from exhaustive, these three angles (political economy/ sociology of development, social movement research, and political sociology) offer complementary but distinct insights into the workings of human rights in the real world. By definition, political economy/development sociology elucidates the world-economic conditions and the IMF, WB, and WTO-inspired state policies that unintentionally foment popular unrest, especially in the Global South. For example, austerity measures and free trade agreements contributed to a wave of protests across Latin America in the 1990s and 2000s. While economic circumstances are not always decisive, they do figure prominently in the age of globalization, not least because they often converge with cultural and environmental circumstances (Appelbaum and Robinson 2005). This book uses the term "rights conditions" to designate the circumstances that give rise to grievances.

For its part, social movement research illuminates not only the manner in which SMOs and their NGO allies frame their grievances in terms of human rights, but also the organizational structures, strategies, and tactics used by SMOs. This book uses the term "rights claims" to capture the concrete demands of SMOs and their allies. For example, the global justice movement, understood as a transnational activist network, has characterized social programs, cultural protections, and environmental remediation as human rights, thereby making claims on national governments.

Finally, political sociology explains not only how evolving rights claims influence policy prescriptions at the international, national, and local levels, but also how recently granted rights – as manifested in IGO and state policies – serve both to enable and to limit social actors at all three levels. This book uses the term "rights effects" to denote the impacts of rights that have been actualized through state policies. For example, various nation-states have recently granted marriage rights to same-sex partners. The conferral of such rights has the effect of facilitating tax breaks, health benefits, adoption and childrearing, and inheritance rights for same-sex couples. Over time, marriage equality could have the cultural impact of encouraging greater acceptance of the LGBT community.

In essence, this book weaves together the three approaches – those of political economy/development, social movement research, and political sociology – in order to shed light on the genesis, evolution, and impact of human rights norms, laws, practices, and institutions. In combining the political economy/development sociology, social movement research, and political sociology approaches, and thereby linking the three concepts described above, the book takes a macro-historical view of the debates and struggles that have defined the trajectory of human rights since 1945. This view emphasizes the utility of analyzing the emergence and propagation of the human rights canon and the policies influenced by it in proper historical context (Lauren 2003).

It is worth noting, however, that the aforementioned three-pronged approach advocated by and employed in this book is not exhaustive. In principle, there are other ways of using sociology to intervene in human rights. In actuality, sociologists examine human rights from a variety of other angles, including the sociology of peace, economic sociology, the sociology of law, the sociology of organizations, the sociology of migration, the sociology of race and ethnicity, the sociology of gender and sexuality, cultural sociology, environmental sociology, the sociology of health/medical sociology, urban sociology, criminology, and social psychology. For example, the sociology of peace might pay careful attention to the role of popular and elite peace advocacy networks in shaping human rights. Economic sociologists might address the operations of transnational corporations and economic regulatory agencies, along with the role of the market in either impeding or facilitating human rights. Sociologists of migration might examine the human rights implications of immigration policies. Sociologists studying race, gender, sexuality, and nationality might look at the implications of personal identity for human rights. Like their counterparts in anthropology, cultural sociologists might take heed of how specific cultures "filter" rights claims. Environmental sociologists might examine how specific ecosystems influence the rights claims of their inhabitants. Sociologists of health and medicine might analyze the connections between health policy and human rights. Urban sociologists might explore differential access to housing and problems with city infrastructures. Like their counterparts in the sociology of law, criminologists might illuminate the treatment of prisoners. Finally, social psychologists might elucidate changes in attitudes about human rights in a given population.

Notwithstanding pronounced theoretical, methodological, and substantive differences, all of these pathways reach the same summit, namely a properly *sociological* excavation of the *social* underpinnings and implications of human rights. Hence the question arises: What do the various approaches to the sociology of human rights have in common with one another? In essence, what many of the approaches share is the use of sociological theories and methods to analyze (a) the social conditions under which grievances are transformed by popular forces and coalitions into rights claims, (b) the processes by which states and other public authorities enact rights-oriented policies and laws, and (c) the political outcomes of human rights legislation (e.g., shifting power relations among social actors and the creation of enduring institutions).

To one extent or another, most sociologists of human rights examine each of these dimensions. Sociologists remind us that knowledge in the area of human rights is produced in a variety of ways: by professors and students in the halls of academia; by UN officials and policymakers in government circles; by NGO staff working in poor and conflict-ridden areas; and by SMO members, community activists, and ordinary people on the streets, in factories, and in fields. It is worthwhile to stress that SMOs, their constituents, and the general public play a significant role in shaping human rights. What counts as human rights in a given society, global context, and historical period is the net result of contention – or better yet, contestation – among different groups with different degrees of power. In a nutshell, this means that consensuses on the nature, scope, and applicability of rights are fluid insofar as they derive from processes of research, debate, dialogue, negotiation, and struggle. This is a profoundly *sociological* problem. In keeping with the spirit of sociology as a discipline, this book explores the *social preconditions* and *social impacts* of human rights – understood as both a form of knowledge, a set of institutions, and an array of practices.

By definition, sociology is an academic discipline devoted to the systematic analysis of human behavior, power relations, and social structures on the global, national, and local scales. Meanwhile, human rights are defined as norms, laws, customs, policies, programs, and institutions that afford protections and entitlements to persons in their home contexts. Notwithstanding changes associated with globalization, the nation-state remains the most important institutional actor in the area of human rights. Since the aforementioned protections and entitlements vary not only among nation-states and communities, but also within social formations (according to race, class, gender, sexual orientation, national origin, and other forms of identity or social standing), rights-oriented sociologists inevitably cross paths with political scientists, anthropologists, and geographers. As a consequence, one of the major tasks of this book is to delineate an expressly *sociological* perspective on human rights. Nevertheless, the resulting sociological perspective serves as a complement to the perspectives offered by the other social sciences (Cushman 2011). Thus, instead of "reinventing the wheel" by reproducing the analyses offered by neighboring disciplines, sociologists aim to capture the specifically sociological aspects of human rights debates, legislation and policymaking, and activism (Brunsma et al. 2012). It is reasonable to expect – and indeed to hope for – cross-pollination among the social scientific approaches to human rights.

Major Concepts in the Sociology of Human Rights

Instead of defending a specific platform or program, this book highlights a few ways of *practicing* the sociology of human rights in research, teaching, service, and conversation. The first way is to offer an analysis of the conditions, whether economic, political, social, or cultural, under which grievances are formulated. This approach addresses the question: How have given circumstances (e.g., the negative impacts of globalization) inspired or compelled exploited, marginalized, and disenchanted groups to articulate their grievances in terms of the human rights canon? In responding to this question, sociologists illuminate *rights conditions* (i.e., the circumstances under which aggrieved groups formulate and express their objectives).

The second way is to present a detailed explanation of how popular forces and their NGO allies refashion existing conceptions of human rights in accordance with their objectives. This approach poses the question: How do activist organizations claim human rights? In answering this question, sociologists shed light on *rights claims* (i.e., the demands for protections and entitlements that aggrieved groups make on authorities). In effect, SMOs and their allies translate grievances into the language of human rights. This process of translation often involves reference to major documents in the human rights canon.

The third way is to offer a rigorous analysis of the stakes, especially in terms of power relations and polices, in a given debate or struggle over human rights. This approach asks the question: Whose actions would be facilitated or limited if a given set of rights were recognized and implemented by the state and other political authorities? In addressing this question, sociologists illuminate *rights effects* (i.e., how the attainment of rights by aggrieved groups changes political institutions and social relations). In essence, the answer to this question involves the outcomes, whether transitory or permanent, of policymaking oriented toward human rights. Doubtless, the biggest "payoff" in rights-oriented activism comes in the form of state policy. In this light, it is worth mentioning two caveats. First, it is difficult to *prove* that a given coalition produced a specific piece of legislation. In the real world of nation-states, there exist levels of mediation between rights claimants and the policymakers who produce legislation, even in democratic regimes (Giugni 1998; Amenta et al. 2010). The second caveat is that state policies can be altered or even abolished over time. Thus, apparent victories for rights-oriented coalitions and their elite partners in political parties are always subject to reversal. Interestingly enough, an illustration of both caveats comes in the form of the Voting Rights Act of 1965 – one of the most important pieces of legislation in the history of the US. On the one hand, it would be a challenge to demonstrate definitively that the civil rights movement precipitated the Voting Rights Act. Clearly, the movement was a major factor. But was it the decisive factor? On the other hand, though widely acknowledged as having been effective in ensuring the franchise for African Americans in the South, the Voting Rights Act has been under fire for some time. In principle, it could be modified or even repealed.

The fourth way to undertake the sociology of human rights is to offer a systematic examination of how different types of rights, whether imagined, under consideration, or actualized, are connected to one another in both theoretical and practical terms. This approach explores the question: For a given right to be implemented, what other rights must be achieved? In handling this question, sociologists elucidate *rights bundles* (i.e., packages of organically linked rights that cut across conventional categories). To explore rights bundles is necessarily to imagine new ways of interpreting or augmenting the existing rights canon, the principal components of which appear in the form of the UDHR, the ICCPR, and the ICESCR (considered in the context of other declarations and resolutions produced by the UN, the putative curator of human rights norms and the most significant actor in the rights-oriented epistemic community). By definition, rights bundling – projecting rights claims into the future either on behalf of or in concert with aggrieved parties – constitutes a normative exercise, since advocates must refer to a vision of a "better world." Within the sociology of human rights, there are different degrees of support for and opposition to such normative exercises. Accordingly, this book proceeds cautiously in exploring rights bundles. On the one hand, the book proposes three rights bundles to address the most significant problems of the contemporary world. On the other hand, the book refrains from speculating about how such rights bundles might be adopted by political parties and SMOs in particular nation-states.

Nevertheless, it remains important for sociologists to grapple with the distinction between the analysis and the advocacy of human rights. While some rights-oriented sociologists engage exclusively in analysis (Deflem 2005), others undertake both analysis and advocacy (Blau and Moncada 2009). In delineating theories and concepts for use in the sociology of human rights, this book urges readers not only to think through the relationship between analysis and advocacy, but also to consider the circumstances under which readers might intervene in the name of one normative vision or another. At the same time, this book refrains from advocating a party platform or SMO program. Instead, the book confines itself to affirming popular participation in the human rights community as the precondition for a more representative and effective agenda.

Having revisited the issue of analysis versus advocacy, we may review the role of the four concepts in this book. Taken together, these four concepts – rights conditions, rights claims, rights effects, and rights bundles – form the building blocks of the approach to the sociology of human rights that is delineated in this book. In other words, these concepts offer crucial insights into the following processes: how the grievances of groups and communities are articulated as human rights; how struggles over human rights contribute, whether directly or indirectly, to the alteration of power structures and social relations; and how different types of rights whether merely proposed or actually achieved, relate to one another conceptually and practically. The third aspect merits an additional comment: Although it is useful for analytic, pedagogical, and political purposes to explore different types of rights separately, it is equally important to recognize the inextricability of human rights in practice.

What does it mean to say that human rights, though separable in theory, are indivisible in practice? The short answer is as follows: If we are to conceptualize such social problems as poverty, social inequalities (based on race, gender, sexual orientation, national origin, or other sources of personal identity), cultural marginalization, and environmental degradation as *interrelated human rights abuses*, we must also conceptualize the policy proposals of community groups, SMOs, NGOs, and UN agencies as *interrelated human rights remedies*. Moreover, in analyzing the policy proposals of such entities, we affirm the *value* of marshaling sociological expertise to make the world a better place. But what constitutes a "better world" remains a matter of debate. Reasonable and well-intentioned persons and groups may disagree on this issue, sometimes vehemently.

Science, Values, and Rights Bundles

Though beyond the scope of this chapter, the issue of the relationship between scientific research and the affirmation of explicit values figures prominently in the sociology of human rights. Accordingly, the issue serves as a major subtext in this book – a theme that recurs in different guises. In a sense, this is inevitable because the object of study comprises the most celebrated and powerful normative frame-work in the contemporary world (Lauren 2003). Despite its pervasive-ness, the rights framework remains highly contested in the Global North and the Global South alike. As a consequence, as practitioners of social science, with its methodological protocol, sociologists must analyze competing interpretations of the human rights canon with a high degree of critical detachment.

Of the four building blocks of a rights-oriented sociology, the concept of rights bundles (i.e., parcels of interconnected rights that elude classification) has the most direct bearing on the relation-ship between social scientific research and the espousal of values. Why is this the case? In essence, teaching students and informing the public about the inextricability of different forms of rights (e.g., civil and political, economic and social, cultural and environmental rights) serves not only to inspire them to think about how rights are implemented through policies, laws, and institutions, but also to recognize the role of both collective and individual human agency in determining what "counts" as rights in a given time and place. To encourage students and the public to participate in human rights education, whether under the auspices of Human Rights Education Associates, Amnesty International, Human Rights Watch, and other NGOs or independently, is necessarily to affirm the normative principle of popular participation (otherwise known as the *right to democracy*). Nevertheless, the question of where such popular par-ticipation should lead is deliberately left unanswered. Similarly, the question of how democracy should be implemented is not explored. The sociological analysis of competing models of democracy deserves treatment in a separate book.

In addition to proposing three rights bundles – longevity, the full development of the person, and peace – this book invites readers to propose their own rights bundles. Accordingly, the book operates from the assumption that all human beings have something to con-tribute to the delineation of a human rights agenda that reconciles universalism with cultural pluralism (Pearce 2001; Donnelly 2003). Devising rights bundles in a controlled setting (e.g., a classroom or a community meeting) is more than a scholarly trial or pedagogical technique. Indeed, the purpose of such an exercise is two-fold. First, it brings home the argument that increased popular participation is crucial for the advancement of human rights not only in the US, but also on a global scale. Second, the exercise solidifies the contention that what "sticks" as human rights in a given time and place, far from being determined in advance, derives from the complex interplay of social and political forces. Instead of being given a priori, any plausible universalism (or globally-binding framework) would need to be grounded not only in a critical assessment of human history, but also in a collective conversation on the character, reach, and efficacy of human rights. It follows that what matters most is extending an *invitation* far and wide for popular participation in delineating the human rights agenda for the coming decades. Extending such an invitation constitutes one of the most significant objectives of the sociology of human rights.

In this light, we may return to the theme of indivisibility – the impetus to rights bundling. Taken together, different types of rights – negative/civil and political rights and positive/economic and social, cultural, and environmental rights – promote longevity, the full development of the person, and peace, three crucial objectives for advocates of human rights. In effect, the objectives of longevity, the full development of the person, and peace constitute rights bundles, packages of rights that imply or necessitate one another. It is worthwhile to consider each bundle in succession. First, the right to longevity – the ability to lead a long, healthy life – assumes access to food and water, clothing, shelter, public hygiene, healthcare, and a functioning ecosystem. Second, as an elaboration of what psychologists call self-actualization, the right to the full development of the person – the capacity to develop one's talents, personality, interests, and tastes – presupposes access to general education and vocational training, information and news, and an assortment of options in defining one's identity. Third, the right to peace – the opportunity to live without fear of physical and emotional harm – presupposes both negative peace (i.e., the absence of war, civil strife, and violent crime) and positive peace (i.e., institutions to eliminate the structural violence that comes from racism, sexism, homophobia, xenophobia, and other forms of prejudice) (Barash 2010).

What can we conclude about these rights bundles? Interestingly enough, the three bundles are intertwined with one another: longevity, which requires measures for ensuring good physical and mental health, provides the framework for the full development of the person; meanwhile, peace, which entails measures for reducing the threat of physical and emotional violence, proves essential for longevity; and finally, the three bundles converge on the proclamation of the universal right to pursue a good life. Furthermore, all three bundles problematize the separation of negative rights (protections provided by governments) and positive rights (entitlements granted by governments through the enactment of policies to alleviate social inequalities and rectify historical injustices). In other words, the three bundles cut across the categories of civil and political rights for individuals, economic and social rights for individuals, and cultural and environmental rights for groups. Finally, all three bundles must be filtered through specific cultural frameworks: while the desire for longevity, the full development of the person, and peace may well be universal, the ways of expressing these aspirations and the mechanisms for bringing them to fruition vary from one cultural context to another.

Globalization and Culture

In this light, we must consider culture in greater detail, not least because the spread of consumerism, as one of the major features of globalization, has created threats to non-Western cultures (Vrdoljak 2013). How is culture, conceptualized as a collection of shared values, symbols, and practices within a group or society, linked to human rights? As we have noted, the class of positive rights includes cultural rights as well as economic and social rights, because the *right to have a culture* belongs to specific groups. In theory, all humans, whether in the Global North or the Global South and irrespective of their position or status within their home countries, are entitled not only to have a culture, but also to inhabit their ancestral lands (where appropriate), to affirm the rituals, practices, and customs of their ethnic group, and to learn a minority language in school (where appropriate). It is immediately apparent that the term "where appropriate" presupposes the existence of mechanisms and protocols for determining who may plausibly claim membership in a protected group or community, an issue that exemplifies the need for cultural pluralism (Messer 1997). By design, the aforementioned entitlements help to preserve the world's cultural diversity, which is an important goal in a globalized age characterized by the spread of consumerism, the homogenization of daily practices, and serious threats to the lifeways of indigenous peoples, peasants, and inhabitants of remote communities (Appelbaum and Robinson 2005; McMichael 2012).

What is happening? Although globalization (defined as increasing economic, political, and social integration and interdependency) has

created new opportunities for transnational dialogue and cooperation in the service of human rights, it has also threatened the world's
cultural diversity (Brysk 2002). For example, satellite television,
the Internet, tourism, and migration serve to transport images and
notions, whether real or mythical, of the lifestyle that prevails in the
Global North (especially in the US) to the Global South, while debt
refinancing and development programs, launched by the IMF/WB
in conjunction with national governments, encourage the pursuit
of consumerism as the essential characteristic of such a lifestyle
(Appelbaum and Robinson 2005; McMichael 2012). In many parts
of the Global South, the images, artifacts, and infrastructure of
consumerism create frictions with other cultural traditions, while
altering the landscape and threatening vulnerable ecosystems in
the process. Accordingly, following the example of rights-oriented
anthropologists, rights-oriented sociologists pay careful attention
to cultural rights in the age of globalization. In doing so, they also
examine the issue of environmental rights not only because cultural
and environmental rights comprise the putative third generation of
human rights, but also because cultural formations and ecosystems
are closely connected to one another in the real world.

This book argues that the best way to handle the political, legal,
and cultural dilemma of a globalized yet divided world is to employ
the tools of sociology in *specifying* how human rights theories, norms,
practices, and outcomes "circulate" across borders in a globalization era marked by intense flows not only of capital, commodities,
and information, but also of labor, refugees, and tourists – in a
word, flesh-and-blood human beings representing different cultures
and, by extension, carrying distinct notions of human rights across
national boundaries (Khagram et al. 2002). In effect, renowned
anthropologist Arjun Appadurai's (1996) analysis of transnational
cultural flows in the age of globalization can be used to shed light
on how concepts of human rights that are transmitted through the
"ethnoscape" (i.e., flows of migrants and travelers), the "mediascape"
(i.e., flows of images in mass media), and the "ideoscape" (i.e., flows
of ideas from governments and IGOs) mutate across geographic
space and with regard to culture. Notwithstanding differences in
wealth and power, concentration of NGO and IGO headquarters,
density of mass media, and access to advanced communications technologies, the new linkages between the Global North and the Global
South are "two-way streets." In other words, the flow of human rights
ideas is neither a process of "diffusion" (in which the norms of the

Global North are copied by the Global South) nor a simple imposition perpetrated by the Global North on the Global South (Khagram et al. 2002). By design, the term "circulation" is employed to capture not only the mutability and malleability of human rights thinking, but also the role of power, especially political power or the leverage of nation-states and their affiliates (executive office-holders, parliaments, courts, law enforcement agencies, and militaries), in either facilitating or obstructing the realization of rights claims advanced by an array of organizations, groups, and individuals.

In the process of considering how rights claims filter through different political, legal, and cultural settings, we acquire a greater awareness of the vast scope of human rights, from the civil and political rights that promote liberty, to the economic and social rights that advance equality, to the collective rights (especially cultural and environmental rights) that encourage solidarity (understood as the feeling of belongingness within and connection among nation-states, peoples, groups, and communities). A significant complication is immediately apparent: while liberty and equality-oriented rights belong to *individuals*, solidarity-related rights belong to *collectivities*. Thus, even the *existing* human rights canon forces us to rethink one of the premises of Western political and legal thought, namely the distinction between the individual and the collective (however conceived). Though present in Western social thought, the concept of solidarity has been articulated differently in Latin America and elsewhere in the Global South. As we shall see, these differences harbor great potential for overcoming the conventional blockages in post-Enlightenment thinking.

In effect, this foreshadows one of the major issues addressed throughout the book. As the widespread invocation of the motto of the French Revolution ("Liberty, Equality, Fraternity!") suggests, it can be useful – for analytic, pedagogical, and political reasons – to place human rights into categories bequeathed to us by the European Enlightenment and subsequently formalized by the UN system and the NGOs operating in its orbit. Once upon a time, scholars, policymakers, and activists alike emphasized the *distinctions* among the putative "three generations" of human rights: first-generation civil and political rights guaranteeing to *individuals* basic freedoms and protections from abuse by state and non-state actors, along with participation in social life; second-generation economic and social rights guaranteeing to *individuals* basic social provisions, a minimum standard of living, a semblance of education and vocational training, a modicum of upward social mobility, assistance throughout the life-course, and relief during economic downturns and natural disasters; and, ultimately, third-generation cultural and environmental rights guaranteeing to *collectivities* (peoples, groups, and communities) life-ways, access to the means of subsistence, and protections for fragile ecosystems.

Deriving from a practical interpretation of the UDHR that stressed the need to compare the performance of different regimes, this tendency was formalized in Vasak's (1977) influential approach. By dividing human rights into these three categories, and hence mimicking the format of the early constitutions of the US, France, and other countries that were influenced by the European Enlightenment, scholars, policymakers, and others have been able to appeal to nation-states for specific pieces of legislation to alleviate political exclusion and an array of social problems. At the same time, the human rights community has come to see the limitations of these categories, especially as globalization has revealed an array of alternative conceptions of human rights emanating from the Global South (Desai 2002). These ideas have found expression not only in social movements, but also in the platforms of political parties and the language of new constitutions (especially in Latin America). This has precipitated a sea change in human rights thinking.

Summary

To reiterate, this chapter has defined the sociology of human rights fundamentally as the systematic use of sociological theories and methods in the analysis of the social conditions under which human rights are imagined, contested, implemented, enforced, and transgressed. Accordingly, rights-oriented sociologists examine rights conditions (i.e., the circumstances giving rise to grievances), rights claims (i.e., the demands for protections and entitlements that aggrieved groups make on governments), rights effects (i.e., alterations in political structures and social relations deriving from the attainment of rights by aggrieved groups), and rights bundles (i.e., parcels of organically connected rights that transcend the conventional categories). Taken together, these four concepts – rights conditions, rights claims, rights effects, and rights bundles – form the foundation of the sociological perspective on human rights. Accordingly, we will employ these concepts throughout the book.

How shall we use the sociological perspective on human rights?

In essence, we shall use this new perspective to illuminate the quest for innovative solutions to enduring social problems on the global, national, and local scales. As we have seen, many social problems have profound ramifications for human rights. This is one of the central arguments of rights-oriented sociologists. Far from negating the work of philosophers and political scientists, sociologists aim to add onto the contributions of researchers in other disciplines, especially anthropologists and geographers who have shed light on the cultural and environmental aspects of human rights. By inclination, training, and custom, sociologists are interested primarily in the social underpinnings and ramifications of human rights. When examined through the sociological lens, human rights appear not only as proclamations inscribed on pieces of parchment or spoken at formal occasions, but also as norms, practices, and structures that serve both to empower and to constrain an array of social actors.

Discussion Questions

- Why are negative rights (protections) more widely accepted than positive rights (entitlements)?
- What are the obstacles to expanding positive rights (entitlements)?
- How do human rights empower and constrain social actors?
- Why do conceptions of human rights vary across historical time and geographic space?
- What does the case of Oxfam International – an NGO devoted to the alleviation of poverty – reveal about cutting-edge human rights thinking?

2 Classifying Human Rights

Whereas chapter 1 introduced the sociological perspective and the fundamental concepts that accompany it, including rights conditions, rights claims, rights effects, and rights bundles, this chapter explores the issue of classification in human rights. Classification is a fundamental part not only of humans' endeavors to render their experiences intelligible, but also of the attempts of scholars, policymakers, activists, and other members of the rights-oriented epistemic community to point out human rights *abuses* and *remedies* across the world. In order to propose campaigns and programs to alleviate human rights violations, analysts and advocates need to either apply the existing rights canon (as manifested in UN documents and many national constitutions) or to suggest changes to the canon. In other words, we need a theoretical touchstone or reference point if we are to ascertain which *types* of rights have been violated and which remedies are available to aggrieved parties. But the results of such inquiries may vary not only according to the classification schema that we invoke, whether that of negative and positive rights, that of the three generations of rights, or some other perspective, but also according to the priorities we place on specific types of rights. And priorities, in turn, vary dramatically from one nation-state and cultural context to another.

For example, many US policymakers and citizens cite the Constitution and accompanying traditions in the legal system in emphasizing negative rights (or protections from physical abuse, humiliation, exploitation, and exclusion perpetrated by state or non-state actors) *over* positive rights (or entitlements to economic structures and social programs that provide citizens with access to the means of subsistence, help them to enter trades or professions, and insulate them from health crises, recessions, and natural disasters). In its role as a global actor and major player in the UN system, the US government often articulates a preference for negative rights (Blau et al. 2008). In sum, it is commonplace for Americans to assert that the rights to life and personal security, due process of law, along with the freedoms of association, assembly, speech, and petition are *genuine human rights* that may not be abridged, while food stamps, unemployment insurance, social security, and Medicare/Medicaid, though public goods, are mere *social programs* that may be either expanded or contracted (or even abolished altogether) according to changing circumstances (especially budgetary constraints).

In contrast, many revised constitutions in Europe, Latin America, and elsewhere contain explicit provisions for positive rights (expressed in publicly-funded programs to implement such economic and social rights as government-funded healthcare, maternity and paternity leave, and daycare). Though the actual programs are subject to change, the principle that motivates the programs remains in place, namely that government ought to provide a range of economic and social entitlements to help citizens make their way through the life course. Thus, it is normal for citizens of these countries to accord equal status to negative and positive rights, with the implicit understanding that negative rights are necessary but insufficient for citizens to lead good lives.

In sum, since the jury is out on the relative merits of negative and positive rights, we must carefully *work through* the issue of classification. Our goal is not to determine how to rank different types of rights – a task that must be left to different power blocs, constituencies, communities, and individuals operating under different state structures and facing distinct political opportunities – but rather to grasp how the classification of rights influences *claims-making* – the process of formulating and articulating demands from authorities (usually governments) for protections (i.e., negative rights, which are usually civil and political in character) and entitlements (i.e., positive rights, which are usually economic, social, and cultural in character).

In examining the advantages and disadvantages of the two schemas, this chapter touches on several recurring issues in the field of human rights: what it means to characterize poverty, social inequalities (stemming from racism, class structure, sexism, homophobia, and xenophobia), social exclusion, bullying and hate crime, cultural marginalization, and environmental degradation not only as social problems, but also as *human rights violations* (when such problems are sufficiently severe, widespread, and systemic); how to reconcile individual and collective rights (where conflicts between the two emerge); how to combine universalism (i.e., the belief that a set of norms should be implemented on a global scale) with cultural pluralism (i.e., the belief that accommodations should be made for particular cultures); why conceptions of human rights vary across historical time and geographic space; and how to extricate the doctrine of human rights (and the related doctrine of development) from Eurocentric assumptions about the origins and pathways of different civilizations (Rist 2009). Far from being exhausted in the current chapter, these issues are revisited throughout the book.

Why Do We Need to Rethink the Categories of Human Rights?

Owing to the prior work of philosophers, political scientists, legal scholars, NGOs (especially those with programs in human rights education), and UN agencies (particularly those tasked with reporting on human rights abuses), sociologists have inherited various ways of classifying human rights. Far from being written in stone, these classifications have resulted from periodic debates on the nature, scope, and applicability of human rights. After reviewing the basic features of the sociological perspective, this chapter elucidates the theoretical, advocacy, and practical implications of the two classification schemas that once prevailed among academics, policymakers, and activists in the domain of human rights: a perspective that contrasts negative and positive rights and a perspective that delineates three generations of rights (first-generation civil and political rights, second-generation economic and social rights, and third-generation group rights to cultural and environmental goods). In the course of the chapter, it becomes apparent not only that the two classification schemas have both advantages and disadvantages for research, teaching, policy-making, and activism, but also that it can be helpful to consider the intersections among different types of rights.

One of the key sociological contributions is the notion of rights bundles (i.e., packages of intersecting rights that meet the exigencies of complex or ambiguous circumstances). Over time, rights bundles may or may not become rights claims, depending on whether and to what extent they are adopted by disenchanted or disenfranchised groups. In order to analyze rights bundles, we need to understand not only how the prevailing classifications of human rights – that of negative and positive rights and that of the three generations of rights – operate, but also why real-world *problems* and *remedies* often escape these classifications. In other words, we need to work through the two classification schemas if we are to capture the convergences of rights in the real world.

How does the process of claims-making work? Irrespective of their social standing or location in the world, aggrieved parties must undertake two essential tasks. First, they must impose an intellectual structure on the rights to which they lay claim, whether by referring to the existing human rights canon or by starting from scratch (and hence resorting to local norms, concepts, doctrines, and texts). This usually involves placing human rights in categories. Second, they must seek allies, whether among other activists, NGOs, UN agencies, the mass media, or even among elites, in their struggles and negotiations with political authorities. This forces community groups and SMOs to find common ground with better-funded and more powerful members of the rights-oriented epistemic community. Thus, from start to finish, claims-making is a matter of reflection, deliberation, negotiation, and compromise. As a consequence, rights claims are routinely subjected to filtration and dilution as they make their way through hierarchies and across societies. With this in mind, let us turn our attention to the issue of classification in social science, an issue that proves paramount for sociologists who examine the circulation of human rights. As we shall see, the issue of classification constitutes a significant preoccupation for participants in the rights-oriented epistemic community.

Though widely recognized within the epistemic community, especially by social scientists of various stripes, the issue of the relevance of the two schemas has not been addressed definitively. The reasons for this are quite apparent. First, notwithstanding their obvious limitations, the two schemas remain useful for the short-handed analysis and advocacy of human rights. Second, to date, no scholarly or organizational entity has succeeded in propagating an alternative schema. Instead, various members of the human rights community, especially such influential NGOs as Oxfam International (in its anti-poverty campaign) and Amnesty International (in its campaign for economic, social, and cultural rights), have demonstrated ways of cutting across the existing categories in targeting multi-causal and multifaceted rights puzzles. Accordingly, this book refers to and builds on the ad hoc efforts of NGOs to move beyond the existing categories in solving rights puzzles.

Sociological Perspectives

In addressing these issues, our goal is to acquire a deeper understanding of how human rights – or more precisely, novel ways of *conceptualizing, institutionalizing,* and *practicing* human rights – "circulate" through the world: between grassroots actors and elite policymakers, between academics and the general public, and between the Global South and the Global North. In a sense, Arjun Appadurai's anthropological analysis of the cultural flows associated with globalization can be employed by sociologists to illuminate the passage of rights norms across national boundaries (1996). The transmission of rights norms from one nation-state and/or cultural formation to another constitutes one aspect of what this book terms "circulation." In this light, it is worth noting that the term "circulation" is more accurate than the term "diffusion" because it is based on the rejection of the notion that human rights precepts inevitably flow from the top to the bottom in the political hierarchy of a given nation-state or from the Global North (i.e., the wealthier and more powerful nation-states) to the Global South (i.e., the poorer, less powerful nation-states) in the interstate system. Owing to the pervasive influence of the European Enlightenment (with its emphasis on reason, critique, and revolution), it is commonly assumed that innovations in human rights usually emanate from the Global North, especially from the pan-European world that includes Western Europe and the United States. Known as *Eurocentrism* (the idea that the West outstripped the non-West in terms of economic development and geopolitical power by virtue of its supposed cultural superiority), this worldview has been subjected to fierce criticism in the fields of political economy (Amin 2010), social geography (Blaut 1993), critical development studies (Rist 2009), and critical globalization studies (Appelbaum and Robinson 2005).

The current work extrapolates the critique of Eurocentrism made by critical development and globalization scholars for use in the field of human rights. There is a historical reason for this decision. Since the US-led post-Second World War reconstruction of the world economy (around the IMF, the WB, and the US dollar) and the interstate system (around the UN), there have been affinities between the terms "development" and "human rights." But owing to exigencies of the Cold War, scholars rarely explored these affinities. More recently, scholars wishing to advance a non-Eurocentric framework for development have embraced contemporary conceptualizations of human rights, often proposing a "right to development" that would involve tailoring programs for specific cultures and permitting the highest degree of popular participation. Accordingly, this book examines a human rights approach to development.

Formed as a consequence of Europe's domination of the rest of the world, the Eurocentric mindset produced a powerful paradox:

> The paradox of the West lies in its ability to produce universals, to raise them to the level of absolutes, and to violate in an extraordinarily systematic way the principles that it derives from them, while still feeling the need to develop theoretical justifications for those violations. The planetary reach of its hegemony, coupled with the dogged attempt to justify itself over the centuries by the means of a sophisticated cultural apparatus in which universality is constantly evoked, constitute a two-fold specificity that clearly deserves to be examined at length. (Bessis 2003: 5)

As Bessis has argued, the double-movement undertaken by the West – from the time of its invention and especially in the aftermath of the Enlightenment – was to position itself as the arbiter of universal values while generating elaborate rationalizations for violating those very values (e.g., in the case of centuries of colonialism, justified according to a "civilizing mission"). It follows that the reclamation of certain Enlightenment principles would entail a complex historical reckoning. However, as the case of human rights shows, much of the Enlightenment project merits preservation (Bronner 2004).

As numerous critics have demonstrated, the Eurocentric worldview, traces of which can be found in policymaking circles, advocacy networks, and the general public (despite the best intentions of many participants), impedes some analysts not only from recognizing the contributions that non-Western civilizations have made to human rights thinking, but also from recognizing the blockages to a genuine universalism. In principle, a *genuine universalism* would entail the equal inclusion of voices from across the world, irrespective of wealth, power, location, or culture. In a world marred by interstate warfare, civil strife, forced migration, poverty, cultural exclusion, and environmental degradation, the stakes are extremely high. If global governance experts and human rights advocates are to propose a globally binding framework for human rights – above and beyond the ambitious but insufficient UN system – they would need to provide for a high degree of cultural pluralism (Held 2004). To that end, they would need to acknowledge that the West, particularly the US and Europe, has exerted disproportionate influence on the human rights canon and the institutional structures that accompany it, including the UN and its affiliates, as well as the array of US and European-based NGOs that inhabit the orbit of the UN. Experts in global governance would also need to accord proper representation to non-Western perspectives on human rights (Gordon 2004).

Having addressed the issue of Eurocentrism, we can shift to the related issue of elitism, namely the assumption that rights-oriented knowledge always emanates from the top of the political hierarchy (usually elected officials and their staffs) or from highly trained experts in the field (usually scholars with positions in universities, think tanks, or foundations). Doubtless, state policymakers and legal professionals (both within and beyond the judicial branch of government) play important roles both in creating political policies that facilitate the pursuit of rights and in codifying rights at the level of law. Nevertheless, popular forces – immersed in political cultures defined, in one way or another, by rights thinking – often produce significant pressures for the expansion of human rights (especially in regimes that are considered democratic). In fact, the push for the re-interpretation of old rights (expressed in national constitutions and UN declarations) and the invention of new rights (expressed in printed pamphlets and electronic manifestoes) often emerges within aggrieved communities and groups – in other words, at the grass-roots level – before spreading to other sectors (through the mediation of NGOs and other allies, as well as with the assistance, whether accidental or intentional, of the mass media).

Lumping and Splitting in the Domain of Human Rights

We have seen why claims-making – the process by which grassroots forces and their more influential allies construct and express the demands that they wish to make of governments – necessitates referring to categories of human rights (whether enthusiastically or critically). In order to offer an answer to the deeper question of why categorization proves crucial to the field of human rights, we need to consider a recurring issue in social science, that of "lumping" (placing similar entities, processes, and ideas in clusters) and "splitting" (drawing distinctions between clusters). In a groundbreaking study of the role of classification in social science, Zerubavel advances the following argument: "Although the world in which we live is essentially continuous, we experience it as discrete chunks: 'strangers' and 'acquaintances,' 'fiction' and 'non-fiction,' 'business' and 'pleasure,' 'normal' and 'perverse'" (Zerubavel 1996: 421). In order to make sense of their interactions with one another and with nature, human beings must use their cognitive abilities to impose a structure on the world.

It follows that the process of demarcating "islands of meaning" consists of "two contrasting yet complementary cognitive acts – lumping and splitting" (Zerubavel 1996). Whereas the process of lumping "enables us to perceive grape juice as similar to orange juice and chimpanzees as similar to baboons," the process of splitting "enables us to perceive grape juice as different from wine and chimpanzees as different from humans" (Zerubavel 1996: 421–2). In essence, Zerubavel demonstrates that lumping (i.e., the first step of relegating things to categories) and splitting (i.e., the second step of heightening the distinctions between categories) are crucial moments not only in individuals' attempts to navigate the world, but also in social scientists' efforts to render intelligible the workings of the economy, the polity, society, culture, and the built environment. As we shall see, this proves particularly important to our efforts to set up and solve rights puzzles.

What does this mean in concrete terms? By convention, social scientists treat economics, politics, social relations, cultural life, and the natural environment as "separate spheres" of the human experience. While doing so serves significant purposes for research and teaching, it is important to recognize that these spheres overlap in the real world. While the social sciences capture different aspects of the human experience, they may on occasion mislead us into reifying the concepts of the "market," "government," "society," "culture," and "environment." In the extreme, reification (the fallacy of treating abstract concepts as if they were real things) can cause us to overlook continuities in the human experience (e.g., the manner in which cultural practices, including the production and consumption of food, are both literally and figuratively *grounded* in how communities and peoples interact with the natural environment). In sum, the theoretical/methodological processes of lumping and splitting have significant implications not only for social science in general, but also for the sociological analysis of human rights in particular.

Indeed, one of the central arguments of this book is that Zerubavel's insights into the processes of lumping and splitting can be applied fruitfully to theory and practice, advocacy, and policymaking in human rights. Drawing on Zerubavel's analysis, we can come to the following conclusion. Irrespective of whether human rights are grounded in physiology (or the universal capacity for suffering and hence the natural need for protection and nurturing), in the intrinsic social character of human beings, or simply in the accumulation of common experiences (across centuries of interactions among civilizations), we must recognize (a) that ways of *thinking about* and *acting on* human rights have varied considerably across historical time and geographic space, (b) that conceptions of human rights, no matter how commonly held, are always filtered through specific cultural frameworks, and (c) that how we classify human rights has a significant bearing on the relations between claims-makers and political authorities (whether in democracies or in authoritarian regimes). The last point proves particularly important for our current purposes. In essence, community groups, SMOs, and their more powerful allies must express their rights claims in a manner that is comprehensible to governments. Otherwise, sympathetic government officials or staff members will be unable to translate rights claims into state policies. As a consequence, it is important for sociologists, especially those who study societies in the Global South, to sift through different classifications of human rights.

As Zerubavel's analysis would suggest, when applied to the issue of human rights, each mode of classification involves lumping (placing seemingly comparable rights into categories) and splitting (highlighting the differences among categories). Although we may object either to the placement of a given right in this or that category or to the exaggeration or minimization of the differences between categories, we must acknowledge the importance of the cognitive and social scientific act of relying on categories to make sense of human rights abuses and remedies in the real world. Why is this the case? In a nutshell, we need to invoke categories, in this instance categories agreed upon by social scientists, policymakers, and activists, in order to render intelligible human rights violations and solutions in the real world. Accordingly, we must operate from the assumption that there exists a "real world," and that social science, alongside other sources of knowledge (including the collective wisdom of indigenous peoples and micro-societies), can help us to make sense of it. Notwithstanding their differences, the two classification schemas rest on the same essential assumption.

Two Ways of Classifying Human Rights

Let us return to our investigation of the prevailing ways of lumping and splitting human rights. In essence, there are two widely accepted ways of classifying human rights.

1. As we have seen in chapter 1 and in the section above, the first schema distinguishes *negative rights* (protections, provided by the government yet checking government power, that ensure a person's life, bodily integrity, dignity, freedom to practice a religion or to refrain from doing so, and freedoms to associate, assemble, speak, and petition the government for redress) from *positive rights* (entitlements, provided by the government through the enactment of social programs, that ensure a person's access to such basic necessities as food, clothing, shelter, healthcare, and cultural practices). In principle, both negative and positive rights are accorded to *individuals*.
2. In contrast, the second schema (i.e., the three-generations framework) attempts to account for the *difference* between individual and collective rights. Implied but not explored in chapter 1, the second schema echoes the celebrated motto of the French Revolution ("Liberty, Equality, Fraternity!") in differentiating three generations of human rights: first-generation civil and political rights ensuring *liberty* to *individuals*, as expressed in the International Covenant on Civil and Political Rights (ICCPR); second-generation economic, social, and cultural rights ensuring *equality* to *individuals*, as expressed in the International Covenant on Economic, Social, and Cultural Rights (ICESCR); and an assortment of third-generation rights (e.g., the rights to self-determination, development, participation in a cultural heritage, and enjoyment of a sustainable environment) ensuring *fraternity* (or to use the preferable gender-neutral term, *solidarity*) among *peoples*, *groups*, and *communities*, as expressed, for example, in the Stockholm Declaration of the United Nations Conference on the Human Environment. We can immediately see the logic operating in the three-generations framework.

Far from being independent of one another, the two classification schemas are rooted in the US-led, post-Second World War reconstruction of the interstate system, the consequent institutionalization of the UN (with its dispute resolution, peacemaking, humanitarian relief, development, and research functions), and the related growth of the NGO sector (as the primary locus of lobbying for human rights). Often characterized as the "human rights revolution," the postwar proliferation of rights talk and the concomitant creation of institutions to evaluate the human rights records of state and non-state actors necessitated widespread agreement on the basic categories. More precisely, such agreement was important for intellectual, advocacy, political, and practical purposes. To a certain extent, this remains the case in the age of globalization. But it is also true that globalization entails innovations in rights thinking.

Owing to their common roots, the two schemas overlap with one another. For example, negative rights (or protections) are normally defined as civil and political rights for individuals, while positive rights (or entitlements) are usually conceptualized as economic and social rights for individuals. Hence the difference between the two schemas consists in (a) the issue of whether or not it is desirable to think in terms of "generations" of human rights (insofar as this implies either a prescribed pathway for the realization of rights or a hierarchy of rights), and (b) the issue of whether to recognize the collective rights, primarily cultural and environmental in character, that comprise the "third generation." Reflecting on the two schemas, many analysts have undertaken a *critical rethinking* of the distinctions between negative and positive rights and/or among the three generations of rights. In the process, such analysts have pointed to the intersections among civil and political rights on one side, and economic and social rights on the other. More complicated is the relationship between individual rights and collective rights, especially when the two sets of rights come into conflict in the real world. As one might imagine, the conflict between individual and collective rights plays itself out in different ways across nation-states and cultural formations. For example, the Declaration on the Rights of Indigenous Peoples, adopted by the UN General Assembly in 2007 in order to support the rights claims of indigenous peoples across the world, entails addressing the complex relationship between the rights of individuals (irrespective of culture) and cultural groups (with the qualifications for membership to be determined by the groups themselves). On the ground, this forces the nation-state to adjudicate competing claims not only for cultural protections, but also for farmland, waterways, forests, and other natural resources.

The negative–positive schema has difficulty accommodating a group or community's access to such environmental amenities as arable land, unpolluted bodies of water, preserved forests, and natural resources that can be used sustainably. This points to a limitation of the negative–positive schema: rights to environmental goods constitute both protections and entitlements; and these rights are accorded not to individuals, but rather to communities, groups, peoples, and, sometimes, to the earth itself (Shiva 2005). By their very nature, collective goods are difficult to divide in an equitable manner. Geared to facilitate the workings of businesses and the demands of mass consumption, contemporary economic practices routinely conflict with traditional lifeways – a problem that has become paramount in the age of globalization (Appelbaum and Robinson 2005).

Though an unintended consequence of the prioritization of the market, itself originally a Western idea that has, through the extensive and intensive expansion of the capitalist system over five centuries, gained traction across the world, the commodification of the commons has dramatically altered the lives of indigenous peoples and micro-societies. In other words, the commons, including the farmlands, forests, and waterways inhabited, used, and sustained by indigenous peoples and micro-societies for centuries, are literally *indivisible*. Yet the interests of transnational corporations and the requirements of consumers often either reduce access to or degrade the commons. As a consequence, traditionally held and managed natural spaces often form the basis for the rights claims of indigenous peoples and micro-societies. Interestingly enough, these rights claims are as much environmental as they are cultural in character. Moreover, these claims imply a different way of thinking not only about civil/political rights and economic/social rights, but also about what it means to be an "individual" who "belongs to" a community, tribe, people, or group. In recent years, the rights-oriented epistemic community has shown an interest in considering the ramifications of non-Western ways of thinking about the relationship between individuals and communities (Gordon 2004).

Let us turn our attention to the three-generations schema and its embeddedness in debates and conflicts in the post-Second World War world. To reiterate, first-generation rights to liberty and second-generation rights to equality are *individual rights*, while third-generation rights to solidarity (achieved through cultural and environmental connections) are *collective rights*. Both in the human rights community and in the general public, there are varying degrees of support for the respective generations of human rights. This is to be expected given differences in political perspective and cultural background, as well as the pressures of power blocs and advocacy coalitions.

More precisely, there is a strong consensus on the legitimacy of first-generation civil and political rights (especially in the US and the European Union) and solid support for second-generation economic and social rights (especially in the European Union and Latin America) within the confines of welfare states (Soohoo et al. 2009). In contrast, there is fierce debate on the legitimacy of third-generation rights, not least because the category remains under-theorized by scholars (owing, in part, to the higher density of universities in the Global North). After all, many of the major innovations in the area of third-generation rights have come from the Global South. Scholars and activists interested in the Zapatista solidarity network and the World Social Forum have transmitted these innovations to the Global North.

Moreover, the three-generations schema has been subjected to vigorous and sustained critique for implying, or at least seeming to imply, a linear progression from one type of rights to another. But this issue necessitates careful thinking. While civil and political rights, especially the rights to association, assembly, speech, and petition, often set the stage for SMOs and their allies to pursue economic and social rights and/or collective rights to cultural and environmental goods, there exists no magic formula for how rights are achieved. This constitutes the essential point. In principle, a given nation-state or society can achieve second- or even third-generation rights *before* achieving first-generation rights. In practice, the world has seen many pathways toward the realization of human rights. Arguably, the ascendance of East Asia in general, and China in particular, demonstrates this point. For example, in the years after Mao Zedong's death in 1976, China used a state-led development program to transform an agrarian socialist country into the industrial workshop of the global capitalist system. In effect, this process of rapid industrialization facilitated outsourcing from the US and other parts of the Global North, contributing to the rise of Wal-Mart and other "big box" stores, along with their retail-driven commodity chains. Going against the grain of the developmentalism recommended by the World Bank and the US government, the Chinese development project brought about a significant rise in the standard of living – measured in strictly material terms – for large segments of the Chinese population. If poverty constitutes a human rights issue, then China's progress in increasing the standard of living can be seen as a relative success in terms of economic and social rights. Yet this process did not have a great impact either on civil and political rights or on cultural and environmental rights in China. What follows is that development, like the realization of human rights, is always an uneven process. In sum, the accumulation of rights proves appreciably more complex than the three-generations schema would suggest. Accordingly, we must turn our attention to the role of popular forces and their better-positioned allies (in NGOs, UN agencies, and universities) in expanding what is thinkable and realizable in terms of human rights.

Social Movements, Policy, and Law

Drawing on social movement research, a body of thought that harbors profound implications for the analysis of human rights, we can make the following observation: whether or not the rights claims of disenchanted communities and groups facilitate, albeit through a complex process of *mediation*, the enactment of policy and legislation on the national and international levels depends upon three major factors. The first major factor is the capacity of the aggrieved parties to frame their demands in a manner that jibes with emerging rights norms (expressed in the aspirational documents produced by SMOs, NGOs, UN agencies, and other entities that serve as moral compasses or reference points), an insight derived from framing theory (Snow and Benford 2000). For example, many SMOs in the civil rights movement framed their demands in the language of the Declaration of Independence and the Constitution, a vernacular that resonated with most Americans and fitted the demands of the legislative process and the court system. The second major factor is the ability of the aggrieved parties to mobilize the resources (including money, technical tools, and talent) to pursue their objectives, an insight produced by resource mobilization theory (Jenkins 1983). The third major factor is the availability and influence of allies within national governments and/or intergovernmental organizations and the resulting political opportunities (or convergences of interests between the aggrieved parties and authorities), an insight that comes from political process theory (McAdam 1985). For example, many civil rights SMOs found a "fit" between their interests and the interests of the more progressive elements within the Democratic Party. While the SMOs wished to codify civil rights through national legislation, the Democratic Party wished to expand its power base by enfranchising African Americans in the South. Other social movement scholars have considered the role of cultural forces (Goodwin and Jasper 2009) and the disruptive power of movements (Piven and Cloward 1978).

It is likely that scholars will isolate other factors that condition the capacity of social movements to advance their rights claims through mediating forces (including such mass media as TV, radio, newspapers, and Internet sites), culminating in the enactment and enforcement of policies. To date, no scholar has produced the multifaceted theory that the puzzle requires. However, the growing literature on social movement consequences and outcomes constitutes a significant step in the right direction (Giugni 1998; Amenta et al. 2010). For its part, the inchoate theory of rights circulation – a thread that runs through this book – builds not only on the aforementioned succession of social movement theories, but also on analyses of transnational norms (Khagram et al. 2002) and cross-cultural flows associated with globalization (Appadurai 1996).

Taken together, the aforementioned theoretical currents in social movement research, especially framing theory, resource mobilization theory, political process theory, and theories of outcomes, illuminate how communities, groups, and their allies use various forms of contentious politics (e.g., gatherings in public squares, marches, sit-ins and full-scale occupations, work slowdowns and strikes, and other forms of non-violent protest that disrupt daily life or ordinary politics) to militate for the implementation of a broader spectrum of human rights (Goodwin and Jasper 2009). For its part, political sociology, another domain that has contributed greatly to the sociological perspective on human rights, elucidates not only how contentious politics (including civil disobedience) can influence policymaking and legislation on the national and international levels, but also how the granting of rights to previously underrepresented populations can alter power relations (Stout et al. 2004).

It is worth noting that the same set of direct action tactics (e.g., occupations, road blockages, and strikes) can be applied differently according to national context and political culture. In countries where public protest is *illegal*, activists often assert the priority of achieving basic political freedoms and expanding access to the public sphere as preludes to making further demands on state authorities. In countries where public protest is *legal*, activists routinely use such civil and political rights as the freedom of assembly, speech, and petition to pursue economic and social rights. Thus, social movement theory suggests that civil and political rights can be seen not only as ends-in-themselves, but also as means to further ends, including the realization of economic, and social rights (i.e., entitlements that entail the creation of social programs to protect populations from food and housing shortages, unemployment, infirmity, and crisis).

Taken together, social movement theory and political sociology offer precious insights into the social struggles that contribute to the implementation of recently invented rights through a complex process of mediation involving political parties and sitting public officials. However, the actual outcomes, in the form of state policies that correspond, to one degree or another, to rights that have been proclaimed by aggrieved constituencies, can rarely, if ever, be traced exclusively to the disruption caused by movements (Giugni 1998; Amenta et al. 2010).

Throughout US history, SMOs and their sympathizers (often members of more privileged sectors of society) have leveraged the basic rights to assemble in public, speak freely, and demand reforms in pursuing other goals (Armaline et al. 2011). For example, workers and their allies in political parties and trade unions have employed these tools to push for a shorter working day, vacation time, safer factories, union representation and collective bargaining, a minimum wage, and a social safety net. Similarly, women's groups and their allies have employed these tools to push for the right to vote, access to education and jobs, reproductive freedom, and legal protection from such transgressions as sexual harassment, sex discrimination, and domestic violence. In the same way, African Americans and their allies have employed these tools to push for voting rights, unimpeded access to the public sphere, admittance to education and jobs, and legal protection from race discrimination. For their part, disabled persons and their allies have employed these tools not only to render public facilities, including government buildings and parks, more accessible, but also to attain reasonable accommodations at school and work. More recently, the LGBT community and its allies have pursued marriage equality and protection from job and housing discrimination in a number of states. Doubtless, the list could be expanded to include the efforts of numerous other constituencies. But a significant *pattern* is already discernible: by reinterpreting the existing canon of human rights, these constituencies have managed to pressure federal, state, and local governments to enact significant pieces of legislation. That being said, the causal connections between popular pressure (more precisely, social movement activity) and political outcomes (in the form of legislation) prove complex and ambiguous (Giugni 1998; Amenta et al. 2010).

What can we deduce from the examples set by workers, women, African Americans, disabled persons, and the LGBT community in the US? Looking at the pattern sketched above, we can draw a few overlapping conclusions. For the sake of clarity, it makes sense to consider each conclusion individually. First, what is *imaginable* as human rights changes over time. Many of the rights enjoyed by the inhabitants of the contemporary US would have been utterly inconceivable to the authors of the Declaration of Independence and the Bill of Rights. Second, the language of human rights can be applied to a wide variety of objectives. The syntax and semantics of human rights are routinely applied to demands not only for political representation and legal protections (often defined in terms of negative rights), but also for social programs (often defined in terms of positive rights). Since social programs are by definition a matter of *political policy*, they are subject to changing political forces (and hence to debates within and among competing political parties). Third, social movements and their allies often contribute, albeit indirectly and through a complex and unpredictable process of mediation, to the expansion of human rights. Movements seek political opportunities – fortuitous circumstances where government officials, whether out of enlightened self-interest or genuine sympathy, prove responsive to popular demands; but these political opportunities often evolve in unexpected ways. Fourth, human rights are normally secured through changes to federal, state, and local law. Thus, political and legal systems serve as venues for the adjudication of rights claims among contending forces. The next logical step for scholars, students, policymakers, and activists in the area of human rights is to explore, both *ex post facto* and in *anticipation* of the future, not only the underlying connections among the rights-oriented struggles of workers, women, African Americans, disabled persons, the LGBT community, and other constituencies, but also the state responses (in terms of policy and law) to these rights-oriented struggles. In this light, it would be interesting to ascertain what transpires in the gap or hiatus between rights-oriented coalitions and state policymakers.

While the efforts of these constituencies have distinctive traits, they are also linked to one another in a broader quest for human rights. Owing to the achievements of feminist, post-colonial, and other critiques of Enlightenment thought, this broader emancipatory project is conceptualized not as a *fait accompli*, but rather as a project to be pursued vigilantly but cautiously under the banner of human rights. As a rule, community groups and SMOs are conscious of the usefulness of the human rights frame as a vehicle for articulating their grievances. Indeed, the famous slogan, "women's rights *are* human rights," illustrates the point perfectly. On the one hand, the demands made by the women's movement for reproductive freedom, pre- and post-pregnancy healthcare, equal employment opportunity, and protection from sexual harassment are *particular to women*. On the other hand, in spanning negative/first-generation and positive/second-generation rights, these demands can be linked to the rights claims of other constituencies, not least because women also have class, race, sexual, national, and other identity characteristics (Naples and Desai 2002). Finally, the women's movement has not only made common cause with other movements (including mobilizations of workers, people of color, and the LGBT community), it has also exchanged ideas about philosophy, organizational structure, strategies, and tactics with its allies. In sum, the actual circulation of human rights, whether from the bottom up, horizontally, or from the top down, points to the need to explore the theoretical and practical connections among different types of rights.

The Circulation of Human Rights

In recognizing the strengths and limitations, uses and abuses, of the two classification schemas, we find ourselves in a better position to understand how the process of circulation works. Having examined the two most commonly used schemas (that of negative and positive rights and that of the three generations of rights) through the sociological lens, we may now turn our attention to the issue of how human rights circulate both within and among societies. What does the circulation of human rights have to do with the two schemas for categorizing human rights? Notwithstanding its apparent complexity, the answer is fairly straightforward: Over time, the circulation of human rights among a variety of social actors – poor and wealthy, weak and powerful, representing different interests, outside and within the state – challenges old distinctions and creates new ones. Notwithstanding the diversity of social actors involved in the process, rights circulation proves to be more systematic than it would seem at first glance. Since the circulation of human rights has been accelerated in the age of globalization – due to the proliferation of advanced communications technologies and the concomitant growth of the global public sphere, large-scale migration across national boundaries, the implementation of mechanisms for monitoring flagrant abuses of human rights, and changes in the interstate system (especially with the post-Cold War reconfiguration) – it is important to re-examine the existing classification schemas with a critical eye. The sociological perspective proves particularly useful in showing how the circulation of rights, a social process described both in this section of the chapter and elsewhere in the book, strains the conventional categories. For its part, the strain on the prevailing categories creates the "space" for *innovations* in the theory and practice of human rights.

As we discovered in chapter 1, in drawing on such fields as political economy/development, social movement research, political sociology, and other fields, rights-oriented sociology reveals the social conditions under which human rights "circulate" among various social actors (including governments, communities, and individuals). In part, we have examined the process of circulation in terms of the passage of rights notions through the ethnoscape (with migrants crossing national boundaries), the mediascape (with the mass media beaming images across cultural frontiers), and the ideoscape (with the ideas of IGOs and nation-states finding expression in transnational forums) (Appadurai 1996). Indeed, migrants are often motivated by the desire for civil and political rights, as well as economic opportunities. Though controlled primarily by transnational corporations and to a lesser extent by national governments, the mass media (TV, radio, newspapers, and Internet sites) are responsible for spreading information about human rights abuses across the world. Finally, IGOs (including the UN, the IMF, the WB, and the WTO) and the nation-states with which they work either institutionalize or fail to institutionalize human rights through the creation of laws, policies, and institutions. It would be easy to find the place of NGOs, SMOs, and other civil society actors within this framework. In sum, we can construct a theory of circulation from a systematic examination of the workings of the epistemic community surrounding human rights. The theory of circulation ties together the major concepts used in this book: rights conditions, rights claims, rights effects, and rights bundles.

But what does circulation mean in concrete terms? In effect, the term "circulation" denotes not only the manner in which rights are *claimed* by grassroots forces, debated in various venues, and either granted or denied by authorities, but also the concrete ramifications of newly-granted rights for society and government (otherwise known as *rights effects*). Sociologists trace the circuits through which each recently reinterpreted or newly invented right must pass: beginning with the right's conceptualization by aggrieved groups or communities, independent activists, SMOs, and NGOs under specified *conditions* (whether economic, political, or cultural); continuing through a series of debates, undertaken in both the mass media and policymaking circles, among supporters and opponents of the proposed right; and culminating with either the implementation or the rejection of the proposed right on the level of state policy or the legal system.

If, through a complex process of mediation, the proposed right is implemented on the level of policy or law and subsequently enforced by the executive branch and/or adjudicated in the court system, it tends to have a *rippling effect* across society, not only by empowering some actors and constraining others, but also by creating new responsibilities for governments and other authorities. Such rights effects are the most tangible outcomes of the circulation process. Spearheaded by the LGBT movement and supported by other constituencies in a number of countries, the push for marriage equality for same-sex couples exemplifies the circulation of human rights. In the pursuit of marriage equality, conceptualized as a civil right that must be accorded to all without regard to sexual orientation, members of the LGBT community have established and supported NGOs (e.g., Marriage Equality USA) not only to engage in outreach and popular education, but also, and more importantly, to use electoral politics (e.g., ballot initiatives and referenda) and court cases to create or reinterpret legislation to grant marriage rights to same-sex couples (http://www.marriageequality.org/). In addition to encouraging lawmakers to legalize same-sex marriage in a number of countries and several US states – a process that has ramifications for laws on employment, healthcare, child rearing, adoption, and inheritance, as well as for access to social programs and services – activists and their allies in political parties have, with the assistance of the mass media and popular culture, succeeded in building support for marriage equality in the general public. In essence, these interconnected rights can be seen as a rights bundle that cuts across the three generations.

In sum, though seemingly a distant vision as recently as the 1990s, the right to marriage equality has become a major fixture in debates across the world. The degree to which the right to marriage equality is implemented will depend on the complex interplay of power blocs in different countries. Moreover, it goes without saying that some national contexts and cultural formations will prove more receptive than others to implementing the right. Finally, the implementation of marriage equality in various settings will likely inspire LGBT communities to propose new rights bundles that exceed existing legislation. Accordingly, we can see that the process of circulation is open-ended.

Summary

In conclusion, this chapter has moved from a theoretical consideration of the role of classification in human cognition and social science
to an assessment of the two prevailing classification schemas in the
domain of human rights: an approach that differentiates negative
rights (or protections from abuses by state and non-state actors) from
positive rights (or entitlements to be granted by the state); and an
approach that delineates the first-generation civil and political rights
that promote liberty, the second-generation economic and social
rights that promote equality, and the third-generation collective rights
that promote solidarity among peoples, groups, and communities.
In the process, we have made two major observations. First, though
easy to use in research, teaching, policymaking, and advocacy, the
negative–positive schema ignores a range of rights that fall beyond
the scope of ordinary entitlements (including collective rights to
cultural and environmental goods that prove difficult, if not impossible, to divide in an equitable manner). Second, though more comprehensive than the negative–positive schema, the three-generations
schema not only underestimates the intersections between first- and
second-generation rights, it also implies linearity or even teleology
in the achievement of human rights. In other words, the three-
generations schema sometimes engenders the misleading assumption that human rights are destined to unfold in sequence, as if the
process were determined by Nature or by some other trans-historical
force. On the latter point, there is no basis for conceptualizing the
actualization of rights in terms of "stages of development" – an issue
that merits further consideration. There are many pathways to the
summit of human rights; and progress toward the summit is by no
means guaranteed in advance.

In order to compensate for the limitations of the three-generations
schema, it is necessary not only to highlight convergences among different forms of rights (both theoretically and empirically), but also to
jettison the assumption that civil and political rights must always be
achieved first and foremost, followed by economic and social rights,
and, eventually, by collective rights to cultural and environmental
goods. Arguably, the assumption that there are stages through
which human rights struggles must pass constitutes a residue of the
Eurocentric and elitist vision of the origins, evolution, institutionalization, and future of human rights, a residue that is closely and
perhaps not coincidentally paralleled in the prevailing conception of

"development" among officials in the IMF, World Bank, and many governments (Rist 2009). As we shall see, the problem of residual Eurocentrism and elitism points to the need to rethink and rework the putative right to development, a theme that will be explored at a few points in the book. While there is almost universal agreement that poverty (understood as the denial of the basic necessities for a long, healthy life) constitutes a serious problem with significant human rights implications, there is little agreement on precisely how one model of development or another would reduce poverty (Rist 2009). Nor is there agreement on whether the term "development" best captures policies designed to rectify poverty. As the saying goes, the "devil is in the details."

Let us return to the central question in this section of the chapter. Why are Eurocentrism and elitism problems? To reiterate, the Eurocentric and elitist vision cannot account for the variable ways that human rights are actualized in different national and cultural contexts. Nor can the Eurocentric and elitist vision explain how human rights notions circulate among different social actors within a given nation-state or between the Global South and the Global North. Nor can the framework in and of itself illuminate the unfolding of a given right from its inception, through the debates and struggles surrounding it, to its indirect and incomplete implementation in the form of public policy or law by nation-state authorities. As a consequence, the three-generations framework should be seen not as a definitive explanation of progress in human rights, but rather as a *heuristic device* that assists scholars, students, policymakers, and activists in making sense of *rights conditions* (i.e., the circumstances that give rise to grievances), *rights claims* (i.e., the reinterpretation of old rights and the invention of new rights by aggrieved constituencies), and *rights effects* (i.e., the empowerment and constraint of social actors through the implementation of rights on the level of the political and legal systems). In addition, the three-generations framework provides both the impetus and the source material for the construction of *rights bundles* (i.e., packages of organically connected rights that cut across the three generations and thereby meet the needs of new constituencies).

In this light, it is worth highlighting that the need for a critical reworking of the three-generations framework defines the structure of the book. In other words, the structure of the book is predicated on the need to explain, slowly and methodically, not only the strengths and limitations of each category, but also the complex web of connections among the three categories. While chapters 3, 4, and 5 work through the three generations systematically, chapter 6 moves *beyond* the three-generations framework in order to explain how rights bundles (i.e., packets of connected rights that cut across the three categories yet form an organic whole) are proposed and/or adopted by networks of SMOs, NGOs, and/or UN agencies. Finally, drawing on the theories and concepts presented throughout the book, the conclusion delineates an agenda for the sociology of human rights.

Discussion Questions

- Why is classification important in the field of human rights?
- What are the strengths and limitations of the negative–positive schema?
- What are the strengths and limitations of the three-generations schema?
- How do social movements contribute to advances in human rights?

3 Civil and Political Rights

After briefly reviewing the issue of how and why to classify human rights, this chapter explores the most widely accepted category of human rights (especially in the US and elsewhere in the Western world), namely the civil and political rights, proclaimed under the banner of liberty, that (a) protect human beings from abuses perpetrated not only by one another, but also by the state itself, (b) allow human beings to participate freely and fully in civil society and political life, and (c) permit human beings to explore and nurture their identities, interests, ideas, beliefs, and values without undue interference from political authorities. In a nutshell, civil and political rights involve not only checks on government power (enshrined in law and ensured by the court system), but also protections provided by the government that allow individuals to flourish in society. For this reason, civil and political rights are often treated as the most "important" rights, an understandable assumption that this book seeks, nonetheless, to challenge.

Preliminary Questions about Civil and Political Rights

As we have seen in previous chapters, human rights are, by definition, *relational*. In other words, while it is useful for explanatory purposes to classify human rights in one way or another, it is equally important to recognize that different types of rights make sense only in relation to one another. Held by the UN in Vienna in 1993, the World Conference on Human Rights affirmed the connection between civil and political rights and other types of rights (http://www.ohchr.org/en/professionalinterest/pages/vienna.aspx). In the process of explaining where civil and political rights fit in relation to other types of rights, this chapter addresses a series of questions: Why are civil and political rights more widely embraced than other forms of rights, particularly in the US and elsewhere in the Western world? Does the pervasive acceptance of civil and political rights, especially among scholars, jurists, and policymakers, derive primarily from tradition? Or does it make sense to accord logical and/or moral primacy to these rights?

In answering these questions, the chapter advances two arguments about the widespread embrace (in principle, if not always in practice) of civil and political rights. The first argument is *historical*: Notwithstanding precedents in the ancient world (e.g., conceptions of human dignity present in religious traditions in the Middle East, India, and China), it was the European Enlightenment and its attendant revolutions in the eighteenth century that forged and propagated the *modern* notion of human rights (Ishay 2008). Owing to the worldviews and interests of the revolutionaries (many of whom were drawn from relatively privileged sectors of their societies) and the limitations of the time period, the crucial documents of these revolutions highlighted civil and political rights. This is clear in the US Declaration of Independence, the US Constitution, and the French Declaration of the Rights of Man and of the Citizen, documents that have exerted considerable influence into the contemporary period. For example, in the 1950s and 1960s, the language of the Declaration of Independence and the Constitution helped civil rights NGOs to frame their demands for both the American public and elite allies in the Federal Government. More recently, the Tea Party movement has framed its demands in terms of the vision of the "founding fathers," which members believe includes support for limited government and expansive gun rights.

In an extremely complex and contradictory manner, Enlightenment thought gained currency in part through power struggles within Western nation-states and in part through colonialism. Though anathema to the project of human emancipation, European colonizers attempted to legitimize the so-called "civilizing mission" in Africa, Asia, the Caribbean, and elsewhere through reference to *political freedom* and *scientific progress* as the supposed hallmarks of Western Civilization. Though critical of the British, French, and Portuguese empires after the Second World War, the US government propagated a developmentalist logic that plotted all countries on a linear path. This had an effect on the nascent UN even though the latter was charged with promoting conflict resolution, peacekeeping, decolonization, nation building, and development, tasks that implied the inextricability of different forms of rights. Since the US and other Western powers were instrumental in founding the UN, it is not surprising that the organization's early documents (including the UDHR) privileged civil and political rights over other forms of rights. But this fact does not nullify the importance of civil and political rights. Moreover, it is crucial to bear in mind that the UN soon achieved a degree of relative autonomy vis-à-vis the US (its host country and biggest source of funding). Having pointed to the right to national self-determination to legitimize their anti-colonial struggles against the UK, France, Portugal, and other European states, formerly colonized peoples exerted considerable influence on the major documents ratified by the General Assembly in the 1960s (Burke 2010). Thus, in effect, the former colonies came to put their own stamps on rights discourse in general and the human rights canon in particular.

It is worthwhile to reflect on the role of decolonization in the formation of the rights-oriented epistemic community. Over time, the newly independent countries in what was then known as the "Third World" pushed for other types of rights. First, they militated for rights pertaining to economic development (understood as either "catching up" to or merely approximating the standard of living enjoyed in the West). Later, they militated for the protection of culture and the environment, especially in light of how the development project threatened cultures and ecosystems through the spread of industrialization and consumerism (Rist 2009). Thus, the resulting human rights canon cannot be seen as the property of the Western world or the Global North. In actuality, the canon is the imperfect and incomplete property of all humankind. Notwithstanding its status as a reference point, the human rights canon remains highly contested by forces across the world.

The second argument is *practical*: Civil and political rights are remarkably useful for social movements and their allies in NGOs and political parties. Clearly, civil and political rights cover a wide range of options: the right to due process of law; the right to associate with whomever one chooses; the right to assemble in public spaces and to use public facilities without discrimination; the right to vote in free and fair elections; the right to speak openly (without fear of harassment or reprisal from authorities); the right to petition the government for redress; the right to practice (or to refrain from practicing) a religion; the right to adhere to the dictates of one's conscience; and the right to privacy and to the sanctity of one's body. In sum, civil and political rights have long served not only as an objective of social movement activity, but also a springboard to further action to make the world a better place. Clearly, civil and political rights continue to serve this function in the era of globalization.

In the US context, these rights, conceptualized both as ends-in-themselves and as means to further ends, have figured prominently not only in the civil rights movement, which sought to accord African Americans and other racial minorities equal participation in social life, school, the workplace, and politics, but also in movements representing the working class, women, the LGBT community, immigrants, persons with disabilities, and other aggrieved groups. Owing to the experiences and accomplishments of these movements, civil and political rights are routinely seen as the most "fundamental" rights in US society (Soohoo et al. 2009). Similarly, the achievement of these rights was the primary objective of the mass movements challenging the bureaucratic socialist regimes in Eastern Europe in the late 1980s. Indeed, these rights have ranked highly among the objectives of movements across the world (Nepstad 2011).

In sum, the reason for the pervasiveness of civil and political *rights claims* is straightforward: In the *absence* of these rights, activists – often facing repression in the form of harassment, blacklisting, beatings, incarceration, exile, or even death – find it difficult to advance their causes. Conversely, in the *presence* of these rights, activists find it easier to pursue other goals (e.g., the realization of economic and social rights for individuals or cultural and environmental rights for groups). In other words, civil and political rights are notable for their *rights effects* – once they are implemented in the form of laws and policies at the level of the nation-state.

Why is this the case? By definition, civil and political rights accord moral and legal standing and protection to aggrieved parties, thereby altering power relations in the nation-state and society. For example, in numerous contexts, including the US, the conferral of the right to vote to the propertyless, women, and racial minorities has placed these populations in a position to empower themselves in other ways. Once granted the right to vote, previously exploited and marginalized groups find themselves in a position to exert direct influence on political parties. In the process of participating in elections, such groups often find elite allies, sympathetic figures in political parties and actual governments. This offers a useful lesson about how different categories of human rights relate to one another. Yet we ought to bear in mind that the progress of rights is neither inevitable nor subject to a preordained pattern. As a consequence, we have both social scientific and normative reasons for extricating the kernel of human rights from Enlightenment assumptions about reason and progress, a point that has been made repeatedly by scholars and activists in the Global South.

The Legacy of the Enlightenment and the Three-Generations Schema

In order to understand the role of civil and political rights, we need to review, albeit briefly, the classification schemas presented in the previous chapter: an approach that distinguishes negative rights (or protections) from positive rights (or entitlements); and an approach that delineates first-generation civil and political rights for individuals, second-generation economic and social rights for individuals, and third-generation collective rights (especially to cultural and environmental goods). In effect, the two schemas overlap because protections tend to come in the form of civil and political rights (as expressed by the UN in the ICCPR), while entitlements tend to come in the form of economic and social rights (as expressed by the UN in the ICESCR and subsequent documents). Arguably, the concept of collective rights (e.g., to such indivisible cultural goods as rituals, food practices, and lifeways, and such environmental goods as farmland, forests, and waterways), which comprises the third generation, would fall into the category of positive rights, not least because the actualization of such rights entails innovative policymaking by states. But the negative–positive schema is less equipped than its counterpart, the three-generations schema, to accommodate the idea of collective rights (i.e., entitlements that are held by entire peoples, groups, or communities).

Since the three-generations schema can account for both individual and collective rights, it has a broader range than the negative–positive schema. Therefore, we may move beyond the negative–positive schema without fear of losing our analytic, pedagogical, political, and practical edge. For the most part, scholarship, policymaking, legal interpretation, and human rights education have used the three-generations schema. Accordingly, it is worthwhile to explore the historical underpinnings of the framework en route to acquiring a deeper understanding of the most commonly embraced type of rights (especially in the US and elsewhere in the Western world), namely the civil and political rights, including the rights to association, assembly, speech, and petition, that have proven conducive since the eighteenth century to further social movement activity. In effect, civil and political rights found their first *modern* articulation in the US Declaration of Independence (1776), the US Constitution (1787), the French Declaration of the Rights of Man and of the Citizen (1789), and other documents associated with the Enlightenment in the pan-European world (Ishay 2008). Yet it is also true that the more radical elements in the American and French revolutionary movements envisaged a broader project of human emancipation that would free slaves, end colonialism, provide equal rights for women, alleviate poverty, and perhaps challenge the reigning economic system (which would later come to be known as capitalism) (Bronner 2004).

In other words, if left to their own devices, American and French radicals would have pursued what are now known as second-generation economic and social rights in one fashion or another. While the more radical elements were held in check during the eighteenth century, the ongoing Industrial Revolution and concomitant process of urbanization created the conditions for greater organization on the part of social movements, especially the working-class movement, which found partial representation in trade unions and labor, social democratic, and socialist parties (Ishay 2008). These radicals set the stage for the articulation of a new set of demands, including those of women, nationalists, and cultural minorities caught in multi-ethnic empires like those of Austria-Hungary and Russia (Ishay 2008). In light of the gains of the US and French revolutions, intellectuals, activists, and ordinary people rightly inquired: Does not the project of human emancipation entail an end to slavery and colonialism, better conditions and compensation for peasants and workers, and equal rights for women? In effect, this question, already on the table before the advent of sociology as a discipline, animated the debates and struggles of the next two centuries. It is not surprising, therefore, that the Enlightenment notion of progress inspired Comte to propose sociology as the science of society. Later, Marx, Durkheim, and Weber, the celebrated "founders" of the discipline, confronted such issues as industrialization, urbanization, individualism, bureaucratization, modernity, and the advent of mass society. Although the early sociologists did not examine human rights per se, they did address an array of social problems that are treated as human rights puzzles in the present day.

In the shadow of the Enlightenment, the political revolutions in the US and France, and the Industrial Revolution, social movements led by opponents of slavery and colonialism, supporters of legislation on the reduction of the working day and factory safety, and advocates of women's rights pursued their objectives throughout the nineteenth and twentieth centuries. This contributed to a spate of legislation that altered power relations in numerous countries (Tilly and Wood 2009). As we have seen, it is difficult, if not impossible, to establish *conclusively* that the movements produced the legislation. Nevertheless, it is safe to say that the movements and their elite allies *facilitated* the ratification of legislation that expanded civil and political rights to previously excluded segments of the population, while opening the door to economic and social rights (Tilly and Wood 2009). In effect, all of these movements involved both a critique and a radicalization of the Enlightenment. They *critiqued* the Enlightenment not only for its *theoretical* privileging of civil and political rights (with white males who owned property serving as the bearers of universalism), but also for its *practical* shortcomings (including the persistence of slavery, colonialism, exploitation in the workplace, and the subjugation of women). At the same time, these movements *radicalized* the Enlightenment not only by extending the project of human emancipation to historically underrepresented, exploited, and marginalized segments of the population, but also by showing the way beyond civil and political rights and toward economic and social rights (Bronner 2004). In sum, these movements took seriously the motto of the French Revolution by refusing to accept the priority of liberty over equality and solidarity. It would not be a stretch to assert that these movements already had an implicit understanding of what would become the standard framework of human rights (Ishay 2008).

How shall we understand the relationship between the European Enlightenment and the eventual human rights canon, established by the UN in the middle of the twentieth century? As we have established previously, the European Enlightenment provided neither the first nor the last word on the body of thought known as human rights. We would be remiss to ignore either the ancient antecedents of or the contemporary innovations in human rights thinking in the non-Western world. What the European Enlightenment did provide, however, was a major breakthrough in state–society relations, with sovereignty shifting from the monarchy to the people. In effect, the aforementioned American and French proclamations provided the grammar and the vocabulary for the post-Second World War documents that serve, to this day, as touchstones for scholars, policymakers, NGOs, and activists worldwide: the UDHR, the ICCPR, and the ICESCR.

Three examples are worth considering. The 1776 US Declaration of Independence contains the celebrated passage: "We hold these truths to be self-evident, that all men are created equal, that they are endowed by their Creator with certain unalienable Rights, that among these are Life, Liberty and the pursuit of Happiness" (http://www.archives. gov/exhibits/charters/declaration_transcript.html). For its part, the first two articles of the 1789 French Declaration of the Rights of Man and of the Citizen read as follows: "1. Men are born and remain free and equal in rights. Social distinctions may be founded only upon the general good. 2. The aim of all political association is the preservation of the natural and imprescriptible rights of man. These rights are liberty, property, security, and resistance to oppression" (http:// avalon.law.yale.edu/18th_century/rightsof.asp). In addition to setting the tone for post-revolutionary governments in the US and France respectively, these influential documents contained the seeds of the three generations of human rights. Moreover, the language of these documents is echoed in the 1948 UDHR: "All human beings are born free and equal in dignity and rights. They are endowed with reason and conscience and should act towards one another in a spirit of brotherhood" (http://www.un.org/en/documents/udhr/). In accordance with its status as the most famous and influential human rights NGO, Amnesty International routinely cites the UDHR.

Decolonization and Human Rights

In the aftermath of a 30-year period that brought unprecedented killing, destruction of property, and economic ruin to large segments of the world, the UDHR, the ICCPR, and the ICESCR were conceptualized by their framers as the three pillars of an International Bill of Human Rights, a project that was envisaged and debated, but never brought to fruition. Not coincidentally, in the post-1945 period, the newly decolonized states influenced the texts of the ICCPR and the ICESCR, thereby setting the stage for more inclusive conceptualizations of human rights in the contemporary world. We will examine these conceptualizations elsewhere in the book, especially in our discussion of cultural and environmental rights for collectivities. For the moment, suffice it to say that, from the 1940s through the 1970s, the Third World – in attempting to use the UN as a forum for steering a middle course between the US and the Soviet Union – placed particular emphasis on the right to national self-determination, which had its roots in the modern revolutions (in the US, France, Haiti, and Latin America) and found expression again in the Woodrow Wilson/US–Vladimir Lenin/Soviet Union rapprochement at the end of the First World War, a convergence that served a symbolic purpose despite the failure of the League of Nations (1919–46) to dissolve European empires, preside over the demilitarization of European states, or provide for collective security. In other words, the UN was designed in part to compensate for the deficiencies of the League of Nations by emphasizing the right to national self-determination for the colonies of Europe, by addressing the gap between the First and Third Worlds, and by dealing with the emerging Cold War antagonism between the US and the Soviet Union. These objectives were facilitated by the implicit agreement between the US and the Soviet Union on the principle of national self-determination and the concept of development (Rist 2009). Needless to say, this implicit agreement did not prevent the superpowers from meddling in the affairs of Third World countries.

Though routinely stipulated as the precondition for civil and political rights (after all, there must be an autonomous nation-state for *citizens* to enjoy their rights), the right to national self-determination constitutes a *collective* right par excellence. Furthermore, the right to national self-determination appears as the "basis" of the UDHR, the ICCPR, the ICESCR, and subsequent UN documents. In the contemporary period, this right has even formed the basis of the right of *peoples* to self-determination, independently of nation-states. In short, the influence of the Third World, now called the Global South, on human rights thinking has been significant. It is crucial for sociologists to consider such non-Western contributions not only to the human rights canon, but also to the UN system and set of NGOs operating in its orbit.

In this light, the sociological perspective highlights the classifications of human rights that prevail not only among scholars, policymakers, UN officials, NGO staff, and activists, but also among ordinary people. As we have discovered, the three-generations schema has proven useful in helping participants in the epistemic community to think systematically about human rights. *Implicit* in the documents of the European Enlightenment and *explicit* in the documents of the post-Second World War period (in which the UN was founded as the principal custodian of human rights), the three-generations schema remains influential in the present day. Nevertheless, as many scholars and human rights educators have noted, the schema has certain limitations when it comes to evaluating and ameliorating real-world human rights abuses, especially such enduring social problems as poverty and the structural violence associated with racism, classism, sexism, homophobia, xenophobia, and discriminatory attitudes toward persons with disabilities. Therefore, it is incumbent upon persons interested in human rights not to jettison the schema altogether, but rather to work through it methodically in order to arrive at a deeper appreciation of rights bundling, the process by which aggrieved parties and/or sympathetic scholars and policymakers formulate rights claims that exceed the conventional categories. An analogy can be made with the role of improvisation in jazz music: one must know the rules well in order to move beyond them. By convention, knowing rules begins with the mastery of first-generation civil and political rights. Near the end of this chapter, we will return to the metaphor of jazz improvisation, as we evaluate where civil and political rights fit in the context of a range of rights.

The Bedrock of the Human Rights Canon?

As we have seen in the section above, the *actual* bedrock of the human rights canon came in the form of the right to national self-determination, a right that appears at the beginning of the UDHR, the ICCPR, and the ICESCR, among other UN documents. In effect, nation-states must be autonomous in order to have citizens. Moreover, citizens, for their part, are the primary bearers of civil and political rights – aside from the most basic protections that are supposed to be afforded to all human beings, regardless of nationality. Nevertheless, civil and political rights (e.g., the rights to vote and participate freely in social life) are widely presented by members of the rights-oriented epistemic community as the most "fundamental" human rights. As we have seen, the reason for the presumed primacy of civil and political rights may pertain to the spirit of possessive individualism that pervades Western cultures. Doubtless, this question deserves a more comprehensive answer, not least because it bears on the capacity of the sociology of human rights to do justice to both individual and collective rights.

At this juncture, we may return to the question that guides this chapter (albeit at a higher level of analysis): Why is the category of civil and political rights the *most widely embraced* and the *least contested* part of the human rights canon? The answer is that claimants (whether entire peoples, SMOs, communities, or individuals) and nation-states (and other political authorities endowed with the task of granting rights) have entertained these rights in a serious and sustained fashion for more than 200 years. To reiterate, there are two major reasons why civil and political rights have been on the docket, so to speak, longer than other forms of rights. First, these rights figured prominently in two immensely influential revolutions in the eighteenth century: the American Revolution against British rule and the French Revolution, in which the bourgeoisie and the popular classes dealt a decisive blow to a declining aristocracy (Ishay 2008). Notwithstanding the limitations of these revolutions (e.g., their failure to enfranchise large segments of the population (including women), abolish slavery definitively, or end colonialism), the two revolutions, in shifting sovereignty from the monarch to the people, exerted a profound influence on the Western world and its colonial possessions. Second, under the influence of the US and other Western powers, civil and political rights were accorded pride of place in the UN system (as reflected in the UDHR and the ICCPR) and the human rights-oriented NGOs that emerged in its orbit (especially Amnesty International, which had as its original purview advocacy on behalf of "prisoners of conscience" in nation-states with authoritarian regimes, along with Human Rights Watch, which specialized initially in monitoring the abusive behavior of the Soviet Union and its satellites in Eastern Europe).

As a noted scholar has shown, the establishment of the UN system and with it the codification of the human rights canon, through a transnational process that included a host of dissenting voices, served as a theater for North–South and West–East antagonisms. Predictably, these antagonisms centered on attempts by the US and other great powers to position themselves as the arbiters of universalism. Thus, when the UDHR was ratified:

> ... the rights stipulated again were proclaimed to be independent from regional or cultural frameworks, despite reservations made by several countries with socialist or Islamic orientation ... the claim whereupon the classical human rights values and norms are universal or even constitute a consensus of mankind, dashes against postcolonial realities that reject the West's hegemony in political and moral terms. (Frick 2013: 17)

Although, as Frick has demonstrated, the founding of the UN was a highly conflictual process, replete with fierce arguments about normative principles, it does not follow that socialist and non-Western countries failed to influence the human rights canon. As we shall see, subaltern forces managed to break through to a certain degree in the post-1945 period and to an even greater degree in the post-Cold War period.

To say that the US and other Western powers placed a premium on civil and political rights, in part because of their own cultural assumptions, in spearheading the founding of the UN is not to say that these rights were considered unimportant in other countries. Nor is it to say that the UN confined itself exclusively to the promotion of civil and political rights. Under the sway of three forces – newly decolonized states in what came to be known as the "Third World," the Soviet Union and its satellites in Eastern Europe, and labor, social democratic, and socialist parties in Western Europe – the UN became a forum for deliberation on a wide range of rights, including second-generation economic and social rights and third-generation cultural and environmental rights (Burke 2010). Nevertheless, it remains commonplace to assert the primacy of civil and political rights over other types of rights. In the contemporary period, this tendency is akin to a habit.

The Role of the UN

Since the UN has, since its inception, served as a meeting place not only for diplomats, but also for scholars and activists, the organization's *knowledge-production function*, both within and beyond the United Nations Educational, Scientific, and Cultural Organization (UNESCO), should not be underestimated. Over time, the UN in general and UNESCO in particular have exerted a decisive influence not only on interdisciplinary programs in human rights, peace studies, and development studies in universities, but also on the research and practices of NGOs. Although a sociological analysis of the UN's knowledge-production function would fall beyond the purview of this book, it remains worthwhile to stress the organization's pivotal role in the formalization and propagation of the norms that have defined the field of human rights for more than six decades. The production of knowledge constitutes an important way in which the UN influences the rights-oriented epistemic community. For our immediate purposes, it suffices to allude to the UN's contribution to our understanding of the connections among different forms of human rights. Commissioned by the UN, the framers of the UDHR had, from the outset, a coherent vision of the ICCPR and the ICESCR as textual specifications of different, but equally important, forms of rights (Glendon 2002). Hence the framers of the putative International Bill of Human Rights believed not only that different types of rights were cut from the same cloth, but also that each type of rights merited specification. The framers recognized that the specification of different types of human rights would fall to future generations. As sociologists are quick to mention, the process of specification has always been fraught with conflict, as different power blocs and cultural formations attempt to influence the implementation of the UDHR, the ICCPR, and the ICESCR. Such conflicts are part and parcel of the circulation of human rights, from their initial conceptualization to their eventual implementation.

The sociological perspective supports two competing yet complementary gestures: the exploration of the inextricability of human rights, to the end of demonstrating that real-world abuses and remedies often transcend the conventional categories; and the specification of various types of human rights, to the end of assisting students, scholars, policymakers, and activists in thinking and speaking clearly about rights claims in the contemporary world. Needless to say, the ultimate goal of the exercise is to afford members of the human rights community greater facility in constructing, deconstructing, and reconstructing rights claims. This is necessary not only because the world consists of 7 billion persons, divided into 193 nation-states (each with a separate political and legal system), thousands of cultures, and numerous ecosystems, but also because the world is constantly in flux (with information, cultural artifacts, money, commodities, and flesh-and-blood human beings crossing borders at a striking rate). Consequently, what is thinkable and actionable in terms of human rights in the age of globalization differs greatly from what was imaginable and practical in terms of human rights during the Enlightenment.

For example, marriage equality for same-sex partners (a rights claim that belongs in the first generation) and the collective rights of indigenous peoples to ancestral lands and waterways (a rights claim that belongs in the third generation) would have been inconceivable and unworkable for the philosophers, politicians, and even the revolutionaries of the Enlightenment. Though indirectly inspired by two and one half centuries of rights-oriented thinking, the rights claims of the LGBT community and indigenous peoples fall beyond the frame of reference of the European Enlightenment. Alas, we might argue, albeit on a philosophical or moral level, that members of the LGBT community and indigenous peoples "possessed" – or "should have been granted" – such rights in the eighteenth century. Such an argument would be both reasonable and just. Nevertheless, neither the identity groups ("LGBT community" and "indigenous peoples") nor the rights claims (the "right to same-sex marriage" and the "right to inhabit indigenous lands") were fully formed in the eighteenth century. To say that it took centuries for these rights to be placed on the docket is not to say that the process was inevitable. There were many twists and turns, accomplishments and setbacks, along the way. Phrased differently, there was a high degree of contingency built into the process. The results of the exercise of human agency in the form of struggles over human rights cannot be predicted in advance. This stands as an important social scientific lesson for advocates of human rights.

Where Do Civil and Political Rights Fit?

Let us situate first-generation rights – civil and political rights that protect individuals from abuses by state and non-state actors, guarantee a modicum of representation in government, and ensure a measure of popular participation in the amenities of civil society – in relation to second-generation economic and social rights and third-generation collective rights to culture and environment. It is useful to consider a concrete case. Previously, we touched on an example of "systematic improvisation" – something akin to the practice of jazz musicians – within the categories of human rights in the form of the renowned NGO Oxfam International's rights-based approach to the problem of poverty in the Global South. We may now revisit the example at a higher level of analysis. In attempting to reconcile three oppositions – universalism and cultural pluralism, globalism and localism, individual rights and collective rights – Oxfam International *bundles together* interrelated rights as an antidote to poverty: the right to have "a livelihood" (presupposing safe working conditions, the ability to use natural resources, and sound ecological practices); the right to "basic services" (including clean water, public hygiene, and education); the right to "be safe from harm" (and hence to be protected from natural disasters, as well as human-made calamities); the right to "be heard" (presupposing a voice in public debates and a role in decision-making processes); and, lastly, the right to "be treated as equal" (presupposing policies and programs to ensure that minorities, whether racial, cultural, or religious, women, and persons with disabilities have equal access to jobs, resources, and information) (http://www.oxfam.org/en/about/why).

For Oxfam, poverty – understood as a rights puzzle – necessitates a multifaceted approach that touches on civil and political rights (e.g., the rights to personal security and bodily integrity, free speech and democracy). Poverty is puzzling to social scientists and policymakers alike because it has proven resistant even to the social scientifically informed policies of welfare states in the Global North and development states in the Global South. The puzzle is particularly challenging in the Global South, which received uneven benefits from the development projects of the post-Second World War period. What is clear, however, is that poverty is a multi-causal problem and it cannot be reduced to purely economic factors. It follows that any plausible remedy for poverty would need to be multifaceted.

Looking closely, we can find traces of civil and political rights in the rights bundle proposed by Oxfam. Among the intertwined rights that Oxfam International has proposed, the "right to be heard" clearly belongs to the category of civil and political rights. It is another way of designating the right to speak freely (without fear of reprisal from government) and the right to political representation (whether direct in the form of referenda or indirect in the form of representation in a legislative body). In a subtler fashion, the "right to be treated as equal" – and hence to be protected from discrimination – effectively presupposes such civil and political rights as the right to have a racial identity, the right to affirm one's membership in a cultural tradition, and the right to practice (or to refrain from practicing) a religion. All of these protections are individual rights.

What can we deduce from Oxfam International's rights-based approach to the alleviation of poverty? Why does Oxfam International's campaign embrace such a range of objectives? In a nutshell, we can conclude that the problem of poverty is not solely an economic matter; instead, poverty can be perpetuated and exacerbated not only by the lack of remunerative activities and social services, but also by cultural destruction (e.g., the literal or figurative separation of persons from their cultures), environmental degradation (e.g., deforestation, the ruination of farmland, and the pollution of lakes, rivers, and oceans), the lack of popular participation in major decisions, and, of course, discrimination on the basis of a range of identity characteristics. Indeed, the last two aspects – the need for proper representation and the importance of ending discrimination – fall squarely into the category of first-generation civil and political rights. It follows that the alleviation of poverty – the central goal of the organization's leadership, members, and collaborators – cuts across the conventional categories of human rights.

In other words, the remediation of poverty would necessitate granting first-generation civil and political rights, as well as second-generation economic and social rights and third-generation cultural and environmental rights to societies, communities, and individuals mired in poverty. While it goes without saying that anti-poverty programs must be tailored for specific conditions on the ground (e.g., political structure, inherited institutions, gender relations, cultural heritage, geographic location, and the degree of environmental destruction), it remains the case that poverty often involves the denial of civil and political rights. Why is this significant? By custom, we tend to define poverty either as the luck of the draw (in an otherwise just system) or as a denial of economic and social rights (in a not-so-just system). But we tend *not* to think about poverty as a violation of civil and political rights. Nevertheless, two points are worth making here. First, groups, communities, and individuals can fall into poverty because of discrimination on the basis of identity characteristics, not to mention because of the privatization of land, forests, waterways, and other natural resources. Second, confinement in a state of poverty can make it difficult for groups, communities, and individuals to benefit from whatever formal civil and political rights they may have. For example, the right to vote in free and fair elections, though a significant achievement that is worthy of being defended, harbors little meaning to persons who remain mired in poverty irrespective of which political party holds power.

What follows from the acknowledgement of the connection between poverty and the violation of civil and political rights? Long conceptualized by scholars, UN agencies, and NGOs as an antidote to poverty, the right to development – understood as planned social change to improve the material wellbeing of a nation-state, society, or community – would need to be articulated with measures not only to preserve cultural traditions and restore the environment, but also to provide the poor with access to the public sphere and proper political representation. Consequently, the right to development – understood properly as a *rights bundle* that includes all of Oxfam International's suggestions – can be connected to demands for good governance (meaning: transparency, accountability, consistency, and fairness) and even democracy (whether indirect/representative or direct/participatory). Clearly, one of the flaws of most development projects in the Global South has been a lack of popular participation in decision-making processes, seemingly a *violation* of civil and political rights. As a consequence, Oxfam International's conception of the right to development goes against the grain of the development projects implemented by the WB in conjunction with national governments.

In this light, scholars and activists have raised the question of whether human beings have, or could plausibly lay claim to, a *right to democracy*. Arguably, when extrapolated to their logical extreme, civil and political rights culminate in the profession of the right to democracy. At the very least, the right to vote in free and fair elections involving multiple political parties figures prominently on most lists of civil and political rights. However, the devil is in the details, since advocates of such a right would need to think through the practical problem of implementing democracy on a global scale, while allowing for a high degree of cultural pluralism. In other words, partisans of global democracy would need to ascertain how to steer an interstate system that features 193 sovereign nation-states – some with representative democracy and others with authoritarian regimes, some wealthy and powerful and others poor and weak, and all with different visions of both foreign and domestic policy – in the direction of democratic global governance. In an intervention in the debate on global governance, a debate that centers on the question of whether to reform or replace the existing IGOs (including the IMF, the WB, the WTO, and even the UN), British journalist and social critic George Monbiot has proposed a World Parliament (defined as an assembly that would be elected directly by the world's population) along with institutions to replace the IMF, the WB, and the WTO (Monbiot 2004).

Moreover, advocates of the right to democracy would need to think through the question of representative versus participatory democracy on a national scale. Citizens of the US and the European Union are accustomed to representative or indirect democracy – a governmental system in which citizens elect representatives (whether presidents, members of Congress, and Senators or members of parliaments and prime ministers) to make decisions on their behalf (Tilly 2007). Finally, advocates would need to take seriously models of democracy emanating from the Global South, including models of participatory democracy that minimize or bypass parliaments. Accordingly, this book points to the need for sociologists of human rights to examine an array of models of democracy.

Summary

In conclusion, this chapter has explored the most renowned category of human rights: the civil and political rights that serve to protect individuals from abuse (whether from the state or from other individuals), facilitate their participation in civil society and politics, and allow them to develop their personalities and express their beliefs. Yet we have investigated the role of civil and political rights with a twist. Instead of taking for granted the separation of civil and political rights from other types of rights, we have done the opposite. In other words, we have examined the intricate connections between the civil and political rights that figured so prominently in Enlightenment thought and the rights claims that emerged subsequently, particularly with the evolution of parliamentary systems that include multiple political parties and nurture the formation and dissolution of coalitions. More precisely, the sociological perspective has demonstrated that civil and political rights are significant not only as ends-in-themselves, but also as means to further ends. In particular, the rights to association, assembly, free speech, and petition are conducive to social movement activity in the name of other objectives.

This chapter has paid particular attention to the prevalence of civil and political rights both in scholarship and in popular discourse. It is a dictate of sociology not to take popularity of first-generation civil and political rights at face value, but rather to analyze the social conditions underneath the phenomenon. It would be worthwhile to explore what the immense popularity of civil and political rights tells us about the US in particular and the West in general. Clearly, the legacy of possessive individualism, particularly prominent in the US and encapsulated in the emphasis on property rights in the legal system, accounts in part for the popularity of civil and political rights. It is hoped that a future study will illuminate how the particularities of the US – its culture, landscape, and geopolitical role – contributed to an American penchant for civil and political rights. But what matters most for our immediate purposes is that civil and political rights figure prominently in the rights-oriented epistemic community *beyond* the US. Hence the question arises: What does it mean to say that civil and political rights comprise the *most widely embraced* and the *least contested* form of rights both in the human rights community and in the world at large? Let us answer the question by a process of deduction. First, it does *not* mean that civil and political rights are *universally* considered more important than other forms of rights. Across the global landscape, we can find evidence of aggrieved parties pursuing rights claims that fall into the second and third generations. Second, it does *not* mean that there is an inevitable progression from civil and political rights to other forms of rights. Historically, the passage from the first to the second and third generations has been anything but a linear process. Outcomes have varied considerably according to the political system, cultural traditions, and ecological conditions that prevail in a given place. Third, it does *not* necessarily mean that other forms of rights cannot be achieved in the absence of civil and political rights. But it *is* a question of *probability*. In other words, it tends to be *easier* on balance to advance other rights claims, including demands for economic, social, cultural, and environmental remedies, in places where civil and political rights have been achieved. Indeed, social movement activity proves easier to pursue in countries that have constitutional safeguards and democratic institutions. More precisely, the first-generation rights to association, assembly, free speech, and petition (for redress from the government) serve to facilitate social movement activity in the name of other rights (including the second- and third-generation rights analyzed in subsequent chapters).

Discussion Questions

- What are the primary functions of civil and political rights?
- Why are civil and political rights so widely accepted?
- What does it mean to say that civil and political rights form the foundation of the human rights canon?
- How are civil and political rights conducive to social movement activity?
- Describe the subtle ways in which civil and political rights are connected to other types of rights.

4 Economic and Social Rights

As the previous chapters have shown, the prevailing classification schema, namely the three-generations framework that was already implicit in the writings of the European Enlightenment and later rendered explicit in the interpretation of the major documents of the human rights canon after 1945, encourages us to treat first-generation civil and political rights as the "foundation" of human rights *in toto*. Yet, as we discovered in chapter 3, the right to self-determination – a collective right that belongs to "nations" and perhaps to "peoples" as well – serves in the UDHR, the ICCPR, and the ICESCR, as the precondition for civil and political rights. The rationale is straightforward: there must be an independent nation-state in order for there to be proper mechanisms in place for the implementation and enforcement of civil and political rights. In a similar vein, we discovered in the last chapter that human rights are always relational; that is, they can only be understood in their complex and dynamic interactions with one another.

First, this chapter examines the complex relationship between liberty and equality in the trajectory of Enlightenment thought, while illuminating the relational character of human rights. Then, this chapter explores a category of human rights that has found acceptance to a greater extent in the welfare states of the European Union and to a lesser extent in the US welfare state and the post-development states of Latin America. Proclaimed under the banner of equality, economic and social rights serve the following purposes:

- to protect human beings from economic crises, bad luck, and natural disasters;
- to provide human beings with the basic necessities of life (including food, clothing, shelter, and healthcare) while assisting them through different phases of life (especially childhood and old age);

- to ensure human beings have access to education, vocational training, the benefits of science and technology, cultural enrichment (whether through popular culture or "high culture"), and other means of self-improvement and upward social mobility (without regard for race, class, gender, sexual orientation, national origin, or other identity characteristics).

In a nutshell, economic and social rights are entitlements (sometimes enshrined in constitutions, but more often enacted through public policy) that nurture the physical, intellectual, personal, and professional development of individuals (Esparza 2011). In essence, these rights are premised on the idea that *individuals* require a range of social supports in order to actualize their potential. Accordingly, it is worth mentioning that cultural rights were originally formulated as second-generation rights for individuals. When applied to individuals, cultural rights involve a person's ability either to enjoy the fruits of cultural life, including music, art, literature, the mass media, and various forms of entertainment, or to "have a culture" (understood as a public allegiance to an ethnic, religious, or language group). Cultural rights received only cursory treatment in the ICESCR. It was only in the 1970s that cultural rights came to be conceptualized as collective rights under heavy pressure from UN delegations based in the Global South (e.g., at the Stockholm Conference on Human Development). Such rights, including the rights to ancestral lands, forests, and waterways, as well as the rights to minority languages and traditions, will be given more detailed treatment in chapter 5.

Economy and Society

Let us explore the issue of economic and social rights (understood as *entitlements* granted by state policymakers). Owing to their status as *social* programs designed to assist *individuals* in the "pursuit of happiness," these entitlements occupy an ambiguous position in contemporary debates, particularly in the US. Yet these debates harbor great importance for the interpretation of the human rights canon in the coming years (Esparza 2011). For example, it would make a profound difference if more scholars, policymakers, activists, and ordinary people in the US came to conceptualize food provisions, housing allowances, unemployment compensation, disability insurance, retirement benefits, and healthcare not merely as *public goods*, but also as *human rights*. Arguably, such a shift would alter the stakes of the debate by bracketing the competing platforms of the two major political parties in the US – the Democrats (who have traditionally proven more amenable to social programs) and the Republicans (who have by convention been less receptive to social programs) – in favor of a discussion of human rights.

In the last few decades in the US, neither the Democrats nor the Republicans have been inclined to discuss human rights at home. Possible exceptions include the recurring debates on the Second Amendment's affirmation of the right to bear arms and gun control, the rights of the unborn versus women's reproductive freedom, and the rights of states vis-à-vis the Federal Government. It is instructive that the ongoing debate on entitlements, including such vaunted programs as Social Security and Medicare/Medicaid, is *not* couched in the language of human rights. Hence the question arises: How can we explain the reluctance of the major political parties to consider human rights on the domestic front? In effect, the major political parties have operated under the assumption that human rights have largely been attained in the US, if viewed as restricted to the *civil and political rights* that protect human beings from abuses, allow them to participate fully in civil society and political life, and permit them to develop their identities. A corollary to this widespread assumption is that the civil rights and women's rights movements achieved all of their objectives.

Accordingly, the two major political parties have tended to think of human rights in relation to development assistance (particularly with the recent emphasis on "good governance" in countries in the Global South) and foreign policy objectives (particularly with the recent emphasis on "humanitarian intervention" in high-intensity conflict zones). The situation may change with the emerging debate between Democrats and Republicans on whether the Voting Rights Act, passed in 1965 as a means of guaranteeing the right to vote – and by extension the full benefits of citizenship – to African Americans, remains important in the present day or whether, alternatively, racial equality in the South has advanced to such a degree that there is no need to monitor states' and counties' compliance with the Voting Rights Act.

Regardless, the discussion is not likely to veer in the direction of economic and social rights. Furthermore, among the smaller political parties, neither the Green Party (with its emphasis on social and ecological justice) nor the Libertarian Party (with its emphasis on civil liberties and free markets) has the capacity to generate a debate on economic and social rights. Finally, neither the Occupy Wall Street movement (with its left-leaning critique of economic inequality and poverty) nor the Tea Party movement (with its right-leaning critique of government spending on social entitlements) has succeeded in placing such a debate on the docket.

The paucity of rights-oriented conversations in the political culture of the US raises the following question: What would it mean, in concrete terms, to conceptualize a social program as the implementation of a human right? To say that a social program expresses or represents a human right is to say that it must be provided, in one fashion or another, by capable governments. Interestingly enough, Amnesty International, an NGO that gained renown by advocating for *civil and political rights* (particularly for "prisoners of conscience" living under authoritarian regimes), has advanced such an argument. Moving beyond its original purview, Amnesty International has launched a campaign in defense of the following economic, social, and cultural rights:

> rights at work, particularly just and fair conditions of employment, protection against forced or compulsory labor and the right to form and join trade unions; the right to education, including ensuring that primary education is free and compulsory, that education is sufficiently available, accessible, acceptable and adapted to the individual; cultural rights of minorities and Indigenous Peoples; the right to the highest attainable standard of physical and mental health, including the right to healthy living conditions and available, accessible, acceptable and quality health services; the right to adequate housing, including security of tenure, protection from forced eviction and access to affordable, habitable, well located and culturally adequate housing; the right to food, including the right to freedom from hunger and access at all times to adequate nutritious food or the means to obtain it; the right to water – the right to sufficient water and sanitation that is available, accessible (both physically and economically) and safe. (http://www.amnesty.org/en/economic-social-and-cultural-rights)

Since Amnesty International advocates these rights on a *global scale*, it not only refrains from specifying the social programs (instituted on a *national scale*) that would be required to bring these rights to fruition, it also acknowledges that different nation-states have different capabilities (e.g., in terms of wealth, power, geopolitical positioning, bureaucratic efficiency, cultural diversity and cohesion, and environmental stability) in delivering such programs to their populations. For example, in theory, the US would have a greater capacity to implement economic and social rights through policymaking than its poorer neighbor Mexico. Yet it may also be a question of political will.

It is highly instructive that Amnesty International has embraced economic and social rights – and hence whatever social programs might bring them to fruition in specific nation-states – as a complement or corollary to civil and political rights. In sum, Amnesty International's introduction of a campaign for economic, social, and cultural rights, like Oxfam International's anti-poverty program, reflects a growing awareness among NGOs, UN agencies, scholars, and other members of the rights-oriented epistemic community of the interconnectedness of different types of human rights. As we have seen throughout this book, the sociological perspective amounts to a holistic vision of human rights not only in their relations with one another, but also in their embeddedness in nation-states, societies, and communities. For this reason, political sociology (i.e., the analysis of state–society relations in a manner that accords governments, elite actors, organizations, and popular forces appropriate treatment) proves crucial to the sociological approach to human rights.

Preliminary Questions about Economic and Social Rights

As we have seen, the celebrated NGO Amnesty International has recently expanded its mandate beyond "bread-and-butter" civil and political rights: the right to due process of law; the right to be protected from unlawful detainment and torture; the right to speak freely; the right to assemble in public; and the right to petition the government for redress. While Amnesty International became famous for advocating for the rights of "prisoners of conscience," it has moved into the advocacy of such second-generation rights as the rights to food, water, housing, education, work, and healthcare. It has also begun to advocate the third-generation rights of minorities and indigenous peoples to enjoy the fruits of *their particular* cultures.

As we will discover in chapter 6, the convergence of Amnesty International and Oxfam International testifies to the increasing popularity of a holistic view that emphasizes the intersections among the different forms of rights (whether individual or collective) in the UN–NGO–SMO nexus. This points to the importance of rights bundling (packaging together different forms of rights in order to meet the needs of new constituencies) in the age of globalization. In effect, in rendering nation-states more porous and in mixing the "domains" of the economy, the polity, society, culture, and environment in unpredictable ways, globalization has created a new set of rights puzzles. Arguably, such puzzles require recourse to rights bundling.

The first step on the road to rights bundling is the consideration of the *space* of economic and social rights. In the process of explaining where economic and social rights fit in relation to other types of rights, this chapter addresses a series of questions: Why are economic and social rights (pertaining to the *equality* of individuals) subject to more vigorous debate, especially in the US, than civil and political rights (pertaining to the *liberty* of individuals)? To what extent does this debate obscure the complexities not only of Enlightenment thought (which articulated the principles of liberty and equality in conjunction with one another as parts of a broader emancipatory project), but also of the US political tradition (which, if only for a brief time, produced cutting-edge notions of economic and social rights with the emergence and expansion of the Keynesian welfare state in the 1930s and 1940s)? What can we learn from attempts by UN agencies, NGOs, and SMOs to place economic and social rights on the same footing as civil and political rights?

In answering these questions, this chapter argues for the utility of exploring not only the admixture of first-generation civil and political rights and second-generation economic and social rights in the wide-ranging struggles of workers, women, nationalists, and others in the nineteenth century, but also the short-lived but nonetheless significant flowering of economic and social rights during the administrations of Franklin Delano Roosevelt (1933–45). While it would be an exaggeration to assert that these historical examples constitute lost roots, it is certainly true that contemporary debates have tended to reify the distinctions among the three generations of rights. Taken together, these historical examples shed light on the complex interconnections between first- and second-generation rights, an issue that has been brought to the fore, once again, with the mass mobilizations of the present day (Esparza 2011). To take an example from the US: the Tea Party movement, with its status as a grassroots entity designed to influence the Republican Party, has placed particular emphasis on civil and political rights. In contrast, the Occupy Wall Street movement, with its status as a grassroots entity that ignores the Democratic Party and appeals directly to the people, has stressed economic and social rights explicitly without ignoring either civil and political rights or cultural and environmental rights. In this sense, the Occupy Wall Street movement bears great similarity to many of the SMOs that appear at the World Social Forum, a testimony to the influence of the Global South on mobilizations in the US (and, indeed, everywhere that the term "occupy" has been claimed).

Liberty, Equality, and the Legacy of the Enlightenment

In order to understand the place of the second-generation economic and social rights that are designed to protect us from calamities (whether economic or natural), guarantee a minimum standard of living, provide for us during different phases of the life cycle, nurture our physical and psychological development, and allow us to enjoy the benefits of culture (including music, art, literature, and film), we need to consider the limitations of first-generation civil and political rights. While both the first- and the second-generation rights spring from the same source, namely, the revolutions that exemplified the European Enlightenment in the eighteenth century, second-generation economic and social rights found their first notable expression amidst the upsurge of working-class activism (spearheaded by revolutionary socialists, parliamentary socialists, and anarchists), opposition to slavery and serfdom, support for women's emancipation, and liberal nationalism (directed against dynasties) in the nineteenth century. In many ways, the nineteenth century, in which sociology as a discipline was founded in Europe, served as a cauldron for experimentation in human rights. Indeed, as a noted political scientist and historian of human rights has demonstrated:

> It was no single event, but rather a succession of political jolts that fed a chain reaction of popular unrest as workers rose to demand economic and political power, liberal nationalists strove for independence from tyrannical dynasties, serfs and slaves struggled to free themselves from bondage, and suffragettes demanded rights for women. Their outrage in the face of social inequity shaped the nineteenth-century human rights debate – a debate that intensified as conservative forces succumbed to the advance of capitalism and as rapid industrialization spawned social conflict. (Ishay 2008: 118)

In effect, Ishay has provided evidence for one of the major theses of this book: social movement activity, especially since the Enlightenment, has greatly expanded what is *thinkable* and *attainable* in terms of human rights. Yet this expansion has always been a complex and ambiguous process. Notwithstanding the significant differences among the constituencies of workers, anti-slavery activists, opponents of serfdom, nationalists, and others, all of these movements made reference to and consciously sought to expand the human rights canon (by citing and reinterpreting the salient texts of the day). Despite their theoretical contradictions and practical short-comings, these movements grappled with the complex relationship between *liberty* (i.e., the focus of what would come to be known as first-generation civil and political rights) and *equality* (i.e., the focus of what would come to be known as second-generation economic and social rights).

Human Rights and the Political Chessboard

Often, these movements struggled for *both* liberty (along with the civil and political rights that bolster it) *and* equality (along with the economic and social rights that sustain it). In other words, the worldwide struggle for civil and political rights remained incomplete when popular forces began to push for economic and social rights. For example, the International Workingmen's Association (IWMA), founded in 1864 to advance the cause of "proletarian international-ism" in the service of a vision of socialism that would guarantee a range of economic and social rights, expressed a wide range of griev-ances in the language of human rights. More precisely, the IWMA pushed for the following: the right to vote for workers (and the prop-ertyless); factory legislation to reduce the length of the working day and improve working conditions; and the abolition of slavery (in the US and elsewhere) and the right to self-determination for oppressed nations (including Poland and Ireland) (Nimtz 2002). Thus, Marx, Engels, and the other leaders of the IWMA operated according to a *holistic view* of human rights.

Doubtless, Marx, his IWMA colleagues, and their successors in the international working-class movement, were often inconsistent on the question of human rights. Nevertheless, Marx's dual status as an activist and scholar (and, for the purposes of universities, a founder of sociology as a discipline) remains relevant. To a certain extent, this holistic vision has been maintained – and perhaps deepened – by some rights-oriented sociologists. Though most rights-oriented soci-ologists would not identify themselves as partisans of Marxist theory, they might well cite Marx and other *totalizing* thinkers as forerunners of a sociological perspective that stresses the following: the *interrelat-edness* of different forms of rights; the *historical* character of rights; and the need to analyze rights on a *global* scale. Holism, historicism, and globalism are important to many rights-oriented sociologists. At the same time, such sociologists must consider the human rights abuses perpetrated by the Soviet Union, its Eastern European satellites (Bulgaria, Czechoslovakia, East Germany, Hungary, Poland, and Romania), and other state socialist regimes. While state socialist regimes made strides in granting economic and social rights, they routinely denied civil and political rights to their citizens. As a consequence, the 1989 revolutions in Eastern Europe were undertaken partly in the name of civil and political rights.

What can we deduce from the overlap of the struggles for first-generation civil and political rights and second-generation economic and social rights? As we discovered in chapter 3, there are both historical and practical reasons for asserting the primacy of civil and political rights. Historically, the Enlightenment revolutions and the governments that were influenced by them prioritized civil and political rights (albeit for the more privileged parts of society). Practically, such civil and political protections as the rights to association, assembly, free speech, and petition facilitate social movement activity in the name of economic and social rights. In other words, SMOs routinely maximize civil liberties in the struggle for higher wages, better working conditions, retirement funds, access to healthcare, and other second-generation rights. Nevertheless, it is important to bear in mind not only that the realization of civil and political rights remained incomplete when the pursuit of economic and social rights began, but also that there exists no universal recipe for how to achieve human rights. In sum, the proclamation, contestation, and realization of human rights is an uneven process both within and among societies. To date, social scientific research has not unearthed a formula for the actualization of human rights.

For this reason, we must take the three-generations framework (explained in chapter 2) with a grain of salt. Already in the nineteenth century, political philosophers, social critics, policymakers, and activists posed such questions as: How meaningful is political freedom in the presence of exploitation at work, extreme poverty, the subjugation of women, slavery, colonialism, and other injustices? Alternatively, how far can equality be expanded without abridging individual liberty? How rapidly should social change take place? Needless to say, conservatives (who wanted to roll back the gains of the Enlightenment), centrists (usually liberals desiring to consolidate the achievements of the Enlightenment in the name of incremental change), and revolutionaries (usually socialists, including the leaders and membership of the IWMA, wishing to radicalize the

Enlightenment in the name of accelerated change) offered vastly different answers to these questions. As a renowned world-systems analyst has shown, conservatism, liberalism, and socialism – the three dominant ideologies of modernity – crystallized as the most palpable responses to the reality of social change:

> In sum, three postures toward modernity and the "normalization" of change had evolved: conservatism, or circumscribe the danger as much as possible; liberalism, or achieve in due time the happiness of mankind as rationally as possible; and socialism/radicalism, or accelerate the drive for progress by struggling hard against the forces that were strongly resisting it. (Wallerstein 2011: 11)

Building on Wallerstein's explanation of the conflicts among the ideologies of conservatism, liberalism, and socialism, this book argues that, though already apparent in the nineteenth century, the tensions and complementarities between negative/first-generation civil and political rights and positive/second-generation economic and social rights became appreciably more prominent with the post-Second World War founding of the UN system, proposal for an International Bill of Human Rights (consisting of the UDHR, the ICCPR, and the ICESCR), and pursuit of decolonization, nation-building, and development in the Third World.

The Two Covenants

The rise of left-wing parties in Western European parliaments and the spread of an anticolonial ethos across the colonized world were reflected in the UN framers' deliberations on the content of the two Covenants. In drafting the blueprints for the International Bill of Human Rights, the framers attempted to capture both the connections and the distinctions between the first and second generations. On the one hand, they argued that all of the rights sketched in the UDHR and delineated more explicitly in the ICCPR and the ICESCR were linked inextricably to each other. On the other hand, they accorded a semblance of autonomy to the ICCPR and the ICESCR, and this was reflected in the debates surrounding the two documents (with different political forces, governments, and power blocs favoring one or the other).

To a certain extent, the interpretation of the two documents was caught in the Cold War rivalry between the US, which favored civil and political rights, and the Soviet Union, which favored economic and social rights. This rivalry played out in the UN, especially as decolonization movements in the Third World faced the dilemma of siding with the US, siding with the Soviet Union, or joining the Non-Aligned Movement (following standard-bearers India, Indonesia, Egypt, Ghana, and Yugoslavia). To make matters more complicated, though aligned with the US against the Soviet bloc, Western Europe proved more receptive than the US to economic and social rights (as expressed in the implementation of an expansive social safety net that moved considerably beyond the policies and programs of the US New Deal) (Levine 1988). Pushed in part by the presence of labor, social democratic, socialist, and, in the cases of France and Italy, communist parties in parliament, this receptiveness was reflected in the policies and programs of Western European welfare states (Esping-Andersen 1990). A sign of the times came in the form of the European Social Charter. Adopted in 1961 and revised in 1966 by the Council of Europe, the Charter advanced housing, healthcare, fair employment, social security, protection from poverty, and protection from disability as *human rights*, and created an institution, the European Committee of Social Rights, to monitor members' compliance with the Charter.

Viewed in sociological perspective, the debate on the nature and scope of economic and social rights reflected deeper shifts in the post-Second World War world. Over time, these historical processes have forced scholars, policymakers, and activists to work through the dilemmas associated with the quest for liberty, equality, and later solidarity not only on a national scale, but also on a global scale. In the abstract world of ideas, it is relatively easy to postulate a dichotomy between liberty and equality. In the concrete world of power struggles and material processes, the quest for liberty often converges with the quest for equality. As we have seen, these issues remain puzzling in the present day.

The Relational Character of Human Rights

As we have noted throughout the book, human rights exist not in abstraction, but rather in relation to the *social contexts* in which they are constructed, propagated, implemented, enforced, and violated. In addition, different types of human rights exist in relation to one another. To say that human rights are relational is not to say that they are not based on anything real. While it is distinctly possible that the rights (whether protections or entitlements) that individuals and collectivities hold dear are grounded in human physiology (and hence vulnerability), human sociability (and hence the proclivity for establishing families, tribes, communities, and societies), or even an intrinsic capacity for empathy, cooperation, and solidarity, it is also possible that rights are founded on little more than the accumulation of social conventions across centuries of conflict and dialogue, dissent and consensus (Turner 2006; Gregg 2012). Irrespective of whether we adopt the essentialist or the social constructionist position (or perhaps an intermediary position), we must acknowledge not only that what is imaginable and actionable in terms of human rights changes throughout history, but also that changes in human rights knowledge, institutions, and practices are not linear. Thus, while we can make sense of how rights have been achieved *after the fact*, our capacities are extremely limited when it comes to *predicting* where human rights will be headed in the future. Our task, then, is to isolate trends and possibilities in the present day. Once we have sketched the existing trends, we will find ourselves in a position to make informed decisions about where to invest our energies. It goes without saying that reasonable persons may disagree on which rights and programs to emphasize.

We have considered the example of the right to same-sex marriage (understood as an addendum to existing first-generation civil and political rights), advanced by the LGBT community in the US and elsewhere. Clearly, the right to same-sex marriage builds on the prior achievements not only of the LGBT movement, but also, albeit less directly, on the achievements of the women's movement (which had pushed for reproductive freedom and the liberalization of divorce laws) and the civil rights movement (which had maintained as one of its demands the legalization of interracial marriage). These movements were devoted to the pursuit not only of liberty, but also of equality. We might also consider the right to free, comprehensive healthcare (understood as an addendum to existing second-generation economic and social rights), often advanced in the US and largely achieved in Europe through single-payer health insurance or even socialized medicine. Clearly, the right to free, comprehensive healthcare builds on the achievements of the New Deal in the US (under the influence of the working-class movement and its elite allies in the Democratic Party) and more far-reaching spates of legislation in Europe (with the burgeoning power of the working-class, trade unions, and labor, social democratic, and socialist parties). Interestingly enough, the rights to same-sex marriage and free, comprehensive healthcare converge on the question of whether to allow LGBT persons to visit their same-sex partners in emergency rooms or to make medical decisions on their partners' behalf.

Let us consider the ramifications of these equality-oriented movements. Neither the right to same-sex marriage nor the right to free, comprehensive healthcare would have been conceivable – let alone implementable – in the nineteenth century. In the first case, the blockage came in the form of the absence of a coherent LGBT identity. In the second case, the blockage came in the form of severe technical limitations in the field of medicine. To this day, conditions, whether cultural, social, political, or economic, are more auspicious in some places than in others for the actualization of the rights to same-sex marriage and free, comprehensive healthcare. As a consequence, appeals to globalism must take national circumstances into consideration, especially political parties, parliaments and other institutions, constitutions, existing policies, and legal precedents.

In lieu of adopting a definitive position on the debate between strict essentialism and strict social constructionism, a matter better left to philosophers (operating in the faculty of the humanities) and psychologists (operating in the faculty of the natural sciences), this book uses sociology to explain how rights claims (i.e., the demands for protections and entitlements that aggrieved parties make on authorities) mutate, accumulate, and produce changes in power relations (known as rights effects) across historical time and geographic space. By definition, the sociological perspective illuminates how human rights are embedded in every type of social formation, from small communities to large societies. While this point is fairly clear in terms of first-generation civil and political rights, it is even more evident in terms of second-generation economic and social rights insofar as the latter are designed to provide social entitlements and protections throughout the life cycle (with children and elderly persons being particularly vulnerable).

To recapitulate, chapter 3 advanced two arguments about the widespread embrace – in theory, if not always in practice – of such first-generation civil and political rights as the right to due process of law, the right to personal security, and the rights to association, assembly, free speech, and petition. On the one hand, these rights figured prominently in the documents produced by revolutionaries in the US and France in the eighteenth century, setting an important precedent for political and legal systems across the world. On the other hand, these rights have proven remarkably useful to social movements and their allies through the contemporary period. By achieving access to the public sphere and participation in political life, popular forces have been able to pursue other objectives. Many of these objectives have appeared in the form of economic, social, and sometimes cultural rights (albeit initially in the form of demands for national self-determination and the protection of ethnic enclaves). Let us turn our attention to the transitory flowering of economic and social rights – cultural rights as such were not yet on the docket – in the US context.

Economic and Social Rights in the US Context

How can we account for the status of economic and social rights in US society? As we have seen, it is commonplace for Americans, whether politicians or ordinary citizens, to harbor a certain amount of suspicion vis-à-vis economic and social rights. More precisely, Americans tend to conceptualize the array of programs associated with the social safety net not as the tangible manifestation of *economic and social rights*, belonging to all citizens, but rather as *public goods* that may be augmented or restricted according to changing circumstances and ideological squabbles. This caused many analysts to overlook the historical climate that produced many social programs, a climate in which it was reasonable, if not common, to *legitimize* the social safety net in terms of human rights. As we shall see, the case of economic and social rights in the US demonstrates that progress in human rights is neither linear nor permanent.

Let us examine the historical circumstances that occasioned a flickering of economic and social rights in the US. With the success of the New Deal in alleviating the Great Depression and the descent of the US into the Second World War, the administration of President Franklin Delano Roosevelt began planning for US leadership on a global scale in the event of an Allied victory over the Axis Powers (Borgwardt 2005). On the global front, the planning involved making the UN a custodian of human rights, a forum for diplomacy, and a mechanism for peacekeeping. On the domestic front, the planning involved codifying the programs of the New Deal as economic and social rights (Levine 1988). The Roosevelt administration failed to secure Congressional support for the "Economic Bill of Rights"/"Second Bill of Rights" proposed in the 1941 State of the Union Address and the 1944 State of the Union Address. In the eyes of the administration, the US missed an opportunity to legitimize existing and future social programs as *enactments of human rights* (Borgwardt 2005).

As two renowned rights-oriented sociologists have noted, it was not unreasonable for the Roosevelt administration to imagine that there existed a political opportunity between popular sentiment (especially among the poor, the unemployed, and the working class) and government capabilities:

> In the early 1940s it was less clear that Americans were opposed to governmental protections. The recovery from the Great Depression was achieved by Keynesianism in the form of New Deal programs, and the socialist economy of the Soviet Union was not yet the object of scorn that it would later become. Franklin Delano Roosevelt . . . contended that it was unacceptable for any American to go hungry, to be without a job, and to be "necessitous." (Blau and Moncada 2009: 99)

Notwithstanding the best efforts of the Roosevelt administration, economic and social rights were formalized neither at the level of the Constitution nor at the level of Congressional legislation. Instead, the social programs of the New Deal in the 1930s, the Great Society in the 1960s, and other periods remained subject to continual debate and adjustment. Whereas the issue would never again receive serious attention in the US, the European Social Charter – a treaty passed in 1961 and revised in 1966 under the auspices of the Council of Europe – would codify economic and social rights in a significant way. In essence, though designed for individuals and enacted, to a certain degree, in US public policy (e.g., food stamps, public housing, Fannie Mae/Freddie Mac, student loans, unemployment insurance, disability insurance, Social Security, Medicare/Medicaid, and the recently passed Patient Protection and Affordable Care Act), economic and social rights are widely perceived by the wealthy, the middle class, the working class, and the poor alike not as the realization of human rights per se, but rather as the provision of public goods. This distinction proves significant for the sociological analysis of human rights.

Hence the question arises: What is the essential difference between human rights and public goods? What is the significance of this distinction? Whereas human rights, including those expressed in the ICESCR, must be brought to fruition to the best of the ability of a given government, public goods may be expanded or contracted according to changes in the political climate and ideological mood. Doubtless, a spirit of individualism and self-reliance has always pervaded political life and civil society in the US. Nevertheless, there was widespread acceptance of the social programs associated with the New Deal and the Great Society until the late 1970s. Since then, many social programs have been scaled back, while others have been subjected to withering criticism. Indeed, the very concept of social entitlements, built into the general definition of human rights that forms the basis of the sociological perspective and serves as the backbone of this book, has been called into question.

In effect, the situation testifies not only to the precariousness of gains achieved merely though public policy, but also to the advantages of formalizing rights claims through constitutional amendments and sweeping parliamentary legislation. In theory, constitutional amendments would be useful in advancing claims for economic and social rights. Promoted by the IMF, the WB, and the WTO and implemented, to one degree or another, by governments across the world, neoliberalism has renewed calls not only for second-generation economic, social, and cultural rights, but also for third-generation collective rights to cultural and environmental goods (Esparza 2011).

While these calls have been faint in the US, they have been prominent in the European Union (especially in Greece, Spain, and other Southern countries facing serious debt crises and hence draconian budget cuts) and Latin America (with an array of popular movements interacting, in very complex and contradictory ways, with left-leaning governments). While American TV has shown images of tear gas clouds covering anti-austerity protesters, there has been little discussion of the social underpinnings and ramifications of budgetary crises. Increasingly, social movements and their allies (especially NGOs) are articulating their demands in terms of: (a) economic and social rights for individuals, (b) cultural and environmental rights for collectivities, and especially (c) rights bundles for individuals and collectivities alike. It is incumbent upon the rights-oriented epistemic community to accord serious attention to these innovations. Cultural and environmental rights for peoples, groups, and communities form the subject matter of chapter 5. Meanwhile, rights bundles (packets of organically connected protections and entitlements that cut across the conventional categories) form the subject matter of chapter 6. Owing to its very nature, the category of collective rights serves as a gateway to rights bundling, not least because the solution to the development puzzle would entail the enactment of economic and social rights for individuals, as well as cultural and environmental rights for groups.

Summary

In conclusion, this chapter has explored a long-standing yet highly contested category of human rights: economic and social rights that serve to protect individuals from catastrophe (whether from economic downturns, personal misfortune, or natural disasters), provide individuals with the essentials of life (including food, housing, and healthcare) while aiding them through different phases of the life cycle, and ensure individuals unimpeded access to personal development, self-improvement, and upward social mobility (through education, occupational training, job opportunities, and cultural enrichment). These rights were widely discussed in US policymaking circles in the 1940s (Borgwardt 2005). But they were never codified through constitutional amendments or sweeping legislation in the US. In contrast, these rights attained a much higher degree of formalization in the welfare states of Western Europe during the post-Second World War period, and under the umbrella of US hegemony. The double status of the US welfare state as a forerunner and laggard in social provisioning constitutes a significant puzzle for political sociologists (Skocpol 1995; Amenta 1998).

The widespread acceptance of these rights, both in the political establishment and across the population, has contributed to the durability of social programs in the European Union. But it has not prevented the stark realities of globalization from taking root there. Expressed in the European Social Charter, the ICESCR, and other major documents, these rights serve as useful reference points for members of the human rights community. As welfare states in the Global North, former socialist states (in former Yugoslavia, Eastern Europe, and the former Soviet Union), and former development states in the Global South have faced budget cuts, popular forces have generated an array of claims for economic and social rights. It remains to be seen if the regimes will have the willingness and the capacity to accommodate these demands.

Discussion Questions

- What are the primary functions of economic and social rights?
- Why are economic and social rights less widely accepted than civil and political rights?
- What is the significance of Amnesty International's campaign for economic, social, and cultural rights?

- Explain the limitations of second-generation cultural rights for *individuals*. Why does this point to the need for third-generation cultural rights for *collectivities*?
- In the US context, what accounts for the widespread resistance to defining social programs in terms of economic and social rights?
- How has the retreat of the state from social provisioning contributed to the resurgence of claims for economic and social rights?

5 Rights to Culture, the Environment, and Sustainable Development

Building on our reflections on the benefits and drawbacks of classifying human rights (presented in chapter 2), we have made considerable progress in our journey through the three-generations framework. Whereas chapter 3 examined the most widely accepted category of human rights (namely, first-generation civil and political rights), chapter 4 analyzed a less widely accepted but still very familiar category of human rights (namely, the second-generation economic and social rights). As we have seen, the first and second generations pertain exclusively to individuals. Yet individuals are also members of families and communities, citizens of nation-states, and bearers of such identity markers as race and ethnicity, class, gender, and sexual orientation. Accordingly, it is important to think through the connection between individual rights and collective rights. In a concrete way, the question of individual versus collective rights bears on what it means for a person to be a member of a group. Yet processes of individuation and collectivization vary dramatically across cultures.

Solidarity or the Ties that Bind

Taken together, first-generation rights ensuring liberty to individuals and second-generation rights ensuring equality to individuals represent the two major facets of the Enlightenment project of human emancipation. Captured succinctly and poignantly in the clarion call of the French Revolution – "Liberty, Equality, Fraternity!" – the processes of liberating the people from authoritarianism and rendering them more equal vis-à-vis one another have, from the outset, been thoroughly intertwined (Ishay 2008). Since the Enlightenment, social movements and their allies have sought civil and political rights not only as ends-in-themselves, but also as means of advancing economic and social rights. But, for reasons that will be examined in this chapter, considerably less attention has been paid to the meaning of the third term, fraternity (translated as "solidarity" in this book for the sake of gender inclusiveness). Thus, the concept of solidarity warrants theoretical formalization and empirical specification because it was present in Enlightenment thought from the outset and yet found its fullest expression only in mobilizations, both within and beyond the confines of the UN system, after the 1970s.

While some scholars might argue that solidarity rights can be seen as the most under-theorized aspect of Enlightenment thought, other scholars might contend that such collective rights fall considerably beyond the scope of anything that would have been thinkable in the eighteenth century. Both of these arguments are reasonable. In either case, it is clear not only that Enlightenment thinkers and their heirs were ill-equipped to handle *collective* rights (as distinguished from *individual* rights), but also that the specific content of rights claims to solidarity – notably, cultural goods, harmony with the environment, and sustainable development – bear the stamp of the late twentieth and early twenty-first centuries. In essence, rights claims to solidarity, defined as the ties that bind together societies, peoples, ethnic groups, and communities, are not only *history-laden*, they are also typically associated with *non-Western cultures*. More precisely, they were formulated and propagated in response to the demise of the project of Third World developmentalism and the resulting need, as globalization refashioned the world, to grapple with growing threats to culture and environment (Burke 2010). A major consequence of the spread and intensification of consumerism has been the homogenization of culture and the destruction of the natural environment (Appelbaum and Robinson 2005). For this reason, third-generation cultural and environmental rights for collectivities figure prominently in the globalization era.

Accordingly, this chapter explores the newest, most complex, most diverse, and most highly contested category of human rights, namely cultural and environmental rights, proclaimed under the banner of solidarity (Clausen 2011; Toussaint 2011). Solidarity rights serve the following purposes:

- to protect and nurture cultural traditions (e.g., ways of providing for material sustenance, rites and rituals, ways of organizing community and family life, interactions with nature);

- to protect and nurture the natural environment (e.g., waterways, farmland, forests, and natural resources);
- to provide for sustainable development (i.e., planned social change to improve material wellbeing through improvements in food production, infrastructure, public hygiene, and medicine, but without damage to the local culture or ecosystem) (Rahnema and Bawtree 1997; Peet and Hartwick 1999; Pieterse 2004).

One may rightly ask what these diverse rights claims have in common. Notwithstanding the apparent disparity of these rights claims, there are significant connections among them (Clausen 2011; Toussaint 2011). In a nutshell, solidarity rights express the rootedness of norms, customs, rituals, and cuisines in the natural environment. For many inhabitants of the Global North, this sense of rootedness has been obscured by consumerism. For many inhabitants of the Global South, this sense of rootedness remains prominent. These connections will become apparent as we consider the history and geography of third-generation rights.

Situating Collective Rights

At first glance, the category of third-generation collective rights might seem like a hodgepodge. As it turns out, this impression testifies less to under-theorization (although theorists have paid insufficient attention to the category) and more to the real-world complexity of these rights. In light of their diversity, intricacy, ambiguity, and novelty, the links among these rights are not immediately apparent. Upon further reflection, however, it becomes clear that there are close connections among the major types of third-generation rights claims: rights to cultural protections; rights to environmental preservation; and the right to sustainable development. By definition, solidarity rights belong not to individuals, but rather to communities, groups, and peoples. These rights involve access to indivisible goods (like cultural heritages, lifeways, ancestral lands and waterways, and the right to benefit from development).

Since the issue of culture in the age of globalization has figured prominently throughout this book, it makes sense to begin with cultural rights. Though often associated either with such "high level" creative endeavors as music, art, literature, theater, and cinema or with such "popular" creative pursuits as folk music, craft making, folktales, and folkdances, culture also has an *earthier* side. In fact, as the Latin root of the English word "culture" (*cultura*) suggests, there is a deep relationship between a collectivity's lifeways and its *cultivation* of the land. Interestingly enough, the ancient Romans spoke of the cultivation of the *spirit* (through the use of elaborate educational techniques) in much the same way as they spoke of the cultivation of the *land* (through the use of elaborate farming techniques). Clearly, this deep-seated connection between spirit and land is evidenced in the origins and evolution of cuisines and eating rituals.

In any event, the relations among cultural amenities, environmental goods, and sustainable development go considerably beyond hunting, gathering, fishing, and farming techniques, seasonal festivals, food rituals, and types of cuisine. In other words, an integral part of the cultural heritage of a society, people, ethnic group, or community consists in its modes of interacting with the natural environment. Moreover, threats to the natural environment, whether from water, soil, and air pollution, excessive extraction of natural resources, deforestation, the damming of rivers, the over-development of cities and suburbs, over-fishing in major waterways, rising sea levels, or climate change, inevitably encroach cultures (Rahnema and Bawtree 1997; Peet and Hartwick 1999; Pieterse 2004). Finally, launched in the 1940s and terminated in the 1970s, the project of Third World developmentalism – though designed with such noble intentions as alleviating poverty and providing a modicum of economic and social protections and entitlements to long-marginalized and newly independent nations – had serious *unintended consequences* in the form of cultural homogenization and environmental destruction (Rist 2009). For a number of reasons, these consequences have reached fever proportions in the age of globalization.

Culture, Environment, and Development

As we will discover, the accumulation of unintended consequences led to systematic attempts to reformulate the right to development with the preservation of culture and environment in mind. Owing to the awesome power of development projects to transform the landscape – both literally and figuratively – these attempts have always been and will always remain fraught with danger: the damming of rivers and flooding of valleys in order to supply water and electricity to over-grown cities; the clear-cutting of old-growth forests to facilitate the cultivation of cash crops; the proliferation of coal-fired power plants and factories billowing smoke into the sky and dumping effluvium into rivers and streams; mining the earth for minerals; and the widespread migration of human beings from the countryside to the city. These processes were regular features of a development project that sought to allow poor countries to achieve a higher level of consumption for their populations.

If the countries of the Global South are to implement a new form of development – defined as planned social change to improve the material wellbeing of a population – they will need to pay careful attention to cultural and environmental impacts. Thus, the puzzle involves carefully picking and choosing which aspects of development (e.g., technology-intensive yet green farming, public hygiene, medicine, and green housing) best meet the needs of a given nation-state, society, or community. In theory, the resolution of the puzzle would consist not only in providing the technical, material, and logistical resources necessary for alternative development, but also in creating the space for expanded and intensified popular participation in decision making. In short, the right to alternative development is linked very closely to the right to democracy (Rahnema and Bawtree 1997; Peet and Hartwick 1999; Pieterse 2004).

The Specificity of Third-Generation Rights

How did we get here? Owing to their Enlightenment lineage, expression in the major documents of the UN and the human rights canon (including the UDHR, the ICCPR, and the ICESCR), and association with *individuals*, first-generation civil and political rights and second-generation economic and social rights have enjoyed widespread acceptance among scholars and practitioners. In contrast, third-generation *collective* rights (to cultural traditions, harmony with the environment, and sustainable development) seem like a random assortment of peculiar rights. But the sense of "randomness" dissipates with further reflection.

This chapter elucidates ways of handling two interrelated human rights problems that have acquired prominence in the age of globalization:

- the endangerment of the lifeways not only of indigenous peoples (particularly in North and South America), but also of minority enclaves (across the world) (Toussaint 2011);
- the degradation of the environment (especially with the super-extraction of natural resources and the accumulation of dirty

factories and dumping sites in the Global South) (Clausen 2011).

Doubtless, these problems are not new to the world. The first problem dates to the conquest of the New World by Europeans in the late fifteenth century (a process that killed, whether by guns or germs, the majority of the indigenous populations). The second problem dates to the Industrial Revolution in the pan-European world in the late eighteenth and early nineteenth centuries, a process that has since spread to all corners of the globe. As we have seen, the issue of the origins and impacts of urbanization, industrialization, and consumerism caused great concern for the putative "founders" of sociology (Marx, Durkheim, and Weber), engendering different responses from each. Hence the question arises: Why have these problems attracted the attention of scholars and activists alike in the globalization era? A noted world-systems analyst, with particular expertise in the role of commodity chains in connecting producers in the Global South to consumers in the Global North, has captured the links among abject poverty, extreme inequality, cultural exclusion, and environmental degradation:

> These days we talk of globalization as a matter of fact, and often with approval. But approval cannot allay the anxiety associated with melting polar ice caps. We are becoming aware that there are limits to our way of life. Ecological limits are natural limits. However, there are also social limits. While over three-quarters of the world's population can access television images of the global consumer, not much more than a quarter can have access to sufficient cash or credit to participate in the consumer economy. We are at a critical threshold: Whether consumer-based development remains a minority activity or becomes a majority activity among the earth's inhabitants, either way is unacceptable for social (divided planet) or environmental (unsustainable planet) reasons, or both (McMichael 2012: 1).

Shared by innumerable experts in social science and environmental studies, McMichael's powerful thesis, namely that the paradigm of development-as-consumerism is rapidly approaching its cultural and environmental limits, merits further reflection. The thesis harbors profound implications not only for the sociology of human rights as a field of academic inquiry, but also for contests over human rights in the real world. Notwithstanding its hegemonic status and entrenchment in our daily lives, the regime of mass consumption is neither sustainable for its principal beneficiaries (i.e., the inhabitants of the Global North and elites in the Global South) in the long term nor generalizable across a world of 7 billion humans in the present day. To make matters worse, the intensive pursuit of development-as-consumerism by such IGOs as the IMF, the WB, and the WTO, most national governments, transnational corporations, and a vast army of current and aspiring consumers has produced the unintended consequence of augmenting the problems of cultural exclusion (through the standardization of culture) and environmental degradation (through the warming of the planet, the depletion of natural resources, and the pollution of water, air, and soil). In short, despite its undeniable appeal as a means of providing a comfortable and entertaining life, consumerism has the effect of threatening the assertion, implementation, and enforcement of cultural and environmental rights. Phrased differently, collective rights to cultural and environmental goods serve by definition to challenge consumerism as an individualistic enterprise.

Versions of Sustainable Development

Doubtless, a certain level of awareness of these problems is reflected in IMF, WB, and WTO programs in sustainable development, the social and environmental responsibility programs of transnational corporations, and the efforts of organizations promoting socially and environmentally responsible consumption (Appelbaum and Robinson 2005). For example, the Body Shop – a popular distributor of cosmetics and other lifestyle products in North America, Europe, the Middle East, and East Asia – has established programs for small producers in the Global South, emphasized natural ingredients, banned animal testing, and funded programs for community development. For its part, Starbucks – the internationally renowned coffee retailer – sells a certain amount of fair-trade and organic coffee. Finally, a number of corporations have created positions in social and environmental responsibility. These examples represent the tip of the iceberg. Clearly, the trend constitutes a sophisticated response to growing social and environmental consciousness, an auspicious situation for human rights advocates.

Such corporations are neither oblivious to nor callous about the negative cultural and environmental effects of consumerism, not only because of pressure from global justice activists in wealthy countries, but also because it is in the corporations' long-term interests to avoid either provoking negative responses from aggrieved cultures or destroying the environment beyond repair. Their efforts at cultural and environmental protection are useful. Nevertheless, their efforts take for granted a *paradigm* based on the pursuit of growth in gross domestic product as the primary objective of economic life (and by extension of life in general). Moreover, though formulated as a right by UN agencies and associated NGOs, the concept of "sustainable development" remains highly contested. The concept is claimed by competing power blocs. For the sake of consistency, we will use the term "sustainable development" to capture one of the major rights claims in the category of the third generation. But we will add the proviso that the concept has evolved considerably since it was introduced to the lexicon of development studies, UN agencies, and NGOs in the early 1970s. Thus, we will emphasize a model of sustainable development that affirms the right to popular participation (or democracy) as the key to avoiding the re-imposition of Western values on non-Western societies (Rahnema and Bawtree 1997; Peet and Hartwick 1999; Pieterse 2004).

At the preliminary juncture of the early 1970s, the term captured a *critique* of the prevailing development paradigm, which emphasized attempting, against all odds, to "catch up" to the standard of living then enjoyed in the US and Western Europe through a strategy of programmed industrialization. In other words, the term represented a repudiation of the culturally and environmentally destructive development that had taken place in the previous three decades. It is worth noting, however, that advocates of the new perspective did not reject development per se. Instead, they rejected (a) economic reductionism (i.e., the notion that the economy constitutes the most important facet of human life), (b) positivism (i.e., the idea that economic theory and development practice could be "value neutral"), and (c) Eurocentrism (i.e., the assumption that the West – and particularly the UK and the US – should serve as the model for industrialization elsewhere in the world) (Rahnema and Bawtree 1997; Peet and Hartwick 1999; Pieterse 2004). In essence, the unholy trinity of economism, positivism, and Eurocentrism was seen as the source of the extreme cultural insensitivity and environmental destructiveness of the prevailing paradigm of development. Thus, the concept of sustainable development represented an important breakthrough in the field of human rights.

Indeed, as we will see in chapter 6, the concept of sustainable development and its offshoots have pointed to the utility of entertaining rights bundles for the following intertwined objectives: longevity (i.e., leading a long, healthy life through access to the basic necessities, public hygiene, and healthcare); the full development of the person (i.e., cultivating one's talents, ideas, and identity without undue encumbrance from authorities); and peace (i.e., living without fear of interstate war, civil strife, crime, or the structural violence associated with racism, classism, sexism, homophobia, or xeno-phobia). In addition to being a keyword for third-generation rights, sustainable development is a gateway *beyond* the three-generations framework to the theoretical and practical gesture known as rights bundling. Accordingly, sustainable development appears in this book not only as an end-in-itself, but also as means of setting the stage for due consideration of rights bundles.

In the present day, the term "sustainable development" is often used synonymously with, or simply dropped in favor of, the terms "alternative development," the "subsistence approach," and "alter-natives to development" (Bennholdt-Thomsen and Mies 2000). It is worth noting that the emerging domain of critical development studies, attuned to the cultural, environmental, and geopolitical specificity of different nation-states and localities in the Global South, provides precise definitions for these approaches to development in the twenty-first century. While the putative right to development was mentioned in chapter 3 (in relation to the civil and political rights implied by Oxfam International's anti-poverty program) and chapter 4 (in relation to the economic and social rights implicit in Third World developmentalism), it will be revisited not only in this chapter (in relation to the collective rights implicit in calls for sustainable development), but also in chapter 6 (in relation to the rights bundles implied in contemporary attempts to re-launch development while taking seriously culture, gender relations, and the environment). Accordingly, it is important to bear in mind that the right to develop-ment (understood as unimpeded access to the material necessities of life achieved through the careful introduction of advances in food pro-duction, public hygiene, medicine, and housing), a theme that runs through the entire book, cuts across the three generations to such an extent that it might be properly considered a rights bundle unto itself. However, we will, for the sake of the current chapter, treat sustainable development as a third-generation right belonging to collectivities (whether nation-states, large societies, indigenous peoples, or small communities). It should be clear, however, that individuals benefit from the right to development in the same way that they benefit from economic and social rights. Moreover, economic and social rights, in turn, figure prominently among the claims advanced by advocates of alternative development.

Let us return to the question of what unifies the category of third-generation rights. Extrapolating McMichael's (2012) argument, we can see the connecting thread that runs through the category of third-generation collective rights to cultural norms and practices, ecological harmony, and sustainable development (or its alternatives, including a more subsistence-oriented approach): the pressing need to rethink the regime of mass consumption and its supports, widespread industrialization, factory farming, and intensive fishing (under the direction of agribusiness conglomerates) (Bennholdt-Thomsen and Mies 2000). Why is it necessary to re-examine the meshwork of global consumerism? In essence, the regime of mass consumption, premised on the exaltation of the individual as consumer, encroaches on such *indivisible goods* as culture and the environment. Though an unintended consequence of the complex and differentiated spread of a way of life based on wage-labor and possessive individualism, two traits that were incubated in the West and exported elsewhere, it is nonetheless significant in its ramifications for the future of the planet. Accordingly, though advanced primarily by aggrieved parties in the Global South, the right to development – and the cultural and environmental protections and entitlements that go along with it – harbors profound implications for the entire world. To phrase it succinctly, everyone should be concerned about the development puzzle. The manner in which the development puzzle finds a solution (or not) promises to have a decisive impact on the cultural and environmental diversity across the world.

Origins of Third-Generation Rights

From the angle of political economy/sociology of development – a major contributor to the sociological perspective on human rights – we have seen how globalization has created the widespread perception of the need for third-generation rights. The reason is that such rights protect the interests not only of vulnerable collectivities, but also of the earth itself. From another angle, like the neighboring field of cultural anthropology, the sociology of culture sheds light on the *cultural impacts* of globalization. Meanwhile, like the neighboring field of environmental studies, environmental sociology elucidates the *environmental impacts* of globalization. The latter point, namely the environmental consequences of globalization, calls for a significant side-note. Some scholars and practitioners from the Global South have asserted that it is not just humanity as a whole and the vast array of cultures that have sprung from the planet that are the bearers of environmental rights. Indeed, these scholars and practitioners have asserted that the earth itself – as an entity, system, or "being" that includes humans and all other living things – should be seen as the bearer of environmental rights (Shiva 1988, 1997, 2005).

Needless to say, if the (potential) rights claims of the earth itself were widely accepted and enforced, any project of development, whether sustainable or otherwise, would be called into question, since every conceivable form of development entails a degree of harm to the environment (whether through the extraction of natural resources, the construction of infrastructure and urban spaces, or pollution from the production, consumption, and disposal of consumer goods). Accordingly, this book sets aside the question of the rights of the earth itself, a right that has been affirmed in recent constitutions (e.g., that of Bolivia). Though a worthy topic, the question of the earth's rights necessitates sustained reflection on the possibility of transcending development and consumerism altogether in favor of a subsistence-oriented lifestyle on a global scale, a subject that challenges the domains of the sociology of human rights, development sociology, environmental studies, social theory, and social/political philosophy. Such theoretical and philosophical inquiries might connect older research on "conviviality" to newer research on subsistence perspectives (Bennholdt-Thomsen and Mies 2000).

It remains for us to consider the historical origins of the rights claims associated with the third generation. Fittingly, the third generation of human rights came to the fore only with the decline of Keynesianism, state socialism, and Third World developmentalism in the 1970s. Notwithstanding profound differences in state capacity, bureaucratic efficiency, respect for civil and political rights, culture, and geography, Keynesianism (in the First World), state socialism (in the Second World), and developmentalism (in the Third World) shared an emphasis on industrialization as the pathway to mass consumption or at least to material wellbeing for the majority of the population (Bennholdt-Thomsen and Mies 2000). In many ways, these state-forms, especially that of the Keynesian welfare state, proved successful in improving the standard of living. This was achieved not only through the facilitation of mass consumption, but also through the enactment of a set of economic and social rights to protect individuals from market failures and catastrophes, while assisting them through different phases of the life cycle. But these state-forms ran their course, permanently altering global economic conditions, cultures, and ecosystems in the process. Amidst the beginning of what would come to be known as globalization, understood as increasing economic, political, social, and cultural integration, the three state-forms fell into disrepair.

It was in the context of the disintegration of Keynesianism, state socialism, and Third World developmentalism that a space was created for third-generation collective rights to indivisible cultural and environmental goods. As it happened, UN delegations from the Global South were particularly instrumental in having these rights claims placed on the docket (Burke 2010). In effect, they wondered aloud: In light of the failure of mainstream developmentalism – a project supported not only by US and WB officials, but also by a large number of elites in the Global South (many of whom had been trained in development economics in the US and the UK) – to overcome poverty without threatening cultures and the environment, what can be done? In pursuit of this question, the UN eventually found itself at odds with the WB and other lending institutions on the question of development. The UN–WB rift has grown considerably in the last few decades, with the UN placing great emphasis on *alternative visions* of development that prove more consistent with the undertakings of Oxfam International and other NGOs charged with the task of addressing the problems of poverty, economic inequality, cultural exclusion, and severe environmental degradation in the age of globalization.

Let us return to the historical context that occasioned the emergence of third-generation collective rights as a major subject for debate among academics, UN officials, NGO staff, and SMO activists. Rights claims to culture, environment, and sustainable development found their first major expression in the 1972 Stockholm Declaration of the United Nations Conference on the Human Environment, and were subsequently elaborated in the 1992 Rio Declaration on Environment and Development and the 2007 Declaration on the Rights of Indigenous Peoples. In recent years, these rights claims have been advanced by members of minority cultures, indigenous peoples, peasants, and others whose lifeways and landscapes have been encroached by global consumerism. In part, these rights claims can be understood as responses not only to the excess of postwar developmentalism, but also to the more recent neoliberal dismantling of the second-generation economic and social rights that had been achieved, to one degree or another, in welfare, socialist, and development states. In part, the new rights claims stem from progress in identity-based movements. As we will discover in chapter 6, this complex and contradictory convergence has precipitated rights bundles that articulate the cultural and environmental rights of *collectivities* alongside the economic and social rights of *individuals*.

In order to understand these rights, we need to acknowledge that individual rights to liberty and equality, though remarkably important for the quality of life of people across the world, prove insufficient to protect such *indivisible amenities* as culture and environment. After all, how can a system fairly and reasonably divide and allocate access to the fruits of cultural life or to the benefits of a clean, well-preserved environment? On the other hand, how can a system ensure the proper management of culture and the environment? Long considered part of the "commons," these collective goods belong to all members of the relevant people, group, or community. However, as two renowned rights-oriented sociologists have suggested, the management of collective goods entails dealing with a complex problem:

> Like public goods, collective goods exhibit non-excludability – none can easily be barred from benefitting – and like private goods, collective goods exhibit rivalrousness – one person's consumption can reduce the chances of others consuming it. Typically, collective goods are natural resources, such as lakes, streams, forests, fishing grounds, saltwater marshes, and the proverbial village commons, where sheep, cows, and goats graze. They are delicate ecosystems where overuse and poor management can easily tip the balance, with the loss of collective good. (Blau and Moncada 2009: 123–4)

As we have seen, Blau and Moncada place particular emphasis on the environmental aspect of collective rights, not least because the environment, as humanity's habitat, constitutes an absolute limit to capitalist development. Though the question of the possibility of a "green capitalism" moves beyond current research in the sociology of human rights, it is clear that capitalism, characterized by the imperative of ceaseless accumulation, is an *infinite* system, always in search of new sources of raw materials and natural resources, fresh supplies of labor, untapped markets, and new dumping sites, residing on a *finite* planet. For this reason, the intensive and extensive expansion of the regime of mass consumption threatens culture and the environment alike (Appelbaum and Robinson 2005; McMichael 2012).

Looking closely at the analysis offered by Blau and Moncada, it is easy to see how cultures are *embedded* in environments. As a consequence, the *cultivation* of healthy persons and communities entails the preservation of the natural environment. In effect, only collective rights to solidarity, defined as the sisterhood/brotherhood/unity that stems from the acknowledgement of common interests and responsibilities, can provide for the proper use, management, and preservation of *indivisible* cultural and environmental goods. In addition, we must recognize that a common thread runs through the rights to culture, the environment, and sustainable development: the need to critically re-evaluate the regime of mass consumption, along with the assumptions, practices, and institutions that make this regime possible (Bennholdt-Thomsen and Mies 2000). It goes without saying that the critical rethinking of mass consumption is easier said than done, especially in the Global North, but also, for the more privileged sectors of the Global South. Needless to say, this is a pressing issue for everyone in the globalization era, not least because the ethos of consumerism, with its glittering appeal, is beamed by fiber optic cables and satellites to the remotest parts of the earth.

Further Questions about Collective Rights

We have seen that, in forcing us to think through such dilemmas as universalism versus relativism, globalism versus localism, collective rights versus individual rights, and the relations among the economy, the polity, society, culture, and environment, the ambiguity of third-generation collective rights is both its greatest strength and its most significant weakness. Arguably, the most significant problem associated with attempts to proclaim third-generation rights is that of how to grant cultural and environmental entitlements to overlapping, and in some cases, *competing* collectivities. But a proper analysis of this problem would entail a separate treatise on global governance, the connections between international and national law, and the similarities and differences among the national political-legal jurisdictions that cover the globe. In addition, it would entail a rigorous analysis of the origins, evolution and applications of the normative principle of *subsidiarity*, which holds not only that, whenever possible, major decisions (e.g., about development) should be made by those who are most affected, but also that power should gravitate to the local level (Iber 2010). Though worthwhile, such tasks would be better left to those political scientists and legal scholars who participate in the rights-oriented epistemic community. It remains possible, however, to use the sociological perspective to re-examine third-generation rights in relation to other types of rights, at the highest level of analysis. This will shed light on commonalities and differences between collective and individual claims making.

For the sake of analytic and pedagogical clarity, this book has devoted considerable attention to the complex relations among the three generations of human rights: first-generation civil and political rights ensuring liberty to *individuals*; second-generation economic and social rights ensuring equality to *individuals*; and third-generation cultural and environmental rights ensuring solidarity to *collectivities*. As we have seen, there are deep-seated connections between the concepts of liberty and equality, not only in Enlightenment thought and social movement praxis since the nineteenth century, but also in the concept of the individual as a *legal subject* and a *bearer of rights* that runs through the UDHR, the ICCPR, and the ICESCR. These connections have created thick entanglements, in the eyes of theorists and practitioners alike, between first- and second-generation rights. Yet it is not the case that the first and second generations do not deal with groups or collectivities at all. For the most part, they deal with *groups of individuals* (with varying degrees of identification with or membership in a group).

However, the distinction is not as clear as it might seem at first glance. Indeed, we have touched on the following groups of human beings: the rights of African Americans and other racial minorities to equal protection under the law and equal participation in civic life and politics; the rights of workers to union representation, decent wages, benefits (including healthcare), safe working conditions, unemployment insurance, and pensions; the rights of women to reproductive freedom and protection from sexual harassment and discrimination, pre- and postnatal care, paid maternity leave, and childcare; the rights of the LGBT community to protection from discrimination and bullying (especially at school and in the workplace) and marriage equality; the rights of migrants to fair wages, safe working conditions, protection from abuse and exploitation, and a pathway to citizenship (Golash-Boza 2012); and, finally, the rights of indigenous peoples and members of minority cultures to speak their languages, practice their religions, observe their customs, preserve their lifeways, inhabit their ancestral lands, and live in harmony with the natural environment. In covering the basic sociological categories of race, class, gender, sexual orientation, and national origin, these rights claims have also spanned, and in many cases, *exceeded* the three generations of human rights. In the process, they have pointed to the *double-status* of human beings as individuals and as members of collectivities (of one sort or another). Taking both the inextricability of the three generations and the double-status of human beings into consideration, we will examine the theoretical and practical exercise of rights bundling in chapter 6.

Summary

In sum, this chapter has explored the most recently elaborated, ambiguous, and highly contested category of human rights: the collective rights that advance the following objectives:

- the preservation of cultural traditions (including ways of hunting, fishing, gathering, farming, and eating, rituals and folkways, modes of conducting daily life, and traditional ways of accumulating and disseminating knowledge);
- the preservation of the natural environment (including bodies of water, farmland, forests, and natural resources);
- the realization of sustainable development (or a suitable alternative to it) through careful technical improvements in food production, infrastructure, housing, public hygiene, and medicine, designed to avoid harm to the local culture or ecosystem.

In the process of exploring the third generation of human rights, we have discovered that there are profound connections among the right to culture, the right to live in harmony with nature, and the right to sustainable development. But these connections entail systematic reflection on the role of consumerism in the contemporary world. Finally, in examining the connections among culture, environment, and sustainable development, we have testified not only to the interconnectedness of the three generations, but also to the double-status of human beings as individuals and citizens of nation-states and members of societies, peoples, groups, or communities. As a consequence, we have set the stage for the culmination of the book, namely the consideration of rights bundles – packages of rights that cut across the three generations while acknowledging the double-status of human beings.

Discussion Questions

- What is distinctive about third-generation rights?
- Why are collective rights less widely accepted than individual rights?

- What are the primary purposes of cultural rights, environmental rights, and the right to sustainable development?
- Under what world-historical conditions did the push for collective rights to culture, environment, and sustainable development emerge?
- How does the category of third-generation rights set the stage for rights bundling?

6   Rights Bundles

Building on the presentation of first-generation civil and political rights in chapter 3, second-generation economic and social rights in chapter 4, and third-generation collective rights (to indivisible cultural and environmental amenities) in chapter 5, this chapter examines the concept of rights bundling, understood as the binding together of rights that fall into more than one generation, as a *corrective* to the deficiencies of the three-generations framework. In effect, the concept of rights bundling has been transplanted from the domain of property law, in which it designates the parcel of rights attached to a piece of real estate (Klein and Robinson 2011). Nobel Laureate economist Amartya Sen's (1999) emphasis on the inextricability of civil and political rights and development projects constitutes a form of rights bundling. Although the *concept* of rights bundling has not been formalized or popularized nearly to the same extent as the three-generations framework, the *practice* of rights bundling – tying together rights claims (i.e., the demands that aggrieved parties make on governments) that fall into different generations – has long been common among UN agencies, NGOs, SMOs, and community groups. Thus, it remains for sociologists of human rights and other scholars to formalize or codify the achievements of these entities, especially such prominent NGOs as Oxfam International and Amnesty International, by tracing the theoretical underpinnings and implications of practical innovations.

Oxfam International, Amnesty International, and Rights Bundling

In effect, we have seen how rights bundling works in the examples of Oxfam International's anti-poverty program and Amnesty International's campaign for economic, social, and cultural rights.

Far from shying away from controversy in the human rights community and the adjoining policymaking circles, Oxfam International and Amnesty International have brazenly embraced "mission creep," the expansion of their mandates beyond the visions of their founders. Yet these expansions have not taken Oxfam International and Amnesty International beyond their charters. The former's anti-poverty program combines the need for access to resources with the need to recognize diverse identities in a participatory framework. Meanwhile, the latter's campaign for economic, social, and cultural rights points to the importance of conceptualizing the right to food and water, the right to adequate housing, the right to the highest achievable level of physical and mental health, the right to an education, rights at work, and, finally, the cultural rights of indigenous peoples and minorities as parts of a whole.

We have seen how two celebrated NGOs have provided useful examples of rights bundling for consideration by social scientists. Rights bundling figures prominently in the UN–NGO–SMO nexus. As we have seen, the nexus is a transnational force field that has *reinterpreted* old rights and *invented* new rights in response to a number of globalization-related processes: changes in the interstate system since the end of the Cold War and the rise of Islamism; the emergence of the post-Fordist work regime; and the implementation of neoliberal policies by a vast array of states. It is increasingly common for aggrieved parties and their allies to move *deliberately* beyond the three-generations framework in formulating their rights claims. Accordingly, it is crucial for rights-oriented sociologists to examine rights bundling in the context of the growing strain on the existing human rights canon. Notwithstanding their profundity and aspirational status, the UDHR, the ICCPR, and ICESCR prove insufficient to the task of covering the full range of human rights abuses and remedies in the early twenty-first century. The political and practical reasons for the strain on the human rights canon merit consideration in future research.

For a number of years, an *implicit* notion of rights bundling has animated coalitions advancing the rights of racial and ethnic minorities, workers, peasants, women, the LGBT community, immigrants, indigenous peoples, cultural minorities, and environmentalists, especially in their attempts to address social problems (including interstate and civil war, poverty, economic inequality, involuntary migration, cultural exclusion and erosion, and environmental degradation) that involve numerous constituencies. Clearly, such problems weigh heaviest on the most disadvantaged and vulnerable populations. For example, the poor (who, by definition benefit the *least* from consumerism), both on a global scale and within specific nation-states, tend to be disproportionately affected by the environmental degradation associated with mass consumption.

It remains useful for different constituencies to make reference to the human rights canon, including the ICCPR, the ICESCR, and more recent declarations on collective rights. At the same time, these constituencies have pointed to the limitations of the three-generations framework in accounting for the problems confronting them in their daily lives. For example, Falcon (2008) analyses the complexities involved with activists and NGOs connecting their notions of racial justice and reproductive rights to a demand that the US comply with the International Convention to Eliminate All Forms of Racial Discrimination. In referring to the human rights canon, constituencies draw from an array of political and cultural traditions, whether to counter residual Eurocentrism or simply to accommodate changing conditions in the twenty-first century, in proposing and defending rights bundles. By design, the resulting rights bundles cater to multiple constituencies, whether within or between societies. This phenomenon seems likely to continue unabated.

Alternative Development

For example, the oft proposed "right to alternative development," a bundle that would rectify poverty and its attendant problems (including disempowerment and degradation of the poor) while favoring progressive gender relations, protecting cultural heritage, and preserving the environment in the Global South, appeals to NGOs, SMOs, and community groups interested in women's rights, cultural rights, and environmental rights (Rahnema and Bawtree 1997; Peet and Hartwick 1999; Pieterse 2004). A recent contribution from advocates of the paradigm of "Women, Culture, and Development" (WCD) provides a case in point:

> A WCD perspective takes into account how practices and discourses of gender, culture, and the South come together in the everyday lives of women in the Third World by integrating production with reproduction and explicitly acknowledging women's agency. Drawing on three modes of enquiry – feminist studies, cultural studies, and Third World and critical development studies – WCD proposes a paradigmatic shift in the relation between women and projects of development at theoretical, political, and policy levels. (Bhavnani et al. 2005: 324)

While the authors do not use the term, they are, in effect, proposing WCD as a rights bundle that would address the problem of poverty, and hence improve material wellbeing, while respecting gender relations, culture, and the environment to the fullest extent possible. In effect, in adopting a holistic perspective, advocates of WCD maintain that there is no good reason to separate the objective of poverty alleviation from the objectives of gender equality (as conceptualized in different cultural frameworks), cultural sensitivity and inclusion, and environmental preservation. Thus, for Bhavnani et al., the right to alternative development (presupposing a range of second-generation economic and social rights for individuals) must be linked to women's rights (usually characterized as first-generation rights for individuals), cultural rights (usually characterized as third-generation rights for collectivities), and environmental rights (usually characterized as third-generation rights for collectivities).

Explicit in the WCD proposal is an emphasis on popular participation in decision-making processes (usually defined in terms of the first-generation rights to vote and undertake political action). In sum, the WCD proposal constitutes a rights bundle insofar as it presupposes: (a) that poverty (defined as the inability to meet basic needs in a manner that is conducive to good physical and mental health) is a human rights abuse that cuts across the three generations, and (b) that human rights remedies to the problem of poverty must address all three generations simultaneously. Moreover, the WCD proposal endeavors to reconcile individual rights with collective rights, universalism with cultural pluralism, and globalism with localism – an ambitious but realizable set of objectives.

Though different in the details, the WCD proposal is in many ways commensurate with the rights-based approach to development proposed by Oxfam International. The difference is that the WCD proposal is more explicitly connected to the concerns of community-based organizations, while the Oxfam International approach is embedded in the orbit of large NGOs undertaking work in the Global South and appealing, to one degree or another, to policymakers in nation-states. In both the WCD and the Oxfam International cases, the sociological analysis of human rights overlaps with the concerns of critical development studies – a field of academic inquiry nurtured by UN-sponsored conferences on the problems associated with mainstream developmentalism (Rahnema and Bawtree 1997; Peet and Hartwick 1999; Pieterse 2004). The deepening convergence among such domains of academic research as the sociology of human rights, critical development studies, critical globalization studies, and peace studies holds great promise for the advocacy of rights-oriented solutions to the world's problems, especially through considerations of the future of global governance (e.g., the possible reform or abolition of the IMF, the WB, and the WTO, and the potential transformation of the UN) (Wilkinson 2005). This convergence is addressed in the conclusion to this book.

For the moment, it suffices to recall that studies of political economy and development have contributed greatly to the sociological perspective on human rights by illuminating the world-economic conditions under which nation-states, societies, groups, and communities: (a) define poverty, cultural exclusion, and environmental destruction as grievances, (b) translate these grievances into rights claims to be made on governments and other authorities, and (c) appeal to UN agencies and NGOs for support. It is this process that creates the *need for* and the *justification of* rights bundling as a research project, a normative impulse, and a practical exercise. Yet is equally clear that political economy/development sociology cannot explain the full range of rights conditions (especially the expressly *political* and *cultural* circumstances that often give rise to grievances), let alone account for rights claims (for which social movement research proves useful) and rights effects (for which political sociology proves useful). In the end, the "pay-off" from human rights advocacy and mobilization comes in the form of rights effects – changes to state policy that improve the lives of ordinary people. Despite encroachments on sovereignty associated with globalization, nation-states remain the most significant guarantors and abusers of human rights.

Angles on Human Rights

Taken together, political economy/development sociology, social movement research, and political sociology can shed considerable light on rights conditions (or the circumstances that give rise to grievances), rights claims (or the expression of grievances in reference to the human rights canon), and rights effects (or the policy outcomes of rights debates and struggles that change power relations in a tangible fashion). But it is also true that other branches of sociology (e.g., cultural sociology and environmental sociology) could aid us immensely in the task of explicating the cycle through which every proposed right must pass. For example, it is clear that cultural sociology is well equipped to illuminate how the suppression of cultural diversity, whether intentional, as in the case of certain authoritarian regimes, or unintentional, as in the case of consumerist societies, precipitates grievances that strain the human rights canon and challenge the human rights community.

Similarly, environmental sociology has the capacity to elucidate how environmental destruction, whether essentially deliberate, as in the case of the callous extraction of natural resources (through mining, drilling, and deforestation), or accidental, as in the case of consumption by unwitting persons, foments grievances that point beyond existing human rights documents. Taken together, cultural sociology and environmental sociology offer precious insights into both the *rights conditions for* and the *rights claims of* nation-states, peoples, groups, and communities in the Global South. This proves significant for our understanding not only of third-generation collective rights (especially in the areas of culture, environment, and alternative development), but also of rights bundles, not least because third-generation rights, given their implications for collectivities and individuals alike and their tendency to be directed at poverty in the Global South and the effects of consumerism across the world, point almost inevitably in the direction of rights bundling.

In sum, the important thing for rights-oriented sociologists and their fellow travelers is to draw on the available theoretical, methodological, and substantive resources in capturing the human rights cycle, from the formation and articulation of grievances to the mobilization of coalitions and the implementation of state policies. This is the rationale for appealing for the creation of new scholarly resources to address the manifold problems associated with debates and struggles over human rights in the contemporary world.

Historical Origins of Rights Bundling

Let us return to a question that was implied, but not fully explored, in the passages above. Why has the practice of rights bundling become increasingly common in the contemporary period? Phrased differently, what is distinctive about the present day? In order to answer this question, we need to trace a sequence of historical processes, from a period defined by Keynesianism/Third World developmentalism and Fordism (1945–early 1970s) to a period defined by neoliberalism and post-Fordism (early 1970s–present) (Frezzo 2009). Using the lens of political economy/development sociology, we can find both continuities and discontinuities in the realm of human rights across the two phases of US hegemony – the period during which the US has exercised a leadership function in the world. As innumerable challenges to US leadership present themselves, it proves useful to look back on the rise, evolution, decline, and transformation of the post-1945 system – the backdrop of the putative human rights revolution.

As part of the post-Second World War reconstruction, the UN became an institutional custodian of human rights. In essence, the UN legitimized and facilitated the processes of decolonization (understood as disengaging from colonial domination, primarily politically, but to a lesser extent economically and culturally), national self-determination (conceptualized as the realization of a fundamental collective right), and development (defined as planned social change in order the improve the material wellbeing) (Arrighi 2010). Within the confines of the Cold War order, these processes defined the "Third World," and altered power dynamics on a global scale (Burke 2010).

Although newly independent countries did not emerge on an equal footing with wealthier, more powerful countries, they did benefit, to a certain degree, from their independent status. Moreover, in giving concrete meaning to the rights to national self-determination and development, the newly independent countries influenced not only the structure and undertakings of the UN system, but also the content of the ICCPR, the ICESCR, the Stockholm Declaration, and other documents in the human rights canon (Burke 2010). In other words, notwithstanding the Western provenance of much human rights *thinking* and the profound influence of the US and other great powers on human rights *institutions*, the UN (or more precisely, the General Assembly, along with certain agencies) served as a cauldron for "Third Worldism," a perspective that criticized both the US and the Soviet Union, and advocated greater cooperation among poor countries.

Meanwhile, in part because of pressure from the working-class movement and its allies (especially trade unions and labor, social democratic, and socialist parties) and in part because of complex political dynamics underlying a policymaking consensus, the welfare states of the First World implemented a range of economic and social entitlements, including collective bargaining, unemployment insurance, disability insurance, social security, and, in some cases, national healthcare (Esping-Andersen 1990). These entitlements were designed not only to mitigate the effects of economic fluctuations, misfortune, and natural disasters, but also to assist individuals through the stages of life (with particular emphasis on childhood and old age). In Western Europe, trade unions and political parties (especially, but not exclusively, those falling onto the left side of the political spectrum) succeeded in defining these entitlements not only as public goods or beneficent policy measures, but also as *economic and social rights*. This was reflected in the 1961 European Charter of Social Rights.

In the US, many of the same policies became entrenched, but neither lawmakers nor ordinary citizens acquired the habit of characterizing economic and social entitlements as *human rights* per se. Far from being a mere semantic issue, the widespread tendency to conceptualize these entitlements, including those that were achieved with a remarkable spate of legislation during the New Deal in the 1930s, merely as public goods, subject to the vicissitudes of policy-making and political alliances, reflected a deep-seated reluctance on the part of Americans to embrace economic and social rights *in principle*. Perhaps it would have been otherwise if President Roosevelt had succeeded in getting an Economic Bill of Rights through Congress (Borgwardt 2005). To this day, economic and social rights remain highly contested in the US context. In contrast, the US has witnessed significant achievements in terms of civil rights for racial minorities, women's rights, and LGBT rights. As in other parts of the Global North, the realization of these rights (in the form of major pieces of legislation) produced significant rights effects by empowering previously subjugated segments of the population, and thereby facilitating new rights claims – an ongoing process that has produced dramatic gains for the LGBT community in recent years.

In the last 30 years, with the widespread implementation of such neoliberal policies as fiscal austerity (cuts to social programs), deregulation (removal of labor, safety, and environmental restrictions), privatization (sale of state-owned enterprises), financial liberalization (lifting of controls on the flow of capital), and free trade (elimination of subsidies on exports and tariffs on imports) by nation-states in both the Global South (formerly known as the Third World) and the Global North (formerly known as the First World), previously achieved economic and social rights have come under fire (Bandelj and Sowers 2010). Criticism of these rights has taken both ideological and practical form, often to significant effect. Thus, with growing inequality and poverty in many parts of the world, coalitions of NGOs and SMOs have resorted to more innovative ways of articulating their demands for economic and social entitlements. Furthermore, amidst more extreme threats to minority cultures and sensitive ecosystems, attributable in part to the spread of consumerism to different parts of the globe, these coalitions have begun to take a greater interest in cultural rights and environmental rights as corollaries to other types of rights. Consequently, we have witnessed the rise of rights bundling in the age of globalization.

Why Do We Need Rights Bundles?

Having explored the social conditions that have created the need for rights bundling, we may trace the theoretical implications of this need. In order to apprehend the role of rights bundles, we must review the strengths and limitations of the three-generations framework. Designed as a comprehensive introduction to the sociological perspective on human rights, this book advances two arguments about the prevailing conventions in the field of human rights. On the one hand, the book emphasizes the importance of mastering the three generations of human rights. Though no longer subject to rigid adherence among scholars, policymakers, and activists, the three-generations framework remains useful for analytic, pedagogical, advocacy, and political purposes. More precisely, the framework is useful for theorizing the purposes of different types of rights: to protect *individuals* from abuses perpetrated by the state, while allowing them to participate fully in social life and politics (first-generation civil and political rights); to protect *individuals* from economic downturns and natural disasters, while guaranteeing them a minimum standard of living and the realization of basic needs throughout the life course (second-generation economic and social rights); and, finally, to guarantee *collectivities*, whether large societies, identity groups cutting across social formations, or small communities, access to cultural and environmental amenities (third-generation collective rights).

On the other hand, the book points to the limitations of the three-generations framework. As many scholars, policymakers, and activists have noted, the three-generations framework is often interpreted as implying not only the historical, logical, and moral priority of first-generation civil and political rights, but also a linear passage from one generation to another. As we have seen, the assumption of the absolute priority of first-generation civil and political rights and the rigid adherence to the three-generations framework derive from residual Eurocentrism in the field. To say that the Enlightenment revolutions in the pan-European world provided a vocabulary and grammar for future rights claims is not to say that the European model works for all nation-states, societies, peoples, and communities. To say that first-generation civil and political rights, especially the rights to association, assembly, free speech, and petition, have been conducive to the claims-making by social movements is not to say that progress is inconceivable in the absence of such rights. In principle, nation-states can achieve rights in any order; and the outcomes depend on a variety of internal and external factors.

First Argument

Let us consider the first argument in greater detail. Why does the sociological perspective stress the need to work through the three generations? Proclaimed under the banner of *liberty* and built into the canonical 1966 ICCPR, first-generation civil and political rights, including the right to life, the right to due process of law, the right to vote, the freedom of religion, and the rights to association, assembly, free speech, and petition, are designed to serve three purposes: to protect humans from abuses perpetrated not only by one another, but also by nation-states; to permit humans to participate freely in social life and politics; and to allow humans to discover and develop their talents, identities, beliefs, and values without encumbrance from authorities. Proclaimed under the banner of *equality* and built into the canonical 1966 ICESCR, second-generation economic and social rights, including the right to an adequate standard of living, the right to a livelihood, the right to belong to a trade union, the right to social security, the right to maternity leave, the right to benefit from scientific research and technological advancement, and the right to participate in cultural life, are designed not only to protect humans from economic fluctuations, bad luck, and natural disasters, but also to fulfill their basic needs throughout the life course (with special emphasis on childhood and old age). Proclaimed under the banner of *solidarity* and appearing in piecemeal form in a number of texts (e.g., the oft-cited 1972 Stockholm Declaration, the 1992 Rio Declaration, and the 2007 Declaration on the Rights of Indigenous Peoples), the broad spectrum of third-generation collective rights, including the right to adequate conditions of life, the right to gain access to natural resources, the right to a clean environment, and the rights of indigenous peoples to their ancestral lands and cultural practices, are designed to represent the interests, protect the landscapes, and preserve the traditions of groups.

In sum, the three-generations framework facilitates systematic thought and action on human rights for scholars, policymakers, UN agencies, NGOs, SMOs, and the general public. In the process, the framework forms the basis for a series of debates: individual rights versus collective rights; universalism versus cultural pluralism; and globalism versus localism. Yet the framework does *not* provide a basis for resolving these debates. Accordingly, it is necessary for members of the human rights community to produce innovations that move beyond the three generations. In the end, members of the epistemic community will determine the specific results of these debates. It is the author's hope that this book will point to a sensible pathway beyond the three generations and into the realm of rights bundling. It is the author's argument that, in forcing claimants not only to *think beyond* the existing boundaries (in order to include cultural and environmental goods), but also to *think through* the relations between collectivities and individuals, third-generation rights hold the key to the eventual transition to rights bundling. As we shall see shortly, this is clear in the case of proposals for alternative development as a remedy for poverty, understood as a nodal point for a variety of human rights abuses (including cultural exclusion and environmental destruction) (Rahnema and Bawtree 1997; Peet and Hartwick 1999; Pieterse 2004).

Second Argument

Let us consider the second argument in greater detail. Notwithstanding its great value as a scholarly, pedagogical, advocacy, and policymaking tool, the three-generations framework has trouble accounting for human rights abuses and remedies that cut across the conventional categories. In the real world, it can be difficult to assess whether a given violation – and by extension the appropriate solution – falls into a specific category. For example, as we have seen above, both the renowned NGO Oxfam International and the scholars who advocate the WCD proposal conceptualize poverty not only as a social problem, but also as a human rights violation. What does it mean to define poverty as a violation of human rights? The essential argument, implicit in both the Oxfam International program and the WCD proposal, runs as follows. Since poverty is a structural problem rooted in the long-term development, evolution, fluctuations, and crises of capitalism as a global system, it requires the implementation of structural remedies not only on a national scale, but also on a global scale. Why have so many countries descended deeper into poverty?

According to a noted expert on global poverty:

> There are many reasons why a particular country may be poor, but one historical situation is associated with the unprecedented global inequality of today: Expansion of the world economy, a key aspect of globalization, has allowed wealthy nations to disrupt weaker nations and take advantage of the people in poorer nations. (Kerbo 2006)

Since the human rights canon serves as a moral compass or reference point for social actors across the world, it provides a useful platform for the articulation of grievances related to poverty, including complaints not only about the denial of basic necessities, but also about lack of access to education, vocational training, and other means of upward social mobility. UN agencies, NGOs, SMOs, and community groups routinely cite the ICESCR and the Rio Declaration in formulating arguments for treating poverty as an abuse of human rights. To construct poverty as an abuse of human rights is to assert that political authorities – whether global, national, or local – have an overriding responsibility to do something about it. This provides the basis for activism and policymaking to alleviate poverty. Needless to say, different national governments have different capabilities when it comes to providing remedies for poverty. For example, the welfare states of the Global North are better equipped to alleviate poverty in their own jurisdictions than are the former development states of the Global South. Moreover, states in the Global North are capable of providing development assistance to their counterparts in the Global South. Thus, what matters most for advocates of a rights-based approach to poverty is placing the problem on the docket for policymakers across the world.

In which ways does poverty violate human rights? If a person is mired in poverty, he or she is appreciably less likely: to lead a long life; to be physically and mentally healthy throughout the life course; to receive the level of education, the vocational training, the amount of information, and the range of options necessary for him or her to develop his or her talents, skills, and identity; and to live in a peaceful environment (i.e., one that is free not only of interstate war, civil strife, and crime, but also of the structural violence that is associated with various forms of prejudice, discrimination, exclusion, and bullying). While the arrows of causation may point in all directions, it is clear that a person's longevity, capacity to develop fully as a person, and ability to lead a peaceful life are severely compromised by poverty. In other words, poverty can be seen as a *condensation point* for a number of human rights issues. Just as psychoanalysts and psychotherapists employ the term "condensation point" to denote an image or symbol on which a number of issues converge, so too may we invoke the term to designate a rights puzzle – a problem with multiple causes and multiple effects. In light of the immense wealth generated by industry and commerce, poverty stands as one of the most significant rights puzzles in the contemporary world.

Poverty as a Human Rights Puzzle

What follows from this understanding of poverty as a condensation point and a rights puzzle? In effect, the grievances attendant to poverty exceed second-generation rights (including the individual's rights to a livelihood, social security, protection from economic and natural disasters, and assistance through different phases of life) and touch on both first-generation rights (including the individual's right to participate equally, regardless of identity or social standing, in decision-making processes) and third-generation rights (including the collectivity's rights to cultural traditions, natural resources, and a clean environment). It follows that poverty, conceptualized as a human rights violation that cuts across the three generations, entails the advancement and implementation of an *anti-poverty rights bundle*. Far from solving the problem in itself, the point of proposing an anti-poverty rights bundle is to encourage and facilitate constructive debate on concrete ways of setting up and solving the puzzle, with the understanding that existing policies (usually placed under the rubric of development) – though often well intentioned and sometimes well conceived – have varied greatly in their efficacy. In effect, the operative assumption is that existing policies have proven only modestly successful in many nation-states because policymakers have not taken stock of the manner in which poverty restricts the realization not only of economic/social rights, but also of civil/political rights and cultural/environmental rights.

Doubtless, this insight, namely that poverty remediation entails policies that address all three generations of rights, proves extremely useful to the UN agencies, NGOs, SMOs, and community groups that participate in debates on how to address poverty without doing harm to threatened cultures and fragile ecosystems. The issue of cultural and environmental destruction has been brought to the fore by three decades of development-as-catching-up (under the Keynesian consensus) and another three decades of development-as-debt-refinancing (under the neoliberal consensus) in the Global South. In other words, two successive forms of development have proven deleterious to culture and the environment (Rahnema and Bawtree 1997; Peet and Hartwick 1999; Pieterse 2004). This insight is also useful to state policymakers, since it falls to national governments to enact, implement, and enforce anti-poverty measures in the real world.

In sum, for sociologists of human rights, the essential argument is that the proposal of a rights bundle (or, in this case, three intertwined rights bundles) could bring all of the relevant social actors (aggrieved parties, community groups, SMOs, NGOs, state policymakers, and UN agencies) into a more productive dialogue with one another. Whether a given rights bundle (or set of rights bundles) gets traction and contributes to the enactment of policy at the nation-state level depends on numerous factors. In that sense, what this book terms "rights effects" – concrete outcomes in the form of implemented policies and the altered power relations and social conditions that come with them – present ample material for the field of political sociology.

Formulating Rights Bundles

Having seen why constituencies across the world have begun to claim rights bundles that meet the requirements of globalization, we may now shift our attention to a related question: How do constituencies and their allies, whether in civil society or in the state, formulate rights bundles? This question harbors considerable analytic, pedagogical, advocacy, and policymaking import. As the examples of Oxfam International's rights-based program and the WCD proposal attest, the formulation of rights bundles involves three basic steps: first, the isolation, whether by grassroots forces or by their SMO, NGO, UN, and scholarly allies, of a grievance that has not been addressed sufficiently by existing rights; second, the demonstration of how the insufficiently addressed grievance cuts across two or more categories of rights; and third, the articulation of a rights claim that operates in each of those categories. In principle, an emerging rights bundle can flow from the "bottom up," "horizontally," or from the "top down." In other words, social actors operating at various levels may propose rights bundles to capture the needs of specific nation-states, societies, peoples, groups, and communities. From there, the rights bundles enter into circulation: After being claimed by aggrieved parties, the rights bundles are debated in various venues, before being either granted or denied by political authorities, usually in national governments. In sum, rights bundles, like more conventional forms of rights, are subject to fierce contestation. Their acceptance or rejection is predicated on the *balance of forces* in particular political and legal contexts.

How are rights bundles granted? In effect, national governments institutionalize rights bundles in the following ways: by passing protective legislation (for individuals and groups) and social programs; through court decisions; and by undertaking constitutional revisions. Examples include: legal changes entitling peasants and indigenous peoples to maintain subsistence communities with their own ways of making decisions (first-generation civil and political rights for individuals), organizing cultural life (second-generation cultural rights for individuals and third-generation rights for collectivities), and using farmland, forests, bodies of water, and natural resources (third-generation environmental rights for collectivities).

Subsidiarity

For many peasant and indigenous communities in the Global South, the demand for relative autonomy from the central government flows from the principle of subsidiarity. This principle figures prominently not only in Catholic social thought and Liberation Theology, but also in the World Social Forum and an array of mobilizations in Latin America. The principle is inextricably linked to the demands for direct democracy, cultural protections, and environmental amenities at the local level (Leite 2005).

In this light, it is conceivable that the principle of subsidiarity – as expressed in a preference for decision making by the "lowest" authority – offers significant clues for reconciling universalism and cultural pluralism (Iber 2010). While such an intuition is entertained in this book, it is a matter for social and political theorists – whether positioned in the social sciences or in philosophy – to work through the ways in which subsidiarity might contribute to the resolution of the universalism-cultural pluralism. For the current purposes of the sociology of human rights (and by extension of this book), it suffices to point to efforts on the part of the manifold SMOs and NGOs that comprise the global justice movement. In effect, the movement's actors are forced to devise ways of expressing a multitude of grievances, citing innovative interpretations of the existing human rights canon, in a diverse array of political and cultural contexts, bridging the divide between the Global North and the Global South. In short, the principle of subsidiarity points to the need for a new architecture of global governance (which would, presumably, transfer some state functions from the national to the global level and other state functions from the national to the local level). In addition, subsidiarity calls for rights bundles that reconcile global and local, Western and non-Western, majority and minority demands. Though vexing for social and political theorists, the implications of subsidiarity create instructive challenges to the accumulated social learning of movements.

An important dilemma facing social and political theorists involves the future of the nation-state. Would it be possible and desirable to transfer state functions from the national to the global and local levels with a view to eventually decommissioning the "nation," an institution that has divided the world into 193 political and legal jurisdictions, each with a particular framework for the realization of human rights? Though we cannot hope to answer this question now, we can keep in mind changes, both accidental and deliberate, in the role of the nation-state in the globalization era. In addition, we can see that while the state per se will always remain the arbiter of human rights, the nation may provide encumbrances to the expansion of human rights in the future. There is clear evidence that nationalism has often presented an obstacle not only to the implementation of human rights within nation-states, but also to peaceful relations among nation-states. In sum, it would be useful for supporters of a new human rights agenda to think through the possibility of decoupling the state from the nation.

Three Rights Bundles

Having seen how rights bundles are formulated, whether by the aggrieved parties themselves or by their allies and sympathizers elsewhere (including within the state itself), we may now turn our attention to a few rights bundles that have been foreshadowed by the book's emphasis on poverty, inequality, cultural exclusion, and environmental degradation as *human rights problems*. Operating from the argument that these seemingly disparate problems are fundamentally connected to one another as features of globalization, this chapter advances three rights bundles: the right to longevity (understood as the right to the protections and entitlements necessary to lead a long, healthy life); the right to the full development of the person (understood as the right to the protections and entitlements necessary to discover and nurture one's talents and identity); and the right to peace (understood as the right to the protections and entitlements associated with an environment free of war, crime, and structural violence).

In essence, these rights bundles – necessitating legislation at the global, national, and local levels (with the national level being by far the most important both now and for the foreseeable future) – would serve to address the interrelated problems of poverty, inequality, cultural exclusion, and environmental degradation. In pointing to the need for concerted action by governments, these bundles must be seen as regulative ideas or normative proposals for how to make the world a better place for its inhabitants. In other words, they are subject to the consideration and review not only of the aggrieved parties, but also of the political authorities (whether in parliaments or other government bodies) to which they appeal. It would remain for community groups, SMOs, NGOs, and UN agencies to debate, modify, and propose these bundles to policymakers across the world. Moreover, it would remain an open question of whether, how, and when states would implement and enforce such rights bundles. Thus, the proposal of rights bundles would serve merely as a starting point for a new circulation process. It goes without saying not only that the results would vary according to the material capacities, political sensibilities, and legal framework of nation-states, but also that the bundles would need to be filtered through specific cultural traditions.

Hence the question arises: What is the purpose of proposing such rights bundles? In advancing these rights bundles, the author hopes not only to suggest concrete ways of handling the drawbacks of globalization (namely, increasing poverty, inequality, cultural exclusion, and environmental degradation), but also to encourage readers, whether students, scholars, policymakers, or activists, to adopt the practice of proposing rights bundles. In principle, any global citizen may participate in such ongoing debates. While it is impossible to predict which rights bundles will "stick" in the sense of achieving a sufficient amount of traction with claimants and political authorities in order to create state policies, it is possible that the growing practice of rights bundling would alter the way global citizens think about and act on human rights. Contributing to a sea change in consciousness is one of the major objectives of the sociological perspective on human rights. Measuring the resulting sea change, of course, will prove challenging.

In this light, let us consider each rights bundle in greater detail. Conceptualized as a means of addressing the problem of stagnant or even declining life expectancy and high levels of infant mortality in most of the Global South and the poorer areas of the Global North, the *right to longevity* presupposes the rights to healthful food, potable water, clothing, shelter, healthcare, and a clean environment. One of the glaring paradoxes of globalization is the persistence of extreme poverty amidst the spread of consumerism (McMichael 2012). In effect, the right to longevity moves considerably beyond the long-accepted right to life by emphasizing the resources and services necessary for good physical and mental health. Accordingly, the right to longevity can be connected to the calls for improved access to healthcare not only in poor countries, but also in the US – an issue addressed, albeit incompletely, in the ongoing debate on the 2010 Patient Protection and Affordable Care Act.

Conceptualized as a means of removing impediments to personal discovery and growth, the *right to the full development of the person* presupposes the rights to a nurturing milieu (whether a family, a community, or some other type of social formation), a rigorous edu-cation from childhood through early adulthood, vocational training, viable job prospects, information, leisure time, and the opportunity to cultivate one's gender, sexual, and cultural identities. In effect, the right to the full development of the person moves considerably beyond the widely accepted freedom of expression by emphasizing the creation of contexts and institutions that allow individuals to flourish. Accordingly, the right to the full development of the person can be connected to calls not only for improved access to education (from Kindergarten through university) and information (through the bridging of the digital divide), but also for expanded mechanisms to encourage individuals, especially in their youth, to uncover and cultivate their talents and identities.

Conceptualized as a means of reducing the most serious threats to physical and mental wellbeing, the *right to peace* – though appar-ently self-explanatory – presupposes not only "negative peace" (i.e., the cessation of interstate warfare, civil strife, and such crimes against humanity as genocide, mass rape, and mass torture), but also "positive peace" (i.e., the overcoming of the structural violence associ-ated with racism, classism, sexism, homophobia, and xenophobia) (Barash 2010). In effect, the right to peace moves appreciably beyond the widely embraced right to personal security by emphasizing the establishment of political policies and institutions that serve not only to decrease the probability of warfare and crimes against humanity, but also to reduce the effects of various forms of prejudice (including discrimination and bullying at school and in the workplace). On the latter point, it is easy to overlook the fact that bullying, though commonly perpetrated by children, violates the universal human rights to dignity and security of person, and sometimes leads to physical violence. Therefore, the debate on bullying in US schools, with its implications for how young people discover and "inhabit" their identities, proves significant for our purposes.

Why are the aforementioned bundles significant for the sociology of human rights? As we have seen, each bundle traverses first-generation civil and political rights for individuals, second-generation economic and social rights for individuals, and third-generation cultural and environmental rights for collectivities in instructive ways. Furthermore, each bundle necessitates the acknowledgement of the material needs and intrinsic sociability of human beings, while appealing for a series of protections and entitlements to be promoted by intergovernmental organizations, states, and organizations performing state-like functions (especially NGOs operating in regions governed by weak, ineffectual states). Among these entities, states are the most important, since they serve as the ultimate arbiters of human rights. Paradoxically, states can be seen as both the most important enforcers and the most significant violators of human rights. Finally, taken together, the three bundles – longevity, the full development of the person, and peace – capture a broad continuum of rights that are thinkable, worthy of debate, and potentially realizable in the contemporary world. Nevertheless, these bundles are far from exhaustive. Thus, one of the purposes of this chapter has been to demonstrate to the reader that the process of rights bundling, understood as something more than an intellectual exercise, can be reproduced by concerned individuals, activists, community groups, SMOs, NGOs, and policymakers with different perspectives, interests, and objectives.

Summary

This chapter has explored the concept of rights bundling as a means of compensating for the deficiencies of the three-generations framework – the schema that prevailed, first implicitly and then explicitly, with the emergence and growth of the UN system and the NGOs operating in its orbit. With a series of changes in the interstate system, including the breakdown of the Soviet Union and its satellites in Eastern Europe (coupled with the widespread discrediting of state socialism as a model for human emancipation) and the concomitant end of the Cold War, along with the decline of the former Third World as a political force, scholars and practitioners examined new ways of conceptualizing and classifying human rights, paying particular attention to popular (as opposed to elite) and non-Western (as opposed to Western) influences on human rights thought and practice. Over time, it became clear that popular coalitions in the Global South, often faced with the legacy of dictatorship, unresolved land inequality, and the marginalization of indigenous cultures, along with the contemporary reality of neoliberal austerity, consumerist encroachments on cultural traditions, and environmental degradation, thought differently about human rights. Moreover, these coalitions began to exert influence over their allies in the Global North, as the examples of the Zapatista Solidarity Network and the World Social Forum attest. The influence of these coalitions on philosophy, organizational structure, strategy, and tactics (and by extension on the conceptualization of human rights) can be seen in the global justice movement in general and the anti-austerity mobilizations (particularly in Southern Europe) and Occupy protests (particularly in the US). Without employing the word, all of these popular mobilizations undertake rights bundling. In sum, these recent developments have inspired scholars and practitioners to examine the ways in which rights claims can and should cut across the three generations.

Notwithstanding the well-documented analytic, pedagogical, and political merits of the three-generations framework, rights bundling is the primary fashion through which old rights are reinterpreted and new rights are invented. This process testifies not only to the malleability of the language of human rights, but also to how rights accumulate over historical time and across geographic space. In other words, rights bundling stands as a living testimony to the historicity and geography of human rights. Whether simple or complex, every rights claim finds expression in a particular time and a specific political and cultural context, and hence comes with a shelf life and a range of applicability. It is increasingly common for diverse constituencies to seek recourse to rights bundling not only to articulate grievances that fall beyond the conventional categories, but also to forge alliances with one another across national boundaries. In this way, rights bundles serve as the glue that binds together the coalitions that appeal to NGOs and UN agencies in pressuring nation-states – along with the intergovernmental organizations (e.g., the IMF, the WB, and the WTO) that presume to regulate them – for new policies in the form of economic, social, cultural, and environmental protections and entitlements.

As we have seen throughout this book, human rights are highly contested, culturally encoded claims that vary considerably across historical time and geographic space. Therefore, the sociological perspective must take into consideration the debates, struggles, cultural issues, history, and geography associated with rights claims. As the theory of rights circulation (presented in chapter 2) would suggest, various aggrieved parties lay claim to the human rights canon, reinterpreting existing rights and inventing new rights, challenging old classifications and, ultimately, creating new classifications. In the process, these forces expand what is *thinkable* and *implementable* in terms of human rights. We have covered numerous examples of post-Enlightenment rights that have become not only imaginable, but also subject to implementation: reproductive rights for women; LGBT rights (including same-sex marriage and the entitlements that accompany it); and indigenous rights to land, waterways, natural resources, and self-determination. It is reasonable to assume that the expression of new identity claims will give rise to the creation of new categories.

Setting aside the question of whether rights are grounded in *human nature* (e.g., the body's capacity for pain, the intrinsic vulnerability of the psyche, and the inherent propensity to form families, communities, and societies) or merely in *human conventions* (negotiated and accumulated over a long span of time as civilizations interact with one another in multifarious ways), it is clear that human rights are subject to a nonlinear evolutionary process (Turner 2006; Gregg 2012). While it would be useful to trace the many twists and turns, points of progress and regress in the history of human rights (from ancient times, through the European Enlightenment, through the period of decolonization, and beyond), this book has emphasized the emergence of human rights norms, policies, laws, and instruments since the end of the Second World War and the advent of US hegemony in 1945 (Lauren 2003; Ishay 2008; Moyn 2012).

In particular, the book has accentuated the events and processes of the last four decades:

- the transformation of the world economy that followed the breakdown of Keynesianism and Third World developmentalism in the crisis of the 1970s and the subsequent emergence of a post-Fordist work regime, characterized by widespread industrial relocation from the Global North to the Global South;

- the restructuring of the interstate system that followed the end of the Cold War and the collapse of the Eastern Bloc and the Soviet Union between 1989 and 1991;
- the rapid growth of global society or the global public sphere, with such profound advances in communications technologies as personal computers, the Internet, and cell phones (Appelbaum and Robinson 2005; McMichael 2012).

Taken together, these changes have created a need to rethink the human rights canon. More recently, the non-violent end of Apartheid in South Africa, the violent fracturing of the multi-ethnic state of Yugoslavia, genocide in Rwanda, 9/11 and other instances of terrorism, the wars in Afghanistan and Iraq, the social movements of the Arab Spring, the NATO intervention in Libya, and the civil war in Syria have generated considerable debate on non-violent versus violent conflict resolution, the uses of economic and political sanctions, humanitarian interventionism, the role of NGOs in monitoring abuses and promoting solutions, and the place of the UN in the system of global governance. Notwithstanding the challenges ahead, conditions are favorable for discovering, publicizing, and, with a little luck, remedying human rights abuses.

Discussion Questions

- How does the WCD paradigm link alternative development to women's rights, cultural rights, and environmental rights?
- Reflect on the three rights bundles proposed in this chapter: longevity, the full development of the person, and peace. Which problems would be resolved if the three rights bundles were implemented? Which problems would be left unresolved?
- To the end of resolving a problem that has not been addressed by the proposed rights to longevity, the full development of the person, and peace, propose a rights bundle of your own. Take the following steps: isolate a grievance that has not been addressed adequately by existing rights; demonstrate how the new grievance involves two or more categories of rights; and invent a rights claim that operates in those categories.

Conclusion: An Agenda for the Sociology of Human Rights

It seems fitting to conclude the book with a few comments on the interrelated subjects of human rights, peace, and development (defined as a project to alleviate poverty in the Global South). Peace, defined both "negatively" and "positively," constitutes one of the rights bundles explored in chapter 6. Meanwhile, the right to development (and its corollary, the right to be protected from such excesses of development as cultural and environmental degradation) have been examined in the context of the third generation. Nevertheless, it is clear that, if reformulated to compensate for the failures of the post-Second World War and globalization periods, development could be considered a rights bundle. Indeed, the development bundle could be placed alongside the bundles proposed in this book: longevity, the full development of the person, and peace.

Let us consider the possible connections between the development bundle and the other bundles. In essence, any defensible project of development in the Global South would be designed not only to increase the longevity of the population (through improvements in food provisioning, public hygiene, and healthcare), but also to promote peace (through the prevention of interstate and civil war and the alleviation of structural violence). Drawing on Article 15 of the ICESCR, which states that all human beings are entitled to enjoy the benefits of scientific research and technological advancement, we may propose a human rights approach to development. Thus, we could look at development from three angles: from academia, the WCD paradigm and the work of Amartya Sen (1999); from the NGO sphere, the Oxfam International program (http://www.oxfam.org/); and from the IGO sphere, the program of the UN Development Group (http://www.undg.org).

In light of past abuses perpetrated in the name of development, such a project would entail much greater popular participation, transparency, consistency, and accountability than shown in the mainstream development programs of the past. To that end, parties interested in advancing the right to development would need to work through the debates on the uses and abuses of scientific and technical expertise, positivism versus relativism, and universalism versus particularism, not to mention the debate on the role of the state in enacting social programs that bring rights (economic and social, cultural and environmental) to fruition.

Human Rights, Peace, and Development

Let us consider the overlapping issues of human rights, peace, and development. In presenting a blueprint for the sociology of human rights, this book has drawn indirectly on the insights of political science, anthropology, and geography. In addition, the book has echoed the most prominent concern in the interdisciplinary field of peace studies: the *moral* and *practical* need for academics to converse with UN agencies, NGOs, and SMOs in exposing and alleviating structural violence in the real world. By convention, the term structural violence refers to institutionalized patterns of inequality, based on class position, identity, personal beliefs, membership in a particular group, or residence in a specific community, that foment human rights abuses (Barash 2010). Drawn from several disciplines, practitioners of peace studies unveil the workings of structural violence, whether on a global, national, or local scale, not only in the interest of advancing scholarship, but also to the end of promoting *positive peace* in the real world. In essence, positive peace entails the creation of structures and institutions that decrease the likelihood of war, social strife, exploitation, discrimination, persecution, and exclusion. Positive peace also involves non-violent conflict resolution, respect for cultural and ecological diversity, and the observance of human rights norms.

In combining *analysis* with *advocacy*, many peace scholars participate in dialogues with UN officials, NGO staff, and SMO leaders (Barash 2010). Owing to differences in power and funding, purview, ideological orientation, and constituency, these entities often disagree about how to achieve positive peace in the real world. Nevertheless, such ongoing debates contribute to the consolidation of norms on the pursuit of peace and justice. Like their neighbors in peace studies, many rights-oriented sociologists aim to put their research into practice, not only through teaching and mentoring undergraduate and graduate students, but also through service to universities, local communities, and the wider public. Regardless of their normative perspectives, theoretical and methodological tools, or substantive concerns, rights-oriented sociologists often stress the connections among research, teaching, and service. Accordingly, this book has been designed not only to promote the application of sociological research in courses and service projects on human rights, but also to inject classroom and service-based observations into scholarship. In sum, in the spirit of service learning – a pedagogical perspective that has become popular in universities across the US – this book has drawn on the insights of human rights education.

Social Science and Human Values

Building on the prior achievements of sociologists who have examined social inequalities (of race, class, gender, sexual orientation, and national origin) and social problems (including poverty, urban decay, crime, and environmental destruction) with the intention of intervening to make society a better place, rights-oriented sociologists steer a middle course between two poles. On the one hand, such sociologists challenge the legacy of positivism – the idea that sociology must emulate the natural sciences while aspiring to remain value neutral (Frezzo 2011). Against positivism, they argue not only that scientific rigor does not necessitate value neutrality, but also that pretensions to objectivity always conceal value-laden assumptions about the purposes of research. Thus, rights-oriented sociologists respect scientific protocol (e.g., by adhering to highly formalized qualitative, comparative-historical, and quantitative methods) without shunning the value of improving social conditions. This is particularly clear in the case of policy-oriented sociologists, whose analyses of the effects of existing programs are designed to contribute to debates on more effective policies. The sociological literatures on the welfare state, healthcare, education, and the prison system provide excellent examples of policy-oriented research with significant implications for human rights.

On the other hand, rights-oriented sociologists contest the lineage of moral relativism – the notion that sociology must shun universalism in deference to a multitude of particular cultures (Frezzo 2011). In opposition to moral relativism, they contend not only that it is possible to find bases, whether natural or socially constructed, for universalism, but also that sociological research cannot be reduced to mere storytelling. Again, the widespread use not only of rigorous *qualitative* and *quantitative* methods by rights-oriented sociologists proves the point. Moreover, this is an example where cross-pollination between disciplines has been helpful. While particularly sensitive, by inclination and by training, to the claims of non-Western cultures and communities, the American Anthropological Association (AAA) established a Committee on Human Rights in 2006 in order "to promote and protect human rights; to expand the definition of human rights within an anthropological perspective . . . to influence and educate the media, policy makers, non-governmental organizations, and decision makers in the private sector" (http://www.aaanet.org/cmtes/cfhr/). The AAA committee's statement points to the role of professional anthropologists in the epistemic community: they are interested in promoting the *anthropological* perspective on human rights among policymakers, NGOs, and the general public. As the case of the AAA suggests, rights-oriented anthropologists are well suited to address not only the tension between universalism and cultural pluralism, but also the question of scientific rigor and human values.

Let us return to the question of sociology. While most contemporary sociologists are neither positivists nor moral relativists, residues of the two tendencies can be found in the discipline (Turner 2006). As a consequence, rights-oriented sociologists have been compelled to spell out their positions on science, values, and the mission of the university. As it stands now, the ISA Thematic Group on Human Rights and Global Justice and the ASA Section on Human Rights – in reflecting the growth of a knowledge movement – have succeeded in formalizing the field. Many participants in the field reconcile a commitment to scientificity with the embrace of normative principles, including popular participation in decision-making processes. A sociologist can avow the value of popular participation *without* supporting the platform of a political party, the program of an SMO, or even a particular model of democracy. It is understood that the details of how to interpret and implement democracy is to be left to the people.

Where does this leave us? In avoiding the poles of positivism and moral relativism, many sociologists adhere to a conception of scientificity that permits the affirmation of values. In doing so, they join anthropologists, geographers, and others who share an interest in (a) harvesting the fruits of scientific research and technological advancement for the benefit of humanity, while (b) protecting humanity from abusive applications of science and technology. At the same time, these scholars espouse a universalism that allows for a high degree of cultural specificity. In the process, they readily acknowledge that, far from being given a priori, universal values must be discussed and negotiated across cultural frontiers. Furthermore, any plausible and defensible type of universalism would need to be filtered through particular cultures. Therefore, what is required is a cross-civilizational, transnational *project* to build a framework for universalism and cultural pluralism.

Needless to say, such a project – entailing as it would the reform of the UN and the concomitant transformation of the interstate system – would not only require a broad consensus among policymakers and their constituencies, it would also entail decades of hard work by sympathetic organizations and activists. Nevertheless, it proves worthwhile to *imagine* such a project. Such exercises in "grounded utopia" – tracing promising trajectories in the present day to their best possible culmination in the future – form an important part of the sociology of human rights.

Rethinking Development

In effect, the quest for positive peace entails systematic thinking not only on ways of reconciling universalism with cultural pluralism, but also on possible remedies for the interrelated problems of poverty, cultural marginalization, and environmental degradation in the Global South. By extension, this entails rethinking development – the idea that planned social change should be implemented to improve the material wellbeing of a given nation-state or community. The right to development, though recently proclaimed by the UN General Assembly with the support of numerous delegations from the Global South, would be subject to vastly different interpretations from one nation-state and cultural context to another. In other words, different nation-states would draw distinct conclusions about what constitutes development (Appelbaum and Robinson 2005; McMichael 2012). Would it involve the expansion of public infrastructure (roads, bridges, tunnels, power plants and electrical lines, water treatment facilities, cell towers and fiber optic cables)? Or would it entail changes in healthcare and public hygiene? Or would it focus on the industrialization of agriculture to maximize crop yields? What kinds of trade-offs would nation-states need to make? How would development – mainstream, alternative, or otherwise – affect local ways of life and fragile ecosystems? Who would make the fateful decisions: intergovernmental organizations, national governments, or the people themselves? Reasonable scholars, policymakers, activists, and ordinary people may disagree on the answers to these questions. But it is incumbent upon the human rights community to address the issue of development in a systematic fashion.

Fittingly, human development is a case where sociology has borrowed heavily from cultural anthropology and social geography, fields that have considered the peoples, cultures, landscapes, and environmental conditions of the Global South. Reflecting the contributions of these disciplines, NGOs and UN agencies often use the Human Development Index (HDI) to evaluate conditions in nation-states across the world (http://hdr.undp.org/en/statistics/hdi). In a similar vein, the Social Science Research Council has an ongoing project devoted to measuring the HDI in regions, states, counties, and cities in the US (https://www.measureofamerica.org). These scholarly innovations hold great potential for policymaking to combat poverty, and such attendant problems as insufficient access to healthcare and education. Current social scientific thinking on the issue of development, conceived as investment in infrastructure, public health and hygiene, selected industries, and agriculture to improve the material conditions of a nation-state, harbors profound implications not only for the theory and practice of human rights, but also for the ongoing debate on global governance.

Global Governance

By necessity, the human rights community devotes considerable attention to the origins, evolution, and future of global governance – the institutional framework for international cooperation among nation-states, diplomacy, trade, and law enforcement. The institutions of global governance – those already in existence (e.g., the UN, the IMF, the WB, and the WTO) and those that have only been imagined (e.g., a World Parliament, a Global Development Fund, a Global Fair Trade Organization, and a Global Environmental Organization) – would be charged with the task of implementing a new development project (Monbiot 2004). Long the domain of international relations and international law scholars, the literature on global governance has benefited immensely from an infusion of ideas from non-academics (including journalists, NGO staff, and SMO leaders).

Rights Conditions, Rights Claims, and Rights Effects

Two existing NGO projects – Oxfam International's multifaceted anti-poverty program and Amnesty International's multilevel campaign for the realization of economic, social, and cultural rights – point in the direction not only of a critical rethinking of development, but also to the need for reformed and perhaps supplemental institutions of global governance (Wilkinson 2005). Furthermore, the research-oriented WCD paradigm, with its emphasis on the need to build gender, cultural, and environmental considerations into development, points in the same direction. Finally, the three rights bundles advanced in this book – the right to longevity, the right to the full development of the person, and the right to peace – converge on the issue of development. Nevertheless, though an important contributor to the sociology of human rights (with the analysis of rights conditions), political economy/development sociology cannot capture either rights claims (a subject for social movement research) or rights effects (a subject for political sociology). In sum, we must explicate all three aspects: rights conditions (whether economic, political, social, cultural, or environmental), rights claims (whether reform-oriented or transformative), and rights effects (whether in the form of altered relations between SMOs and political parties, new state policies, or changed power relations in civil society).

Doubtless, the problem of poverty, which, as Oxfam International has demonstrated, routinely denies individuals and groups not only economic and social rights (including nutrition, public hygiene, shelter, and healthcare), but also civil/political rights and cultural/environmental rights, constitutes only one condensation point for sociologists of human rights. In principle, rights-oriented sociologists can isolate numerous other condensation points in pursuit of a more expansive research agenda.

A Research Agenda

Where shall we go from here? How should the sociological analysis of human rights proceed? How might other researchers, whether operating from similar or distinct assumptions about the relationship between scientific protocol and the affirmation of values, build on the contributions of the present text? In offering provisional answers to these questions, the author hopes to set the stage for a focused discussion on possible pathways for a rapidly expanding field. As with all emerging domains of inquiry, the sociological study of human rights must pursue a *via media* between two poles. On the one hand, rights-oriented sociologists would do well to expand into areas that they have not yet addressed in detail. These areas include health/medicine, education, and other aspects of social provisioning that have been subjected to budget cuts in welfare states, former socialist states, and former development states across the world. On the other hand, rights-oriented sociologists must take measures to solidify the field around core theories, concepts, and substantive issues, not least because the widespread propagation of human rights notions risks dampening the power of the new field. In navigating a middle course, the author proposes a four-plank agenda for the sociology of human rights in the near future. For the sake of economy and clarity, the author resists the temptation – natural in a field that has implications for efforts by governments to address a wide array of social problems – to delineate a more expansive agenda.

The first plank affirms the utility of drawing on approaches other than the ones featured here (namely, political economy/development sociology, social movement research, and political sociology), especially those of cultural sociology and environmental sociology, in generating empirical research on: (a) the conditions that foment rights-oriented grievances among poor, exploited, marginalized, threatened, or otherwise vulnerable constituencies, groups, and communities, including issues pertaining to collective identity and collective access to life-sustaining resources, and (b) the actual processes by which aggrieved parties deliberate on interpretations of the human rights canon en route to making explicit claims on state policymakers. Building on the acknowledgement of the need for a deeper consideration of the cultural and environmental factors that condition rights claims, the second plank consists of a call for a definitive theory of rights circulation to account for the emergence, contestation, evolution, implementation, and enforcement of human rights. In conjunction with the theorization of rights circulation, the third plank involves extending the analysis of epistemic communities – originated by scholars of international organizations – to capture the role of popular forces (including community-based organizations and SMOs) and their allies (especially NGOs) in interpreting and altering the human rights canon. Finally, the fourth plank consists of a call for rights-oriented sociologists to intervene more directly in the debate on the origins, evolution, decline, and future of the welfare state, especially in the US, as a provider of economic and social rights in the form of workers' protections and provisions, healthcare, and education. Let us examine the four planks in greater detail.

First Plank: Cultural and Environmental Sociology

Though designed to introduce readers (whether students, professors, or members of the general public) to the sociological analysis of human rights, this book can be seen as an attempt to solidify the nascent field around three intertwined approaches: political economy/development, which illuminates *rights conditions* (i.e., the circumstances that precipitate grievances over human rights abuses); social movement research, which elucidates *rights claims* (i.e., the results of efforts by SMOs and their NGO allies to translate their grievances into the language of human rights through reference to the human rights canon); and political sociology, which explicates *rights effects* (i.e., outcomes of human rights struggles in the form of state policies, programs, and institutions). In sum, each approach is linked to a specific concept; and each concept, in turn, is designed to isolate and explain a *moment* of the circulation process.

In principle, the author could have considered other possible approaches to the new field. For example, as previous chapters have noted, cultural sociology (with its potential to demonstrate how threats to culture inspire rights struggles) and environmental sociology (with its potential to show how ecological problems motivate rights struggles) have much to offer to the analysis of both rights conditions and rights claims, while the sociology of law (with its capacity to illuminate how laws, courts, and other legal institutions facilitate and constrain social actors in the name of rights) offers insights into rights claims and rights effects. In practice, for the sake of precision and clarity, the author chose to allude to the other approaches without developing them fully (e.g., in the discussion, in chapter 5, of the imperative to incorporate a concern for cultural and environmental preservation into alternative development projects in the Global South). Nevertheless, it would be worthwhile for scholars to explore the applications of cultural sociology, environmental sociology, and the sociology of law for the analysis of human rights.

Second Plank: A Theory of Rights Circulation

When woven together, the three approaches that figure prominently in this book – political economy/development sociology (with its attentiveness to macroeconomic policies and material conditions), social movement research (with its sensitivity to the organizational structures, strategies, tactics, and framing techniques of SMOs and their NGO partners), and political sociology (with its insights into the workings of political parties and the undertakings of state policymakers) – offer an *inchoate theory* of the circulation of human rights. The components of the theory are as follows. Under certain conditions, grassroots forces and their affiliates mobilize to seek redress for their grievances. Citing the human rights canon, with its attendant strengths and limitations, these coalitions transform their grievances into rights claims. Having been expressed as more or less plausible interpretations and/or extrapolations of the existing human rights canon, these rights claims are debated in various arenas (including government bodies and the court of public opinion). Under particular circumstances, these claims gain traction among state policymakers. Whether acting out of ideological conformity, humanitarian sympathy, or out of a strategic or even Machiavellian desire to co-opt popular forces, policymakers translate rights claims into legislation. Finally, if the legislation endures for a specified period of time, its outcomes (or rather, its rights effects) become clear: protections and/or entitlements in the form of laws, policies, programs, and institutions may improve the fortunes of the aggrieved and/or alter power relations among contending forces. Far from happening once and for all, the cycle is repeated. Rights claims may circulate across a range of social actors from the "bottom up," "horizontally," or from the "top down"; and rights claims may cross international frontiers, with or without the mediation of international NGOs or UN agencies. In sum, the process of circulation is both structured and open-ended.

While this book has provided the *elements* of a theory of circulation – in part as an *antidote* to the theory of diffusion and in part as a *supplement* to theories of resource mobilization, framing, political opportunity, and outcomes – it has not formalized such a theory. The next step would be for a scholar to delineate a general theory of rights circulation. In all likelihood, such a theory would need to be adapted to different types of political regimes (democratic or authoritarian) and diverse cultural configurations (spread across the Global North and the Global South). Yet it seems plausible that a theoretician could discern, describe, and explain a general pattern of the emergence, contestation, implementation, and enforcement of human rights. Such a theory would greatly facilitate cross-national and cross-cultural research on frameworks for implementing human rights, thereby bridging the gap between the literature on transnational norms and the literature on global governance (Wilkinson 2005).

Third Plank: The Epistemic Community

Involving a range of social actors, operating both in concert and in competition with one another in interpreting and applying the central insights of the human rights canon, the process of circulation points to the need for a thoroughgoing analysis of the human rights community, an important arbiter of norms in the realm of human rights. For many years, UN officials and NGO staff have employed the term "community" to denote a transnational network of scholars, policymakers, and others devoted to the advancement of human rights. Notwithstanding its handiness as a metaphor, the image of a mythic village of concerned global citizens, gathered together to adjudicate rights claims, proves insufficient not only to the task of explaining how rights-oriented knowledge is *produced* and *propagated*, but also to the task of capturing the *disputes, contradictions,* and *ambiguities* inherent in a network that includes an array of power blocs and represents conflicting constituencies.

To the end of moving toward a more precise description of the network, this book draws on the concept of an "epistemic community," an import from the literature on international organizations and cooperation among nation-states. As a prominent scholar in this literature has noted, epistemic communities include professionals (whether academics, policymakers, or others) who share common normative principles and objectives (impelled by an implicit understanding of human welfare), a common comprehension of how academic research influences policy outcomes, a shared understanding of what constitutes valid knowledge (especially in the natural and social sciences), and a common desire for successful policy outcomes (especially at the level of the nation-state) (Haas 1992).

In effect, Haas has cleared the ground for a solid explanation of the human rights community. Building on the framework offered by Haas, this book shows how, notwithstanding the prominence of academics and legislators within it, the rights-oriented epistemic community incorporates the *social learning* of aggrieved constituencies across the world. In every nation-state, the social learning of particular groups inflects not only the conceptualization of human rights, but also the attendant policies, laws, and institutions produced in the service of new rights. In sum, in modifying the definition of an epistemic community, this book follows both a social scientific imperative (to explain the workings of human rights) and a normative impulse (to employ human rights in making the world a better place). The next step for the sociology of human rights is to elaborate a theory of the rights-oriented epistemic community.

Fourth Plank: Welfare States

As any political sociologist would attest, the literature on the welfare state, both in the US and elsewhere in the world (especially in Western Europe), is voluminous, insightful, and useful for policymaking purposes (especially in the areas of poverty alleviation, healthcare, and education) (Esping-Andersen 1990; Pierson et al. 2013). Thus, in urging rights-oriented sociologists to intervene in the ongoing debates on the rise, evolution, decline, and possible supersession of the welfare state (as a set of institutions designed to regulate the economy and mitigate risks for the population), this book also advances a caveat to avoid re-inventing the wheel. It is crucial for rights-oriented sociologists to ascertain precisely how they might intervene in debates with immediate ramifications for policymaking, and hence for the actual allocation of protections, entitlements, and social goods to citizens. Hence the question arises: What do rights-oriented sociologists have to offer to the literature on welfare states? The answer to this question involves the manner in which the debates are *framed*. Far from being a mere semantic issue, the framing of the welfare-state debate harbors profound epistemological implications for sociological research on policymaking, especially in nation-states that feature an array of competing political parties and democratic institutions.

To recapitulate an argument that appears previously, the widespread "retreat of the state" from social provisioning – one of the most important components in the platform of neoliberalism (or what some elite economists have called "market fundamentalism") – has created a space for the affirmation of social programs (for poor people, workers, children, the elderly and infirm, and others) not merely as social goods – to be granted and taken away at the whims of policymakers or with fluctuations in the economy – but rather as the actualization of human rights. This makes a significant difference. To say that a given social program (e.g., social security, unemployment insurance, or food subsidies) constitutes the implementation of a human right is to say that the program may not be abolished (unless it is to be replaced by a comparable measure with a similar or improved expectation of success). While the distinction between a rights-oriented program and an ordinary policy matters for both social scientific and normative reasons, it suffices, in the present book, to emphasize the former. However, research is needed not only on cases in which aggrieved constituencies and their allies conceptualize social programs as human rights, but also on cases in which policymakers in welfare states move in the same direction. This points to the contrast between welfare state provisioning in the US and Western Europe. Long the subject of inquiry by political sociologists (and political scientists working in the field of comparative politics), the paradoxical status of the US as both a *pioneer* and an *outlier* in social provisioning among welfare states holds considerable promise as a research topic for the sociology of human rights.

Though grounded in the theories, concepts, and substantive examples presented throughout the book and representative of the utility of the sociological perspective for the analysis of an array of subjects – from policymaking in welfare states, former socialist states, and former development states to global governance, and finally, to the role of transnational norms in modulating the complex and contradictory interactions of IGOs, nation-states, NGOs, and SMOs – these research planks do not exhaust the potential of the new field. As this book has shown, the sociological perspective on human rights serves as a useful lens for examining the causes, effects, and possible policy solutions to a vast range of social problems. Fittingly, sociologists from diverse backgrounds and working in universities across the world are addressing social problems in terms of human rights. In the process, these researchers are contributing not only to the codification of the field as an autonomous mode of inquiry, but also to the propagation of a vision that combines a thoroughgoing belief in the social scientific protocol with a commitment to humanist values. Numerous examples of the efficacy of the sociological perspective appear in Brunsma et al.'s *The Handbook of Sociology and Human Rights* (Paradigm Publishers, 2012), which shows how every section of the ASA might contribute to the analysis of human rights. In light of its capacity for self-reflection and self-criticism – not to mention the diversity of its participants and the global reach of its subject matter – the new field has the research tools necessary for tackling such enduring dilemmas as globalism versus localism, the policymaking functions of the nation-state in the globalization era, and universalism versus cultural pluralism.

Final Thoughts

First, we addressed the constructive challenge of reconciling a commitment to scientific rigor with the embrace of humanist values. Then, we examined a research agenda to meet that challenge. Now, we close with a brief reflection on the need for greater popular participation in debates on the nature, scope, policy applications, and power effects of human rights in nation-states across the world. As the contributions of community-based organizations and SMOs show, the epistemic community built around human rights would benefit immensely from increased input from the general public. In addition to having a wealth of knowledge to contribute to the epistemic community, members of the general public (whether aggrieved or not) have a significant stake in the outcomes of these debates. For example, in countries that do not have single-payer, national healthcare programs, it would make a difference if the general public pushed policymakers to define the *"highest attainable level of health"* (as Amnesty International and other NGOs phrase it) as a universal human right. Similarly, where state funding for free, high-quality education is lacking, it would be useful for citizens to emphasize the universal human right to the *"highest attainable level of education"* (as NGOs might put it). Finally, in areas suffering from cultural erosion and environmental degradation (as well as poverty), it would be helpful for the public to affirm the universal human right to a protected culture and a clean environment (as Oxfam International's anti-poverty program would have it).

Taken together, these rights – to healthcare, education, and cultural and environmental preservation – represent responses to the *interrelated problems* of poverty, economic inequality, cultural exclusion, and environmental destruction. Closely connected to one another, these rights demand *bundles of legislation* from nation-states. Only popular forces have the capacity to pave the road to such bundles. As a corollary to the right to democracy, everyone has the *right* to participate in the delineation, interpretation, and implementation of the human rights canon on the global, national, and local levels. Let this book serve as an invitation to readers and their communities to take seriously the right to democracy – not only as an end in itself, but also as a means of achieving a range of objectives en route to a better world.

Suggestions for Further Reading

Owing to its status as a new field of academic inquiry, the sociology of human rights has yet to acquire a set of canonical texts. Nevertheless, a number of books have established the groundwork for sociological research and teaching on human rights. For the sake of economy, this section lists a sample of books, as opposed to articles, published in the last several years that have exerted an influence on the delineation of the field's parameters. Thus, the reader should note that the list is far from exhaustive. Many of the authors mentioned below have contributed other publications to the cause. Moreover, numerous other authors — some characterizing themselves as sociologists of human rights and others preferring different designations – have helped, whether directly or indirectly, to solidify the field. The list is presented in chronological order.

Vulnerability and Human Rights (2006), a collection of essays by Turner, advances the groundbreaking argument that shared vulnerability constitutes the basis of human rights. In the process, the book establishes the foundation for a sociological approach to human rights.

As its title suggests, *Human Rights: A Primer* (2009), by Blau and Moncada, offers a sociological interpretation of the major theories, concepts, and substantive issues in the domain of human rights. In encapsulating the contributions of their previous publications, Blau and Moncada advance a theoretical and practical framework for affirming the inextricability of different types of rights – civil and political, economic and social, cultural and environmental.

Sociology and Human Rights: A Bill of Rights for the Twenty-First Century (2011), a collection of essays edited by Blau and Frezzo, pursues three interrelated objectives. First, it sketches, albeit briefly, the contours of the sociology of human rights as a field of academic inquiry. Second, it illuminates each of the three generations of human rights. Third, it proposes various ways – theoretical and practical – of bringing cutting-edge conceptions of human rights to the US context.

Human Rights in Our Own Backyard: Injustice and Resistance in the United States (2011), a multi-author volume edited by Armaline, Silfen Glasberg, and Purkayastha, contributes to the delineation of the sociology of human rights by: (a) advancing the concept of the "human rights enterprise" to capture the totality of debates on and struggles over rights-oriented knowledge, policies and laws, institutions and organizations, and practices, (b) pointing to the role of popular forces in influencing the trajectory of human rights (irrespective of whether they appeal to the state for redress), and (c) illuminating the particular status of human rights in the US.

A more recent authored volume by Armaline, Silfen Glasberg, and Purkayastha is *The Human Rights Enterprise: Political Sociology, State Power, and Social Movements* (2014) which presents an accessible framework for understanding human rights sociologically as a terrain of struggle over power between states, private interests, and organized movements.

Though not confined to sociology, *The Handbook of Human Rights* (2011), a large collection of essays edited by Thomas Cushman, contains a few expressly sociological chapters. In addition, it contains chapters that would prove useful to readers interested in contrasting the sociological approach to human rights to approaches offered not only by other social scientific disciplines (especially political science), but also by humanities disciplines (especially history and philosophy). In sum, the book captures the theoretical, methodological, and substantive pluralism of human rights.

The Handbook of Sociology and Human Rights (2012), a large collection of essays edited by Brunsma, Iyall Smith, and Gran, examines the rapid growth of interest in human rights in academic sociology. To the end of documenting a major epistemological event in sociological research, the book collects essays exploring the connection between every section of the ASA and human rights.

Internet Resources for Consultation

Throughout the book, allusions are made to the major documents of the human rights canon – promulgated under the auspices of the UN and used by policymakers, NGOs, SMOs, community-based groups, and other members of the rights-oriented epistemic community as moral and political touchstones. Readers who are interested in consulting these documents may refer to the following Internet sources (presented in chronological order of publication):

- **Universal Declaration of Human Rights (UDHR), 1948**: As the first pillar of the putative International Bill of Human Rights (IBHR), the UDHR delineates the framework for the entire human rights canon. In effect, the promulgation of the UDHR set the stage not only for subsequent documents, but also for advocacy and policymaking from the post-1945 period through the present day. See: http://www.un.org/en/documents/udhr/
- **International Covenant on Civil and Political Rights (ICCPR), 1966**: As the second pillar of the IBHR, the ICCPR delineates the framework for first-generation civil and political rights for individuals. See: http://www1.umn.edu/humanrts/instree/b3ccpr.htm
- **International Covenant on Economic, Social, and Cultural Rights (ICESCR), 1966**: As the third pillar of the IBHR, the ICESCR delineates the framework for second-generation economic, social, and cultural rights for individuals. See: http://www.ohchr.org/EN/ProfessionalInterest/Pages/CESCR.aspx
- **Stockholm Declaration of the United Nations Conference on the Human Environment, 1972**: As a supplement to the IBHR documents, the Stockholm Declaration sketches the contours of third-generation rights to cultural preservation, environmental protection, and development for collectivities (nation-states,

peoples, groups, and communities). See: http://www.unep.org/Documents.Multilingual/Default.asp?DocumentID=97&ArticleID=1503

- **United Nations Convention on the Elimination of All Forms of Discrimination against Women (CEDAW), 1979**: Though not mentioned explicitly in this book's treatment of rights of women (cutting across the three generations), CEDAW has figured prominently as a reference point for scholars, NGOs, and SMOs oriented toward the advocacy of *women's rights as human rights*. See: http://www.un.org/womenwatch/daw/cedaw/
- **United Nations Declaration on the Rights of Indigenous Peoples (DRIP), 2007**: As a supplement to the Stockholm Declaration, the DRIP delineates an array of cultural and environmental rights for indigenous peoples across the world. See: http://www.un.org/esa/socdev/unpfii/documents/DRIPS_en.pdf

Throughout the book, references are made to rights-oriented NGOs. In particular, this book has emphasized the role of Amnesty International, Human Rights Watch, and Oxfam International. Readers who are interested in the charters, purviews, and undertakings of these NGOs may wish to consult their websites (presented below in alphabetical order).

- **Amnesty International**: Founded in 1961 to advocate on behalf of "prisoners of conscience," UK-based Amnesty International has, over time, greatly expanded its purview to include advocacy of economic, social, and cultural rights (among other forms of rights). Amnesty International has become one of the largest and most renowned rights-oriented NGOs in the world. This book contains several references to Amnesty International's campaign for economic, social, and cultural rights as an example of how rights-oriented NGOs respond to the demands of globalization. See: http://www.amnesty.org/en
- **Human Rights Watch**: Founded in 1978 under the name "Helsinki Watch" to monitor Soviet compliance with the Helsinki Accords, the organization that would become US-based Human Rights Watch expanded its purview first to monitor human rights abuses across Eastern Europe, then to undertake the same task in Central America, and finally to advocate for the implementation and enforcement of a broad range of human rights, including protection from inhumane treatment (in the form of torture and capital punishment), protection from land mines, children's

rights, women's rights, and LGBT rights across the world. See: http://www.hrw.org/

- **Oxfam International**: Founded in 1942 under the name "Oxford Committee for Famine Relief" to persuade the British government to allow food to be shipped to Axis-occupied Greece, the organization that would become UK-based Oxford International expanded its purview after the Second World War to include famine relief and poverty alleviation across the world. In the process, Oxfam International adopted a values-based approach to fighting poverty, connecting a range of human rights (including the right to equal treatment under the law and the right to peace) to the right to the basic necessities of life. This book offers a substantial analysis of Oxfam International's current anti-poverty program as a sophisticated example of rights bundling to alleviate a multi-causal and multi-faceted human rights abuse. In addition, this book connects Oxfam International's anti-poverty program to the need for a coherent expression of the right to alternative development. See: http://www.oxfam.org/

Terminology

To the end of contributing to the formalization of the sociology of human rights, a process to which the ASA Section on Human Rights and the ISA Thematic Group on Human Rights and Global Justice have been devoted for several years, this book has not only modified existing terminology (drawn from previous social scientific research, along with the undertakings of NGOs and UN agencies), but also introduced new terminology and theoretical tools for use by students, scholars, policymakers, activists, and members of the general public. In principle, such terminology harbors the potential to assist current and aspiring participants in the rights-oriented epistemic community to set up and resolve rights puzzles, to interrogate existing policies (for their successes and failures in implementing human rights), and to propose new policies (to meet the requirements of diverse constituencies in the age of globalization). For the sake of clarity and precision, this section offers concise definitions of the pivotal terms employed throughout the book.

Human Rights: For the sake of precision and clarity, sociologists define human rights as the set of protections and entitlements "possessed" by the entirety of the world's population, without regard for race, class, gender, sexual orientation, nationality, religious affiliation or non-affiliation, ability or disability, age, or other identity characteristics. While protections involve checks against the power of the state and other social actors to harm individuals and collectivities, entitlements involve social programs and laws granted by the state and other political authorities to individuals and collectivities. By convention, human rights are divided into three categories: first-generation civil and political rights (guaranteeing individuals protection from abuse, representation in politics, and participation in social life); second-generation economic and social rights (guaranteeing individuals a range of programs in health, education, and welfare); and third-generation cultural and environmental rights (guaranteeing collectivities access to indivisible cultural and environmental goods).

Human Rights Canon: Collection of authoritative texts (treaties, declarations, and pronouncements) that serve as the moral and political touchstones for UN agencies, governments, NGOs, SMOs, community groups, and other social actors seeking to legitimize their campaigns, programs, policies, institutions, and practices vis-à-vis widely accepted norms. These include the 1948 UDHR, the 1966 ICCPR, the 1966 ICESCR, the 1972 Stockholm Declaration on the Human Environment, the 1992 Rio Declaration on Environment and Development, and the 2007 Declaration on the Rights of Indigenous Peoples, and other UN documents. In essence, aggrieved constituencies, their organizational partners, and/or sympathetic elites ground their rights claims in exegeses of canonical texts. Over time, in pointing to the strengths and weaknesses of the existing texts, these coalitions influence the content, interpretation, and implementation of the human rights canon.

Human Rights Community: Transnational network of scholars, UN officials, NGO staff, state policymakers, and other figures marshaling social scientific expertise and other forms of knowledge in the service of human rights in the real world. Extrapolating the concept of an "epistemic community," this book examines the conceptions of scientificity, values, and policy objectives shared by participants in the transnational network built around human rights. In addition, drawing on the concept of "social learning," this book explores the role of popular forces, including community-based organizations and SMOs, in influencing the epistemic community in its efforts to reinterpret and/or transform the human rights canon.

Rights Bundles: Normative proposals, generated by members of the human rights community (whether aggrieved parties and their allies, policymakers, or concerned citizens), that cut across the three generations of human rights: first-generation civil and political rights (promoting liberty) for individuals, second-generation economic and social rights (advancing equality) for individuals, and third-generation cultural and environmental rights (expressing solidarity) for collectivities. The term "rights bundle" is borrowed from the academic field of property law, in which it is used to designate interrelated rights that are attached to a parcel of real estate (Klein and Robinson 2011). By definition, rights bundles consist of packages of organically connected rights that are designed not only to compensate for the deficiencies of the existing human rights canon, but also to inspire innovations on the part of policymakers. In arguing that the existing human rights canon – though useful as a reference point – must be updated to fit the globalization era, this book advances three rights bundles: the right to longevity (understood as the right to the nutrition, public hygiene, healthcare, and other entitlements necessary for physical and mental health); the right to the full development of the person (understood as the right to the education and vocational training, information, leisure time, and lifestyle options necessary for discovering and nurturing one's talents, interests, and identity); and the right to peace (understood as the right to inhabit a space that is free not only of warfare, but also of the structural violence stemming from institutionalized racism, class structure, sexism, homophobia, and xenophobia).

Rights Circulation: To the end of explaining the cycle though which human rights go – from the proposal phase to the implementation phase, with many twists and turns in between – this book elaborates a preliminary theory of rights circulation. Notwithstanding its important role in this book, the theory of rights circulation requires further specification by sociologists of human rights. As it stands now, the theory covers the essential moments of the circulation process, from the generation of a grievance under specified rights conditions (whether economic, cultural, environmental, or otherwise) to the translation of the grievance (through allusions to the human rights canon) into recognizable and actionable rights claims (e.g., for development policies that protect cultural and environmental goods), and, finally, to the implementation and enforcement of state policies with tangible rights effects (i.e., changes in power relations).

Rights Claims: Demands on state policymakers (or other legitimate political authorities) made by aggrieved parties (whether by communities, groups, or peoples) and their collaborators (whether community-based organizations, SMOs, NGOs, or UN agencies), articulated in the language of human rights. As a rule, rights claims presuppose either the reinterpretation of the existing human rights canon or invention of new rights. Rights claims are usually designed to inspire or compel policymakers to create new legislation. In evaluating rights claims, this book draws primarily on an approach offered by the field of social movement research and, to a lesser extent, on an approach offered by the sociology of law.

Rights Conditions: Circumstances, whether economic, political, social, cultural, or environmental, that give rise to demands that aggrieved parties express as rights claims on political authorities. Drawing primarily on an approach offered by the field of political economy/development sociology, this book places great emphasis on the role of poverty, "under-development," and economic inequality. Yet the book stipulates that there is no reason to assert the primacy of putatively economic factors a priori. On the contrary, there are good reasons for acknowledging not only that other factors (including expressly political ones associated with party politics and parliamentary coalitions) prove crucial, but also that most rights claims result from multiple causes. Thus, with its special treatment of the proposed "right to development" as an antidote to the twin problems of abject poverty and unbridled consumerism, this book explores the roles of cultural exclusion and environmental destruction in precipitating rights claims. In the process, the book points to the utility of cultural sociology and development sociology in explaining how threats to cultural and environmental diversity create the conditions for new rights claims.

Rights Effects: When rights claims are granted by state authorities – usually through the drafting, ratification, and implementation of new legislation – they tend to empower some constituencies while constraining others. Though anything but a zero-sum game, the conferral of rights on certain constituencies inevitably alters relations among contending parties and between claimants and the state. These palpable changes in power relations are called rights effects. Owing to the vicissitudes of policymaking, rights effects may be reversible; alternatively, rights effects may give rise to such altered conditions that new debates and struggles emerge (albeit at a "higher" level). In assessing rights effects, this book draws primarily on an approach offered by the field of political sociology.

Rights Puzzles: Enduring or intractable social problems, including poverty, inequality, exploitation, institutionalized discrimination on the basis of identity, cultural destruction, and environmental devastation, that befuddle policymakers and yet harbor significant implications for the theory and practice of human rights. By training and inclination, sociologists – like their counterparts in the other social scientific disciplines – are geared for puzzle solving. And puzzles can appear in innumerable guises. Thus, rights-oriented sociologists describe why a given social problem should be conceptualized as a rights puzzle; explain why the problem defies conventional solutions; and demonstrate how state policies, if implemented successfully and enforced consistently, would solve the problem.

Right to Democracy: Interestingly enough, the right to democracy, understood in terms of popular participation in decision making at the level of the nation-state, appears only implicitly in the main documents of the human rights canon (e.g., the UDHR, the ICCPR, and the ICESCR). Far from being an oversight, this omission reflects both the precarious compromise among Western and non-Western, capitalist and socialist countries that permitted the founding of the UN system and a genuine desire on the part of the framers of the three documents to avoid imposing – or seeming to impose – a Western conception of democracy on the rest of the world. Thus, the three pillars of the putative IBHR contain fleeting references to the importance of voting rights and active citizenship, along with accountability and transparency in government. But the right to democracy – whether the representative democracy that prevails in most countries in the Global North (in which citizens elect policymakers to make decisions for them) or the direct democracy practiced, albeit on a much smaller scale, by the Movement of Landless Rural Workers in Brazil, the Zapatistas in Mexico, and other groups (in which participants make all decisions collectively) – has reached its full elaboration only in the age of globalization. For the purposes of this book, the right to democracy is closely connected to the right to development, under the argument that increased popular participation in decision making would ensure that any development project would avoid the mistakes of Eurocentrism, elitism, economism, cultural insensitivity, and callous disregard for the environment.

Right to Development: Asserted in conflicting ways by community-based organizations, SMOs, NGOs, UN agencies, and social scientists, the right to development can be seen as both a critique and an extrapolation of post-1945 efforts to assist governments in the Third World (later known as the Global South) in raising the standard of living for their populations. In effect, advocates of alternative development, defined as planned social change to improve the material wellbeing of populations without doing cultural or environmental damage, have proposed ways of picking and choosing which aspects of development (e.g., green farming and fishing, infrastructural improvements, public hygiene, and medicine) are worth pursuing. In accordance with the anti-poverty program of the celebrated NGO Oxfam International and various scholarly proposals that point in the same direction, this book stresses the need not only to overcome cultural and environmental insensitivity, but also to increase popular participation in decision-making processes (under the assumption that greater democracy, transparency, and accountability would reduce the incidence of cultural exclusion and limit damage to fragile ecosystems).

Sociology of Human Rights: A growing field in academia that uses sociological theories and methods to elucidate: (a) the circumstances – whether economic, political, social, cultural, environmental, or otherwise – under which aggrieved parties and their allies formulate rights claims, (b) the fashion in which rights-oriented policies are implemented by national governments and other political authorities, and (c) the political effects of human rights legislation and institutions (in the form of changing power relations among a range of social actors). To date, the sociology of human rights remains a theoretically and methodological pluralist field, covering a range of theoretical schools and methods (including qualitative, comparative-historical, and quantitative). While this book draws on three major sociological approaches to the debates and struggles surrounding human rights – political economy/development, social movement research, and political sociology – it could have highlighted other approaches (especially cultural sociology and environmental sociology).

Universalism versus Cultural Pluralism: While universalism is a normative position advocating the implementation of a globally binding framework for human rights, cultural pluralism is a normative position embracing the protection of non-Western, minority, and indigenous cultural traditions. One of the major dilemmas confronting the theory and practice of human rights is as follows: How can we reconcile these two normative impulses? In other words, how can we build a human rights regime that implements and enforces certain rights everywhere, while allowing for the preservation and nurturing of cultural diversity? As this book has suggested, the resolution of this dilemma entails the creation of a "filter" that determines not only which rights merit universalization, but also which cultural practices warrant protection. By definition, the debates on and struggles over third-generation collective rights to cultural and environmental amenities bear directly on the problem of universalism and cultural pluralism. In addressing this problem, aggrieved parties in the Global South and their NGO allies in the Global North have produced significant innovations in human rights thinking.

References

Amenta, Edwin. 1998. *Bold Relief: Institutional Politics and the Origins of Modern American Social Policy*. Princeton, NJ: Princeton University Press.

Amenta, Edwin, Neal Caren, Elizabeth Chiarello, and Yang Su. 2010 "The Political Consequences of Social Movements." *Annual Review of Sociology* 36: 287–307.

American Anthropological Association. Committee on Human Rights: http://hdr.undp.org/en/statistics/hdi

American Association for the Advancement of Science, Science and Human Rights Coalition: http://srhrl.aaas.org/coalition/index.shtml

American Sociological Association, Section on Human Rights: http://www.asanet.org/sections/humanrights.cfm

Amin, Samir. 2010. *Eurocentrism*. New York: Monthly Review Press.

Amnesty International. Human Rights Reports: http://www.amnesty.org/en/human-rights/human-rights-by-country

Amnesty International: http://www.amnesty.org/en/economic-social-and-cultural-rights

Anderson, Carol. 2003. *Eyes off the Prize: The United Nations and the African American Struggle for Human Rights, 1945–1955*. Cambridge: Cambridge University Press.

Appadurai, Arjun (1996). *Modernity at Large: Cultural Dimensions of Globalization*. Minneapolis, MN: University of Minnesota Press.

Appelbaum, Richard P. and William Robinson, eds. 2005. *Critical Globalization Studies*. New York: Routledge.

Armaline, William T., Davita Silfen Glasberg, and Bandana Purkayastha, eds. 2011. *Human Rights in Our Own Backyard: Injustice and Resistance in the United States*. Philadelphia, PA: University of Pennsylvania Press.

Armaline, William T., Davita Silfen Glasberg, and Bardana Purkayastha. 2014. *The Human Rights Enterprise: Political Sociology, State Power, and Social Movements*. Cambridge: Polity Press.

Arrighi, Giovanni. 2010. *The Long Twentieth Century: Money, Power and the Origins of Our Times*. London: Verso.

Avalon Project. Declaration of the Rights of Man and of the Citizen: http://avalon.law.yale.edu/18th_century/rightsof.asp

Bandelj, Nina and Elizabeth Sowers. 2010. *Economy and State: A Sociological Perspective.* Cambridge: Polity Press.

Barash, David P., ed. 2010. *Approaches to Peace: A Reader in Peace Studies,* 2nd edn. Oxford: Oxford University Press.

Bennholdt-Thomsen, Veronika and Maria Mies. 2000. *The Subsistence Perspective: Beyond the Globalized Economy.* London: Zed Books.

Bessis, Sophie. 2003. *Western Supremacy: the Triumph of an Idea?* Translated by Patrick Camiller. London: Zed Books.

Bhavnani, Kum-Kum, John Foran, and Molly Talcott. 2005. "The Red, the Green, the Black, and the Purple: Reclaiming Development, Resisting Globalization." In *Critical Globalization Studies,* ed. by Richard P. Appelbaum and William I. Robinson. New York: Routledge.

Blau, Judith and Mark Frezzo, eds. 2011. *Sociology and Human Rights: A Bill of Rights for the Twenty-First Century.* Thousand Oaks, CA: Sage Publications.

Blau, Judith and Keri Iyall Smith, eds. 2006. *The Public Sociologies Reader.* Lanham, MD: Rowman and Littlefield.

Blau, Judith and Alberto Moncada. 2009. *Human Rights: A Primer.* Boulder, CO: Paradigm Publishers.

Blau, Judith, David Brunsma, Alberto Moncada, and Catherine Zimmer. 2008. *The Leading Rogue State: The U.S. and Human Rights.* Boulder, CO: Paradigm Publishers.

Blaut, J.M. 1993. *The Colonizer's Model of the World: Geographical Diffusionism and Eurocentric History.* New York: Guilford Press.

Borgwardt, Elizabeth. 2005. *A New Deal for the World: America's Vision for Human Rights.* Cambridge, MA: Belknap Press.

Bronner, Steven Eric. 2004. *Reclaiming the Enlightenment: Toward a Politics of Radical Engagement.* New York: Columbia University Press.

Brunsma, David, Keri Iyall Smith, and Brian Gran, eds. 2012. *The Handbook of Sociology and Human Rights.* Boulder, CO: Paradigm Publishers.

Brysk, Alison, ed. 2002. *Globalization and Human Rights.* Los Angeles, CA: University of California Press.

Burke, Roland. 2010. *Decolonization and the Evolution of International Human Rights.* Philadelphia, PA: University of Pennsylvania Press.

Claude, Richard. 2002. *Science in the Service of Human Rights.* Philadelphia, PA: University of Pennsylvania Press.

Clausen, Rebecca. 2011. "Cooperating Around Environmental Rights." In *Sociology and Human Rights: A Bill of Rights for the Twenty-First Century,* ed. by Judith Blau and Mark Frezzo. Thousand Oaks, CA: Sage Publications.

Cushman, Thomas. 2011. *The Handbook of Human Rights.* New York: Routledge.

Deflem, Mathieu. 2005. "Public Sociology, Hot Dogs, Apple Pie, and Chevrolet." *The Journal of Professional and Public Sociology* 1(1), Article 4.

Deflem, Mathieu and Stephen Chicoine. 2011. "The Sociological Discourse on Human Rights: Lessons from the Sociology of Law." *Development and Society* 40(1): 101–15.

Desai, Ashwin. 2002. *We Are the Poors: Community Struggles in Post-Apartheid South Africa*. New York: Monthly Review Press.

Donnelly, Jack. 2003. *Universal Human Rights in Theory and Practice*, 2nd edn. Ithaca, NY: Cornell University Press.

Esparza, Louis. 2011. "Ensuring Economic and Social Rights." In *Sociology and Human Rights: A Bill of Rights for the Twenty-First Century*, ed. by Judith Blau and Mark Frezzo. Thousand Oaks, CA: Sage Publications.

Esping-Andersen, Gøsta. 1990. *The Three Worlds of Welfare Capitalism*. Princeton, NJ: Princeton University Press.

Falcon, Sylvanna. 2008. "Invoking Human Rights and Transnational Activism in Racial Justice Struggles at Home: US Antiracist Activists and the UN Committee to Eliminate Racial Discrimination." *Societies without Borders* 4(3): 295–316.

Frezzo, Mark. 2009. *Deflecting the Crisis: Keynesianism, Social Movements, and US Hegemony*. Cologne: Lambert Academic Publishing.

Frezzo, Mark. 2011. "Sociology and Human Rights in the Post-Development Era." *Sociology Compass* 5(3): 203–14.

Frick, Marie-Luisa. 2013. "Universal Claims and Postcolonial Realities: The Deep Unease over Western-Centered Human Rights Standards in the Global South." In *Human Rights in the Third World: Issues and Discourses*, ed. by Subrata Sankar Bagchi and Arnab Das. Lanham, MD: Lexington Books.

Giugni, Marco. 1998. "Was it Worth the Effort? The Outcomes and Consequences of Social Movements." *Annual Review of Sociology* 24: 371–93.

Glendon, Mary Ann. 2002. *A World Made New: Eleanor Roosevelt and the Universal Declaration of Human Rights*. New York: Random House.

Golash-Boza, Tanya. 2012. *Immigration Nation: Raids, Detentions, and Deportations in Post-9/11 America*. Boulder, CO: Paradigm Publishers.

Goodale, Mark. 2006. "Toward a Critical Anthropology of Human Rights." *Current Anthropology* 47(3): 485–511.

Goodwin, Jeff and James M. Jasper. 2009. *The Social Movements Reader: Cases and Concepts*, 2nd edn. Oxford: Blackwell Publishing.

Gordon, Neve, ed. 2004. *From the Margins of Globalization: Critical Perspectives on Human Rights*. Lanham, MD: Lexington Books.

Gregg, Benjamin. 2012. *Human Rights as a Social Construction*. Cambridge: Cambridge University Press.

Haas, Peter M. 1992. "Introduction: Epistemic Communities and International Policy Coordination." *International Organization*, 46(1): 1–35.

Hajjar, Lisa. 2005. "Toward a Sociology of Human Rights: Critical Globalization Studies, International Law, and the Future of Law." In *Critical Globalization Studies*, ed. by Richard P. Appelbaum and William I. Robinson. New York: Routledge, pp. 207–16.

Held, David. 2004. *Global Covenant: The Social Democratic Alternative to the Washington Consensus*. Cambridge: Polity Press.

Human Rights Education Associates: http://www.hrea.org/index.php?base_id=273&language_id=1

Iber, Simeon Tsetim. 2010. *The Principle of Subsidiarity in Catholic Social Thought: Implications for Social Justice and Civil Society in Nigeria*. New York: Peter Lang Publishers.

International Sociological Association, Thematic Group on Human Rights and Global Justice: http://www.isa-sociology.org/tg03.htm

Ishay, Micheline R. 2008. *The History of Human Rights: From Ancient Times to the Globalization Era*. Berkeley, CA: University of California Press.

Jenkins, J. Craig. 1983. "Resource Mobilization Theory and the Study of Social Movements." *Annual Review of Sociology* 9: 527–53.

Kerbo, Harold R. 2006. *World Poverty: Global Inequality and the Modern World System*. New York: McGraw-Hill.

Khagram, Sanjeev, James V. Riker, and Kathryn Sikkink, eds. 2002. *Restructuring World Politics: Transnational Social Movements, Networks, and Norms*. Minneapolis, MN: University of Minnesota Press.

Klein, Daniel B. and John Robinson. 2011. "Property: A Bundle of Rights? Prologue to the Property Symposium." *Econ Journal Watch* 8(3): 193–204.

Lauren, Paul. 2003. *The Evolution of International Human Rights: Visions Seen*. Philadelphia, PA: University of Pennsylvania Press.

Leite, José Corrêa. 2005. *The World Social Forum: Strategies of Resistance*. Chicago, IL: Haymarket Books.

Levine, Rhonda. 1988. *Class Struggle and the New Deal: Industrial Labor, Industrial Capital, and the State*. Lawrence, KS: University of Kansas Press.

Marriage Equality USA: http://www.marriageequality.org/

McAdam, Douglas. 1985. *Political Process and the Development of Black Insurgency, 1930–1970*. Chicago, IL: University of Chicago Press.

McMichael, Philip. 2012. *Development and Social Change: A Global Perspective*, 5th edn. Los Angeles, CA: Sage Publications.

Messer, Ellen. 1997. "Pluralist Approaches to Human Rights." *Journal of Anthropological Research* 53(3): 293–317.

Monbiot, George. 2004. *Manifesto for a New World Order*. New York: New Press.

Moyn, Samuel. 2012. *The Last Utopia: Human Rights in History*. Cambridge, MA: Belknap Press.

Nandy, Ashis. 1995. *The Savage Freud and Other Essays on Possible and Retrievable Selves*. Oxford: Oxford University Press.

Naples, Nancy and Manisha Desai. 2002. *Women's Activism and Globalization: Linking Local Struggles and Transnational Politics.* New York: Routledge.

National Archives and Records Administration. Constitution: http://www.archives.gov/exhibits/charters/constitution.html

National Archives and Records Administration. Declaration of Independence: http://www.archives.gov/exhibits/charters/declaration_transcript.html

Nepstad, Sharon Erickson. 2011. *Nonviolent Revolutions: Civil Resistance in the Late 20th Century.* Oxford: Oxford University Press.

Nichols, John T., ed. 2007. *Public Sociology: The Contemporary Debate.* New Brunswick, NJ: Transaction Publishers.

Nimtz, August. 2002. "Marx and Engels: The Prototypical Transnational Actors." In *Restructuring World Politics: Transnational Social Movements, Networks, and Norms,* ed. by Sanjeev Khagram, James V. Riker, and Kathryn Sikkink. Minneapolis, MN: University of Minnesota Press.

Oxfam International: http://www.oxfam.org/en/about/why

Pearce, Tola Olu. 2001. "Human Rights and Sociology: Some Observations from Africa." *Social Problems* 48(1): 48–56.

Peet, Richard and Elaine Hartwick. 1999. *Theories of Development.* New York: The Guilford Press.

Pierson, Christopher, Francis G. Castles, and Ingela K. Naumann, eds. 2013. *The Welfare State Reader.* Cambridge: Polity Press.

Pieterse, Jan Nederveen. 2004. *Development Theory: Deconstructions/Reconstructions.* London: Sage Publications.

Piven, Frances Fox and Richard A. Cloward. 1978. *Poor People's Movements: Why They Succeed, How They Fail.* New York: Vintage Books.

Piven, Frances Fox and Richard A. Cloward. 1998. *The Breaking of the American Social Compact.* New York: New Press.

Rahnema, Majid and Victoria Bawtree, eds. 1997. *The Post-Development Reader.* London: Zed Books.

Rawls, John. 1999. *A Theory of Justice.* Cambridge, MA: Harvard University Press.

Rist, Gilbert. 2009. *The History of Development: From Western Origins to Global Faith.* London: Zed Books.

Sen, Amartya. 1999. *Development as Freedom.* New York: Anchor Books.

Sen, Amartya. 2009. *The Idea of Justice.* Cambridge, MA: Belknap Press.

Shiva, Vandana. 1988. *Staying Alive: Women, Ecology and Survival in India.* London: Zed Books.

Shiva, Vandana. 1997. *Biopiracy: the Plunder of Nature and Knowledge.* Cambridge, MA: South End Press.

Shiva, Vandana. 2005. *Earth Democracy: Justice, Sustainability, and Peace.* Cambridge, MA: South End Press.

Sjoberg, Gideon, Elizabeth A. Gill, and Norma Williams. 2001. "A Sociology of Human Rights." *Social Problems* 48(1): 11–47.

Skocpol, Theda. 1995. *Protecting Soldiers and Mothers: The Political Origins of Social Policy in the United States*. Cambridge, MA: Belknap Press.

Smith, Jackie. 2007. *Social Movements for Global Democracy*. Baltimore, MD: Johns Hopkins University Press.

Snow, David and Robert D. Benford. 2000. "Framing Processes and Social Movements: An Overview and Assessment." *Annual Review of Sociology* 26: 611–39.

Social Science Research Council. Measure of America: https://www.measu reofamerica.org

Soohoo, Cynthia, Catherine Albisa, and Martha F. Davis. 2009. *Bringing Human Rights Home: A History of Human Rights in the United States*. Abridged edition. Philadelphia, PA: University of Pennsylvania Press.

Stout, Kathryn, Richard Dello Buono, and William J. Chambliss, eds. 2004. *Social Problems, Law, and Society*. Lanham, MD: Rowman and Littlefield.

Tilly, Charles. 2007. *Democracy*. Cambridge: Cambridge University Press.

Tilly, Charles and Leslie Wood. 2009. *Social Movements, 1768–2008*. 2nd edn. Boulder, CO: Paradigm Publishers.

Toussaint, Laura. 2011. "Promoting Cultural Rights." In *Sociology and Human Rights: A Bill of Rights for the Twenty-First Century*, ed. by Judith Blau and Mark Frezzo. Thousand Oaks, CA: Sage Publications.

Turner, Bryan. 1993. "Outline of a Theory of Human Rights." *Sociology* 27(3): 489–512.

Turner, Bryan. 2006. *Vulnerability and Human Rights*. University Park, PA: Pennsylvania State University Press.

United Nations Development Group: http://www.undg.org

United Nations Development Program. Human Development Reports: http://hdr.undp.org/en/statistics/hdi

United Nations. Universal Declaration of Human Rights: http://www. un.org/en/documents/udhr/

United Nations. Vienna Declaration: http://www.ohchr.org/en/profession alinterest/pages/vienna.aspx

Vasak, Karel. 1977. "Human Rights: A Thirty-Year Struggle: The Sustained Efforts to Give Force of Law to the Universal Declaration of Human Rights." *UNESCO Courier* 30: 11.

Vrdoljak, Ana, ed. 2013. *The Cultural Dimension of Human Rights*. Oxford: Oxford University Press.

Wallerstein, Immanuel. 2011. *The Modern World-System IV: Centrist Liberalism Triumphant, 1789–1914*. Berkeley, CA: University of California Press.

Waters, Malcolm. 1996. "Human Rights and the Universalization of Interests: A Social Constructionist Approach." *Sociology* 30(3): 593–600.

Wilkinson, Riordan, ed. 2005. *The Global Governance Reader*. London: Routledge.

World Social Forum. 2013. Charter of Principles: http://www.fsm2013.org/en/node/204

Zerubavel, Eviatar. 1996. "Lumping and Splitting: Notes on Social Classification." *Sociological Forum* 11(3): 421–33.

Index

advocacy, analysis and, xviii–xix, 151
Afghanistan, 149
agenda
  global governance, 155
  human values and social sciences,
    152–4, 163
  research, 156–62
  rethinking development, 154–5
  rights, peace and development, 151–2
  scientific research and humanist
    values, 163
  sociology of HR, 150–63
American Anthropological Association,
  xv, 153
American Association for the
  Advancement of Science
  (AAAS), xxiii, xxiv
American Political Science Association,
  xv
American Sociological Association
  (ASA), xv, xix, xxiv, 1, 24, 153,
  162, 169
Amnesty International
  annual reports, 14–15
  bundling rights, 128–9
  debates, 34
  economic, social and cultural rights,
    54, 96–7, 128–30
  health, 163
  HR education, xxiii, 44
  origins, 84
  résumé, 167
  rights education, 44
  UDHR and, 81
analysis, advocacy and, xviii–xix, 151

ancient Rome, 114
ancient world, 75
anthropology, xvii, 7, 19, 36, 153, 155
Apartheid, 149
Appadurai, Arjun, 47, 55
Arab Spring, 149
Armaline, William, 23–4
Association of American Geographers,
  xv
Austria-Hungary, 79

Bessis, Sophie, 56
Bhavnani, Kum-Kum, 130–1
Blau, Judith, xviii, xix, 107, 123
Body Shop, 117
Bolivia, 121
bottom-up approach, 24
Brazil, Landless Rural Workers'
  Movement, 32, 173
Brookings Institution, xvi
Brunsma, David, 24, 162
Bulgaria, 36, 101
bundles of rights
  alternative development, 130–2
  Amnesty International, 128–9
  angles on human rights, 132–3
  anti-poverty bundle, 140–1
  collective rights and, 108
  concept, xx, 4, 34–5, 170–1
  culture and universalism, xxi
  development, 128, 130–2, 150, 156
  examples, 5
  formulating bundles, 21, 141–2
  indivisibility, 45
  interconnectedness of rights, 97

bundles of rights *(cont.)*
  nation-states and, 163
  need, 136–40
  normative framework, 43–6
  origins, 133–6
  Oxfam, 34–5, 87–90, 128–9, 141
  rights claims and, 53–4
  sociology, 42–3
  subsidiarity, 142–3
  three proposed bundles, 44, 45–6,
    143–6, 156
Burke, Roland, 2

canon
  1st and 2nd generation rights, 115
  civil and political rights, 83–5
  concept of the individual, 125
  Enlightenment and, 80
  insufficiency, 129
  major documents, 12–15
  markers, 17
  meaning, x, 7, 11–15, 170
  rethinking, x–xii
  Western influence on, 56–7, 76, 130
  See also specific conventions
Catholicism, 142
CEDAW (International Convention on
    the Elimination of All Forms of
    Discrimination against Women),
    167
China, development, 63–4
Chipko movement, xii
circulation of rights, 65, 68–70, 158–60,
  171
civic engagement, service learning and,
    xxii–xxiv
civil and political rights
  1st generation rights, 53
  1989 revolutions and, 101
  common acceptance, 25
  decolonization and, 76, 81–3
  Enlightenment legacy, 75–6
    three generations schema, 78–9
  individual rights, 60, 61
  legitimacy, 63
  place in rights scheme, 87–90
  poverty and, 87–90
  power relations, 77–8, 80

  preliminary questions, 74–8
  primacy, 74
    bedrock of rights canon, 83–5
    historical reasons, 75–6, 101
  relational rights, 74–5
  rights effects, 77
  sociological perspective, 74–92
  theoretical abstraction, 19
  UN role, 85–7
  US policy, 51–2, 63, 64, 76, 77, 91,
    95
  usefulness to social movements,
    76–7
Civilian Conservation Corps, 16
classification of human rights
  circulation of rights, 68–70
  civil and political rights, 27–9
  collective rights, 33, 60, 62–3
  cultural and environmental rights,
    32–3
  economic and social rights, 30–2
  elitism, 57, 72
  Eurocentrism, 55–7, 72
  generations. *See* three-generations
    framework
  individual rights, 60, 61, 62–3
  lumping and splitting, 57–9
  negative rights, 27–9, 51–2
  positive rights, 30–3, 52–3
  positive v negative rights, 60–4
  rethinking, 53–7
  rights claims and, 52
  significance, 51–4
  social movements and, 64–8
  sociological perspective, 26–33, 55–7
  two ways of classifying, 60–4
Claude, Richard, xxiii
Clinton, Bill, 29
Cold War, 13, 14, 36, 55–6, 82, 102–3,
  134
collective rights
  bundling rights, 108
  classification of rights, 33, 60, 62–3
  competing collectivities, 124–5
  connecting thread, 120
  Enlightenment and, 112
  origins, 120–4
  positive rights, 78

precondition for civil and political
  rights, 93
situating, 113–14
specificity of 3rd generation rights,
  115–17
See also cultural and environmental
  rights
colonialism, xi, 2, 10, 56, 75, 76, 79, 80,
  101, 116
commons
  commodification, 62
  culture and environment, 123
community. *See* human rights
  community
Comte, Auguste, 35, 79
consumerism, 47, 62, 112, 116–17, 120,
  124, 133
Council of Europe, 103, 107
criminology, Durkheim and, xvii
critical development studies, 131–2
cultural and environmental rights
  3rd generation rights, 53, 120–4
  competing collectivities, 124–5
  connecting thread, 120
  culture, environment and
    development, 114–15
  debated rights, 25, 33
  global consumerism and, 120
  Global South, 47, 76
  globalization threat, 112, 113–14
  group rights, 33
  indigenous peoples, 62
  original formulation, 94
  positive rights, 32–3
  research agenda, 158
  situating collective rights, 113–14
  sociological perspective, 111–27
  solidarity, 111–13
  specificity, 115–17
  theoretical abstraction, 19
  versions of sustainable development,
    117–20
culture
  embeddedness, 123–4
  etymology, 114
  globalization and, 46–9, 55
  rights. *See* cultural and environmental
    rights

sociology, 120–1, 132–3
universalism and, xx–xxi, 6, 8, 53,
  154, 174–5
Czechoslovakia, 36, 101

Declaration on the Rights of Indigenous
    Peoples (DRIP, 2007), 137, 167,
    170
decolonization, 13, 14, 76, 81–3, 85,
    134
democracy
  education and, 9
  right to, 90, 173
  subsidiarity and, 142
Demos, xvi
developing countries. *See* Global South
development
  abuses, 151
  alternative development, 115, 119,
    130–2, 133, 138, 173–4
  bundling rights, 128, 130–2, 150, 156
  China, 63
  Cold War period, 82
  critical development studies, 131–2
  culture, environment and, 114–20
  development-as-consumerism, 47,
    116–17
  neoliberal views of, 72
  post-WWII, 14
  rethinking, 154–5
  right to, 56, 60, 89–90, 150, 154,
    173–4
  rights, peace and development, 151–2
  rights puzzle, 108, 115, 120
  sociology, 121
  Third World developmentalism, 112,
    114, 121–2, 133–4, 148
  US policy, 75–6, 122
  versions of sustainable development,
    117–20
  waves, 140–1
  women and, 130–1
development of the person, 44, 45,
    143–4, 145, 156
disability movement, 66
divorce, 104
Durkheim, Emile, xvi–xvii, 35–6, 79,
    116

East Germany, 36, 101
economic and social rights
  2nd generation rights, 53, 111
  debated rights, 25, 33
  Enlightenment legacy, 99–100
  importance, 98
  liberty and equality, 99–100
  politics, 94–7, 100–02
  positive rights, 30–2
  preliminary questions, 97–9
  purposes, 93–4
  relationalism of rights, 103–6
  sociological perspective, 93–110
  theoretical abstraction, 19
  UN Covenants and, 102–3
  United States, 31–2, 94–7, 98, 106–8,
    135
  Western Europe and, 103
  women's rights and, 131
economic reductionism, 118
education rights, 9, 163
Egypt, Non-Aligned Movement, 103
elitism, 57, 71–2, 173
Engels, Friedrich, 100
Enlightenment
  civil and political rights and, 75–6,
    78–9, 101
  classification of rights, 48, 49
  emancipatory project, 98
  liberty and equality, 99–100, 125
  non-European world and, xxi, 55,
    136–7
  progress, 2
  radicalizing, 101–2
  rights gaps, 67, 86–7
  scope of rights, 111–12
  solidarity and, 112
  universalism, 56
environmental rights. See cultural and
    environmental rights
environmental sociology, 133
epistemic community, 9–10, 12, 54, 69,
    160–1, 163
ethnoscapes, 47, 69
Eurocentrism, xxi, 2, 53, 55–7, 72, 118,
    130, 173
European Committee of Social Rights,
    103

European Social Charter (1961), 103,
    107, 135
European Union, debt crisis, 29, 108

fair trade, 117
Falcon, Sylvanna, 130
Fordism, 133
France
  colonialism, 76
  constitutional model, 49
  Declaration of the Rights of Man
    (1789), 2, 75, 79, 81
  Revolution
    fraternity, 111–12
    influence, 84, 105
    liberty, equality, fraternity, 48, 60,
      80, 81, 111
fraternity. See solidarity
free trade, 37, 135
Frick, Marie-Luisa, 84

generations. See three-generations
    framework
Ghana, Non-Aligned Movement, 103
global justice movement, 38
Global North
  African values v Western values, 1
  civil and political rights, 91
  consumerism, 113, 116–17, 124
  cultural flows to Global South, 55
  cultural pluralism and, xxi
  democratic rights, 90
  Eurocentrism, xxi, 2, 53, 55–7, 72,
    118, 130, 173
  ICCPR and, 13
  life expectancy, 145
  North-South divide, 14
  outsourcing, 37, 63
  perception of human rights, viii–ix
  popular coalitions, 147
  popular protests, 36
  power, 9
  social movements, 10
  solidarity, 48
  welfare states, 29, 31, 88, 139
Global South
  3rd generation rights and, 63
  alternative concepts of HR, 49

bundling rights, 133
civil and political rights and, 76
classification of human rights, 59
contributions of non-elites, 11
contributions to HR development,
    2–3, 82, 99
cultural and environmental rights,
    32–3, 47, 76, 94
cultural flows from Global North, 55
democracy and, 90
development. *See* development
development of consumerism, 47
elites, 122
environment, 155
good governance, 95
life expectancy, 145
North-South divide, 14
outsourcing to, 37
Oxfam. *See* Oxfam
popular coalitions, 147
popular protests, 36, 37
proxy wars, 13
rootedness, 113
scholars, 120–1
solidarity, 48
terminology, 3
unequal power, 9
globalization
    circulation of rights, 68–70
    critical globalization studies, 132
    cultural/environmental rights and,
        112, 113–14
    cultural flows, 46–9, 55
    definition, 46–7
    global governance, 155
    global public sphere, 68, 149
    human rights and, xi, 9
    issues, 5
    poverty and, 145
    rethinking rights and, 61
    rights bundling, 136
    rights puzzles, 98
Great Depression, 14, 16, 30–1, 106–7
Great Recession, 29, 108
Great Society programs, 31, 107
Greece, 29, 108, 168
green capitalism, 123
group rights. *See* collective rights

Haas, Peter, 10, 12, 160
Haiti, 81
Hajar, Lisa, 1
Helsinki Accords, 167
Heritage Foundation, xvi
history, human rights and, xv, 75–6, 101
Holocaust, 14
Hoover Institution, xvi
Human Development Index, 155
human dignity, ancient world, 75
human rights
    bundles. *See* bundles of rights
    canon. *See* canon
    claims. *See* rights claims
    classes. *See* classification of human
        rights
    conditions. *See* rights conditions
    definition, 169–70
    dilemma, 7–8
    effects. *See* rights effects
    invitation to, 6–7
    revolution, 61
human rights community
    classification of human rights and, 54
    epistemic community, 9–10, 12, 54,
        69, 160–1, 163
    influence, 18
    meaning, 8–11, 170
Human Rights Education Associates,
    xxiii, 44
Human Rights Watch, 14–15, 34, 44,
    84, 167–8
humanitarian interventions, 95, 149
Hungary, 36, 101

identity-based movements, 123
ideoscapes, 47, 69
IMF
    bundling rights and, 147–8
    concept of development, 72
    development-as-consumerism, 47,
        117
    institutionalization of rights, 69
    neoliberalism, 36–7, 108
    reforming, 90, 132
    sustainable development, 117
    US reconstruction of world economy,
        55–6

immanent critique, xii
India, xii, 75, 103
indigenous peoples, 61–2, 86–7, 96, 115,
    119, 122, 137, 167
Indonesia, Non-Aligned Movement, 103
Industrial Revolution, 79, 116
interdisciplinarity, xvii, 5–6
International Convention on the
    Elimination of All Forms of
    Discrimination against Women
    (CEDAW), 167
International Convention to
    Eliminate All Forms of Racial
    Discrimination (ICERD), 130
International Covenant on Civil and
    Political Rights (ICCPR, 1966)
  classification of rights, 78
  context, 13–15, 102–3
  decolonization and, 81
  globalization and, 34
  HR canon, 12, 170
  implementation, 86
  individual rights, 60
  insufficiency, 129, 130
  interpreting, 17
  liberty banner, 137
  primacy, 84
  ratification, 13
  self-determination, 82, 83
  Third World and, 134
  vision, 85
  website, 166
  Western values, 13
International Covenant on Economic,
    Social and Cultural Rights
    (ICESCR, 1966)
  context, 13–15, 102–3
  cultural rights, 94
  decolonization and, 81
  equality banner, 137
  globalization and, 34
  HR canon, 12, 170
  implementation, 86
  individual rights, 60
  inspiration for social programs, 17
  insufficiency, 129, 130
  interpreting, 17
  poverty campaigners and, 139
  ratification, 13
  scientific research, xxiii, 150
  self-determination, 82, 83
  Soviet values, 13
  Third World and, 134
  vision, 85
  website, 166
International Sociological Association
    (ISA), xxiv, 1, 153, 169
International Workingmen's
    Association (IWMA), 100, 101–2
Iraq, 149
Ishay, Micheline, 99
Islamism, 129
Iyall Smith, Keri, xix

Jim Crow, 16, 23
Johnson, Lyndon, 16

Kerbo, Harold, 139
Keynesianism, 30, 98, 121–2, 133, 140,
    148
knowledge of human rights, xv–xviii

League of Nations, 14, 82
Lenin, Vladimir, 81–2
LGBT movement
  Enlightenment gap, 86–7
  equality, 38, 66, 70
  same-sex marriage, 38, 66, 87, 104–5
  successes, 135
Libya, 149
life expectancy, 145
longevity, right to, 44, 45, 143, 145, 156

McMichael, Philip, 116, 120
Mao Zedong, 63
market fundamentalism, 161
market rationality, 37
marriage, same-sex partners, 38, 66, 69,
    87, 104–5
Marx, Karl, xvi–xvii, 35–6, 79, 100, 116
mediascapes, 47, 69
Medicare/Medicaid, 52, 95, 107
Mexico, Zapatista movement, 10, 32, 37,
    147, 173
Moncada, Alberto, xviii, 107, 123
moral relativism, 152–3

nation-states
   bundling rights, 163
   civil and political rights and, 77–8, 80
   HR failures, 15
   post-WWII US reconstruction of
      system, 60–1
   retreat, 29, 37
   role, 7–8
   social policy and law, 15–18
   subsidiarity and, 143
National Science Foundation, xvi
National Security Agency, 28
NATO, 149
natural resources, 34, 61, 87, 89,
      113–17, 121, 123, 133, 137, 140,
      142, 148
negative rights
   civil and political rights, 27–9
   positive rights and, 60–4
   US policy, 51–2
neoliberalism, 36–7, 108, 133, 141, 161
New Deal, 16, 31, 106–7, 135
Non-Aligned Movement, 103

Occupy movements, 10, 29, 96, 98–9,
      147
outsourcing, 37, 63
Oxfam
   anti-poverty campaign, 54, 87–90, 88,
      119, 122, 128–30, 156, 174
   bundling rights, 34–5, 87–90, 128–30,
      141
   debates, 34
   development approach, 97, 150, 156
   five universal rights, 34–5, 87
   nation-states and, 131
   poverty as violation of human rights,
      138
   résumé, 168

peace
   definition, 150
   right to, 44, 45, 144, 145–6, 156
   rights, peace and development, 151–2
Pearce, Tola Olu, 1
Poland, 36, 101
Portugal, colonialism, 76
positive rights

collective rights, 78
cultural and environmental rights,
      32–3
economic and social rights, 30–2
Europe and Latin America, 52
negative rights and, 60–4
positivism, 36, 118, 151, 152, 153
post-colonialism, 67
post-Fordism, 37, 129, 133
poverty
   anti-poverty bundle, 140–1
   causes, 138–9
   civil and political rights and, 87–90
   definition, xii, 89
   Oxfam anti-poverty program, 54,
      87–90, 88, 119, 122, 128–30, 174
   paradox of globalization, 145
   rights puzzle, 87–8
   violation of human rights, 89, 138–40,
      156
   See also development
property law, xx, 4, 128
Public Citizen, xvi
public sociology project, xix

RAND Corporation, xvi
Rawls, John, xii
Reagan, Ronald, 29
relationalism of rights, 74–5, 103–6
relativism, 152–3
research agenda, 156–62
Revolution Theology, 142
rights bundles. See bundles of rights
rights claims
   agenda, 156
   bundling rights and, 53–4
   classification of rights and, 52
   filtering process, 48
   meaning, 4, 19, 38, 171–2
   mediating forms, 65
   process, 54
   social movements, 5
rights conditions, 4, 19, 38, 156, 172
rights education, xxiii, 44
rights effects, xiv, 4, 19, 38, 41, 77, 156,
      158, 172
rights puzzles, 19–21, 54, 87–8, 98,
      140–1, 172–3

Rio Declaration (1992), 122, 137, 139, 170
Romania, 36, 101
Roosevelt, Franklin Delano, 16, 31, 98, 106–7, 135
Russia, ethnic minorities, 79
Rwanda, 149

scientific research, xxiii, 150, 152–4
self-determination, 2, 60, 82, 93, 100, 134
Sen, Amartya, xii, 128, 150
service learning, xxii–xxiv, 152
sexual orientation. See LGBT movement
Shiva, Vandana, xii
Sjoberg, Gideon, 1
slavery, 79, 80, 99, 100, 101
social constructs, 26
social learning, 10–11, 143, 160, 170
social movements
    civil and political rights and, 76–7, 101
    classification of human rights and, 64–8
    direct action, 65
    Global North, 10
    globalization and, xi
    identity-based movements, 123
    influence, 18, 23
    post-Cold War, 36–7
    research, 5, 38
    rights bundling, 128
    role, 3–4, 40
    shaping human rights, 40
    UN-NGO-SMO nexus, 34–5, 97, 129
    United States, 3
    See also specific movements and NGOs
social rights. See economic and social rights
Social Science Research Council, xvi, 155
social sciences
    human values and, 152–4, 163
    interdisciplinarity, xvii, 5–6
    knowledge of human rights and, xv–xviii
    pluralism, xviii, xix

socialism, 100, 102, 121–2, 146–7
sociology, origins, xvi–xvii, 35–6, 79, 100, 116
sociology of HR
    agenda, 150–63
    angles, 37–40
    defining, 35–43, 174
    dilemma in human rights, 7–8
    fundamental questions, 4–6
    human rights canon. See canon
    human rights community, 8–11
    invitation to human rights, 6–7
    major concepts, 41–3
    normative framework, 43–6
    origins, 36–7
    perspective, 23–6
    social policy and law, 15–18
    thinking sociologically, xiii–xv, 1–21
solidarity, 48, 111–13, 137
South Africa, 149
Soviet Union
    dissolution, 36, 146–7, 149
    human rights abuses, 101
    Human Rights Watch and, 84
    United Nations and, 85
    US relations, 13, 14, 81–2, 102–3
Spain, Great Recession, 29, 108
Starbucks, 117
Stockholm Declaration (1972), 94, 122, 134, 166–7, 170
subsidiarity, 124, 142–3
sustainable development
    culture and, 114
    earth's rights, 121
    meaning, 113
    right to, 126
    Stockholm Declaration, 122
    versions, 117–20
Syria, 149

Tea Party, 75, 96, 98
Third World. See Global South
three-generations framework
    classification of rights, 60–4
    Enlightenment legacy, 78–9
    limitations, 71–3, 128, 136–40
    origins of 3rd generation rights, 120–4

rethinking, 53, 101–2
rights bundling and, 129
specificity of 3rd generation rights,
    115–17
usefulness, 19–20
trade unions, 66, 79, 96, 104, 134–5, 137
transnational corporations
commodification of the commons, 62
environmental responsibility
    programs, 117
mass media ownership, 69
neoliberalism and, 36–7
role, 8
Turner, Bryan, 1

UNESCO, 85
United Kingdom, 76, 118, 122
United Nations
3rd generation rights, 122
academic research and, xiv–xv
civil and political rights and, 85–7
custodian of human rights, 82, 106,
    134
Declaration on the Rights of
    Indigenous Peoples (2007), 61,
    122, 137
Development Group, 150
expansion of system, xxi
HR canon, 7, 11, 12–15, 17
inequality and, xi
influence, 8
institutionalization of rights, 27, 48,
    60–1, 69
International Bill of Human Rights
    (IBHR), 12–15, 81, 85–6, 102
knowledge-production function, 85
origins, 76, 82, 84, 85
reforming, 90, 132
right to development, 154
rights bundling, 128
sustainable development, 118
Third World influence, 2, 82
UN-NGO-SMO nexus, 34–5, 97, 129
United States and, 76
World Bank rift, 122
World Conference on Human Rights
    (Vienna, 1993), 74
See also specific conventions

United States
Bill of Rights, 67
bullying in schools, 146
civic engagement and service
    learning, xxii–xxiv
civil and political rights, 25, 51–2, 63,
    64, 76, 77, 91, 95
civil rights movement, 14, 16, 23, 64,
    77, 104, 135
Constitution (1787)
    civil rights, 25
    Enlightenment legacy, 75
    landmark, 79
    model, 49
    negative rights, 29, 51–2
    privacy, 28
Declaration of Independence (1776)
    Enlightenment legacy, 75
    historical context, 67
    landmark, 2, 79
    pursuit of happiness, 80–1, 94
development policy, 75–6, 122
economic and social rights, 31–2,
    94–7, 98, 106–8, 135
feminist movement, 14
Great Depression, 16, 30–1
Great Society programs, 31, 107
HDI, 155
healthcare, 32, 52, 95, 107, 145, 158
hegemony, 134
human rights violations, federal
    prosecutions, 28
humanitarian interventions, 95
ICERD and, 130
marriage equality, 70, 104
New Deal, 16, 31, 104, 106–7, 135
NSA monitoring, 28
Occupy movement, 10, 29, 37, 96, 98,
    147
outsourcing to China, 63
reconstruction of state system, 60–1
reconstruction of world economy,
    55–6
Revolution, 81, 84, 105
social learning, 10
social movements, 3, 66–7
Soviet relations, 13, 14, 81–2, 102–3
strategic interests, 13

United States *(cont.)*
    Tea Party, 75, 96, 98
    United Nations and, 76
    voting rights, 42, 66, 77, 95
    welfare state, 29, 30, 32, 98, 107,
        157–8, 162
Universal Declaration of Human Rights
        (UDHR, 1948)
    civil and political rights, 84
    context, 13–15
    Enlightenment legacy, 81
    globalization and, 34
    HR canon, x, 12, 13–15, 170
    implementation, 86
    interpretations, 49
    self-determination, 82
    universalism, 84
    vision, 85
    website, 166
universalism
    constructing, 27
    cultural pluralism and, xx–xxi, 6, 8,
        53, 154, 174–5
    Enlightenment, 56
    moral relativism and, 152–3
    Oxfam five universal rights, 34–5, 87
    UDHR, 84
urbanization, 35, 79, 116

values
    International Covenants, 13
    scientific research and humanist
        values, 152–4, 163
    Western v African values, 1
Vasak, Karel, 49
voting rights, 42, 77, 89, 90, 95, 100

Wallerstein, Immanuel, 102
Waters, Malcolm, 1

Weber, Max, xvi–xvii, 35–6, 79, 116
welfare states, 29, 30–2, 52, 88, 93, 103,
        107, 134–5, 139, 157–8, 161–2
Western values. *See* Global North
Wilson, Woodrow, 81–2
women, CEDAW, 167
Women, Culture and Development
        (WCD), 130–1, 137, 141, 150, 156
women's movement
    critique of Enlightenment, 67
    Enlightenment, 99
    human rights framework, 67–8
    LGBT movement and, 104
    tactics, 66
    US assumption, 95
Works Progress Administration, 16
World Bank
    bundling rights and, 147–8
    development-as-consumerism, 47,
        117
    development concept, 72, 90, 122
    institutionalization of rights, 69
    neoliberalism, 36–7, 63, 108
    reforming, 90, 132
    sustainable development, 117
    UN rift, 122
    US reconstruction of world economy,
        55–6
World Conference on Human Rights
        (Vienna, 1993), 74
World Social Forum, 10, 32–3, 37, 63,
        98–9, 142, 147
World Wars, 14
WTO, 36–7, 90, 108, 117, 132, 147–8

Yugoslavia, 36, 103, 149

Zapatistas, 10, 32, 37, 147, 173
Zerubavel, Eviatar, 57–9

Printed in the USA
CPSIA information can be obtained
at www.ICGtesting.com
JSHW012028211223
54119JS00012B/166